Heal Your Heart

Free Your Mind!

9 Steps to Break Free *from Struggle in Your Relationships & All Areas of Your Life!*

Brandy Faith Weld

After you buy your book, go to the following link and put in your Amazon receipt number to receive your Free Gifts worth $1,100.00, to help you

Heal Your Heart and Free Your Mind:

www.HealYourHeartFreeYourMindBook.com/Bonuses

ISBN: 1505590655
ISBN-13: 978-1505590654

DEDICATION

In light of your Light

A Beautiful Gift to All that You Touched. I dedicate this book to my mother, Barbara Weld, whom I loved more than life itself. You were my best friend and soul mate, and I am so very grateful for the sacrifices you made for my soul's growth and evolvement. You were an *Angel* embodied, always caring about and looking after all in our family! I feel honored to have had the opportunity to be your daughter! I will love you for eternity and look forward to seeing you again on the other side.

And Dad, thank you for going on this healing journey with me! Thank you for going outside of your comfort zone to participate in this internal work. Thank you for being one of my Healing Angels and for being willing to play the roles that you did for my soul's growth and evolvement! I love you and I am eternally grateful.

TABLE OF CONTENTS

Foreword by Bob Doyle

Throughout my years in the personal development industry, I have read countless numbers of books on the subject of personal transformation. From among these, there are only a few that I consider to be truly important works capable of genuinely transforming the planet.

Heal Your Heart ~ Free Your Mind............ is definitely one of those books!

Brandy Faith Weld has truly pinpointed exactly why we as humans have the challenges that we do, in virtually all areas of our lives — and it all starts with our relationships.

I have done enough personal work in my life to know what a key role our relationships play in our quality of life, particularly with our parents– but I have reached an entirely different level of understanding after reading this book.

As a Law of Attraction teacher since 2002, I am well aware of how powerfully we each create our own experience in response to our energetic communications with the rest of the Universe. But what determines the quality of that communication?

When people learn about the Law of Attraction (what Brandy brilliantly refers to as the Law of Reflection in this book), they often excitedly try to use all the tools and techniques they hear about to "magically" transform their lives– but are more often than not met with frustration. Because what they are trying to attract doesn't show up according to their personal time table, they are inclined to disregard the Law of Attraction/Reflection entirely.

This book explains exactly why people don't get results even when they seem to be doing all the right things.

It's all about what Brandy refers to as "charges." These are energetic patterns that are created even before we are born, that run within each of us, that truly have the power to shape our destiny– and mostly in very disempowering ways.

The good news is that when you understand where these charges come from, you can actually do something about them!

That work is what this book is all about.

What I can tell you for sure is that if you complete the processes set forth in this book– actually take them on fully, and complete them– you will become an extremely powerful *intentional* creator, manifesting your own destiny. I say *intentional* because all of us are powerfully manifesting all the time, whether we know it or not. The problem is that we're running on energetic autopilot, unaware of the energy systems (the charges) that are really running the show. This book shows you how to turn off the auto-pilot and finally take control.

But here's what's really unfortunate. The odds are slim to none that you will actually complete these processes as a result of just reading this book. Unfortunately, MOST people don't take action on the books that they read, no matter how much they get out of them. When it comes to actually doing what it takes to facilitate the transformation they *say* they truly want, they simply don't do it. And it's not really their fault. People are unfortunately programmed to sabotage themselves and they don't even know it.

It also doesn't matter how people appear to the outside world. They may profess to believe in the power to create their lives by design. And it may seem, to all observing, that they are happy, successful, and living passionate and exciting lives. However, we need only look at the recent string of celebrity suicides and overdoses to begin to understand that there are very powerful energetic forces at work in our lives, which, if left unchecked, can literally kill us. These were people who, from the outside, seemed to have it all, and yet they carried powerful charges that created feelings of unworthiness, self-loathing, fear, worry, sadness, anger— the list goes on and on.

Brandy's powerful book can genuinely prevent things like this from happening by getting to the root of how all this negative programming starts in the first place, and providing a huge collection of tools and processes that absolutely will help you to clear out all the charges that are negatively impacting your ability to live a life you love.

But again, you have to act on what you read — and so few do.

Without knowing it, you are — in this moment– at one of the most important crossroads of your life.

As you read this book and are given a specific instruction of something to do.... such as a writing exercise or a meditation exercise etc., and you make the decision NOT to act on it, I invite you to notice exactly what is happening in your mind as you make that decision. Don't just be at the mercy of the thought that holds you back. Observe it. Allow your curiosity to speculate honestly on what pattern within you tells you not to do something that you know will be good for you.

Ironically, by actually doing what Brandy suggests, that pattern can be eliminated forever, and you can truly become unstoppable— because now YOU are consciously at cause for the actions you take, rather than at the mercy of years of subconscious programming that have been unconsciously driving you.

When it comes down to it, this book is about the power of your capacity for unconditional love... not only for others, but for yourself. The aspects of ourselves that we share with the world, through who we "be," are such a small fraction of what makes us who we are. Still, we are looking for love and approval from others based on that "version" of us that we feel safe to share. But in the end, how can someone truly love us unconditionally if we don't share with them who we truly are because of our own shame or fear about those parts of us that we consider negative?

This book is a pathway to unconditional self-love, which opens the door to possibility of that TRUE love from others that we all deeply desire. But it all starts with loving ourselves first.

And from that place, you can truly create whatever you can imagine.

I want the *world* to read this book. Starting with you!

I dare you.

Peace, love, and bliss to you all!

Bob Doyle
#1 Bestselling author of ***Follow Your Passion Find Your Power*** and featured teacher in the mega hit movie ***The Secret.***

How to Get the Most Out of This Book...

Congratulations on taking the first step to freeing yourself from the struggles of the past, be it from relationships or other areas of your life. This book is based on a revolutionary eight-day program that has transformed thousands of lives around the world! Our goal is to help as many people as possible break free from the struggle and pain that they have experienced in life, and guide them to now living a joyful, love-filled, peaceful life that feels almost magical!

Through this book you will gain a greater understanding of how everything works, and the truth of why your relationships and life are the way they are at this moment. By gaining this awareness and following the process I will be guiding you through, you will now be able to see what has been limiting you from living the life of your heart and soul's intention. You will break free from patterns and anything that has been blocking you from having great relationships and living your best life ever!

To try to recreate as much as possible the powerful experience our participants have at our live events, we have incorporated a great deal of technology into this book. Throughout the book you will find url's with QR codes beside them that will lead you to a specific web page through your Smartphone or Tablet. **Download a free QR Code Reader from your App Store now** and open up the App and hold the viewer over the code (making sure to get the image only within the reader box and not any of the text around it) to scan it whenever you see a QR Code in the book that looks like this:

Did you download it and test it? If not, do that now. These QR codes are a very important part of the journey! We have incorporated vital audio clips to lead you through the powerful processes in this book. Whenever you see a url or a QR code, make sure you go to that url/code, preferably with your Smartphone or Tablet (you could type the url into your computer's browser as well), to either listen to the audio file with your headphones directly from the website or download it into your MP3 playing device. It is very important and crucial to the process that you listen to these audios when guided to. Do not skip any of them, and please make sure you are listening to them with headphones. In these audio clips, we are using a sound technology to bypass your conscious mind and directly reach your subconscious mind, where all of what has been troubling your heart and mind resides, so that we can assist those "troubles" in moving out.

For your safety, do not listen to these audio clips while you are driving. Also, do not listen to them with headphones if you are pregnant, wear a pace-maker or if you are prone to seizures of any kind. This sound technology will put you into a hypnotic trance state.

As another great option, you can have all of the information at your fingertips when you download our free app at www.AppCatch.com through your Smartphone or Tablet browser. Simply type "**Eternal Love**" into the search bar on the top right-hand side of the page to find our App. When it comes up, tap on the red heart labeled *Eternal Love*, click the "**Install**" link and follow the directions that pop up for how to add the App's launch button to the home screen of your device. Then find the red heart with the words *Eternal Love* beneath it on your home screen, and you will have everything you need at the push of a button!

I also highly recommend getting a journal that is dedicated to this most important journey you're about to go on. Although there is a workbook included, you will find there is a lot more information you will want to capture that won't fit within the confines of this book. In the end, this journal will become something very sacred to you that you will want to have as a keep-sake for your life's defining moments.

To live a life free of the struggles you have been experiencing, commit to yourself to complete all of the exercises in this book, in the order they have been given. Do not read ahead and do not read further until after you have completed each exercise assigned. Everything is designed in a precise order to get you to your desired outcome. Jumping ahead will not help or serve you in reaching your intended goal. My only desire is for you to be able to live the joyful, love-filled and peaceful life of your heart and soul's intention, and to be free of any struggles that have been limiting you from that, thus far.

Also, for all of you grammarians out there: I want to forewarn you that this book has a lot of run on sentences that start with "And" and "So". I understand this might frustrate you and bring to mind all kinds of— well, let's just say, "thoughts". And that's great! I will just ask you to notice them and make those "thoughts" a part of the inner journey you're about to go on. When the time is right, ask yourself, "Where do these *'thoughts'* come from?

Did I pick them up from someone else? My mom? My dad? A grandparent?" Just know that I am aware of these grammatical errors....... and they are there on purpose, for a conversational tone and a dramatic effect. I hope that you won't allow it to distract you from feeling the emotions that this book is intended to bring up for you. Our intention is to get past your very intelligent, guarded mind, and your intellects' *'need to be right'*. The solutions to your problems are not in the mind. They are in your heart. And we are about to learn how very powerful the heart is, indeed!

So let's begin this most important journey now.....

Preface

What is Your Marathon?

Would you like to?

➢ Experience more love in your life
➢ Experience less conflict and more internal peace
➢ Have a greater relationship with your life partner
➢ Grow stronger relationships with your family, friends and coworkers
➢ Be free of old hurts, patterns and limiting beliefs
➢ Enjoy greater health
➢ Experience more magic, joy and abundance in your life
➢ Understand how you have created your life thus far and transform it into the life of your dreams
➢ **Live Your Life's Dream, Purpose and Soul's Intention**

What is Your Marathon?

This is the question that has driven me.

It all started one day, when a friend of mine from Australia came to town to stay with me for a week, while he pursued his life goal and purpose. He was just about to turn 40 years old when he decided to put all of his belongings in storage to pursue his dream of beating a **Guinness World Record** — running the most marathons in one year. That meant he needed to run 160 marathons in a year's time. Meaning, he had to run at least three marathons a week on average. Do you know how long a marathon is? It is 26 miles and 385 yards or 42.195 kilometers. He was running this distance at least three times a week!

The real madness is that he would finish his marathon, take a shower, eat, then fly out that evening to his next location. He'd arrive late that night or sometimes in the wee hours of the next morning, get himself to some kind of accommodation, sleep for just a few hours and have to be up by 5 a.m. to get to his next start time— which was normally around 6:30 a.m.

Then he did it all over again the next day!

For example, this was his crazy schedule when he came to stay with me in the Los Angeles area: he flew a red eye from Tel Aviv to Washington DC, got off the plane and immediately ran a marathon. Then he hopped back on a plane that evening to arrive in Los Angeles, got himself to his accommodations and to sleep around 2 a.m. He arose again at 5 a.m. for a 6:30 start time for the LA Marathon. Upon finishing, he had a snack, took a shower, ate some *drunch* (dinner + lunch), socialized with me, went to sleep at about 11:00 p.m., and woke up again at 5 for another 6:30 a.m. start time! And he continued to do this every day for the entire week!!! He then flew north to Oakland, CA after his last race of the week in LA, and completed his big *Century Mark* run (his 100th marathon) the very next morning! After he conducted interviews with the media about his Century Milestone that afternoon, he got up the next morning and ran again for the next seven days in San Francisco. Crazy!

Crazy Dedication and Determination That Is!!

Needless to say, this goal, this dedication and the spirit behind it really inspired and motivated me to take action in my own life. I still remember the tears rolling down my cheeks as I stood on the sidelines cheering my friend on, as thousands of others were cheering for their friends or family members who were living out their life goal, and celebrating it together at the end. This moment illuminated the human spirit's desire to have a dream or set a goal, and its tenacity in making that vision come true. It reminded me that everything we have around us today was once only someone's vision and dream. With tears in my eyes, I thought to myself, "Wow, look at all of these dreams and goals being achieved and coming true today! Look at all of the pride, joy and celebration they are all sharing!"

This unstoppable dedication and determination led me to ask this question: **What is _my_ marathon?**

What do I want to accomplish and achieve before I die? I may not want to run a marathon, but I do have a vision and a dream that would be equivalent to someone else's marathon. And why am I not living it now? Why aren't I getting focused on my goal, creating a plan and doing the work to make it happen?

These thoughts brought the remembrance that once, I was working towards my marathon, for both my mother and myself. At the time, I was driven more by the desire to make it come true for her. You see, my mother was a talented artist who loved nature and inspiring, supportive thoughts. She had a dream to blend her art and her passion for nature with inspirational words, to create gift cards. But she lacked the confidence in her art to bring it forth. With my passion for spiritual growth, along with my desire to make a difference in the world, I created a project that my mother and I could work on together, to display her gift and launch her dream. To launch both of our dreams; which was to create a series of spiritual personal development books for children, filled with my mother's illustrations.

As we worked on our vision, my mother struggled to be satisfied with her drawings and she would go back to the drawing board incessantly, preventing her from really finishing any of her work. I would call her and tell her how much I loved her drawings and encourage her to finish them. I did that continuously, until that fateful day. A day that I will never forget...... a day that changed my life as I knew it — forever.

"Your mother is not doing well," my father said. "We have an appointment with the doctor in the morning for a CAT scan. If you want to join us, you are welcome." Fear consumed me instantly. I paced back and forth across my living room all night long, agonizing, "No God, please nooooooooo! *Not my mother*! Please don't take my mother. I can't live without her. I don't want to live in this world without her!"

That day, the doctor told my mother that she had an inoperable brain tumor that had grown through the cortex and had taken over both sides of her brain, and that she only had three months to live. It was an unfortunate death sentence that came true; she lived just a couple days longer than that three month prognosis.

I was inconsolable. My entire family was wrought with pain. My mother was quite the matriarch of the family. She was always so thoughtful and took care of everyone. She was an earth angel and I loved my mother more than life itself. She was my soul mate, my best friend, my confidant and my one safe place. I was angry at God. I was angry at the world. I blamed so many for my mother's death and deeply regretted all of the mistakes I had made with her myself.

Her dream died that day. A soul's life purpose and passion never got fulfilled before its passing, simply because my mother didn't have enough confidence in herself or in her gifts.

I let my dream die with her on that day as well.……..

Until now. **This is my marathon**. You are holding it in your hands right now. You are reading its words. All inspired by my friend's courage to go for his dream, no matter what obstacles he might face. No matter what others' limiting beliefs were, or how they tried to discourage him, he was running for *The Cause* in honor of his mother and step-mother's deaths from cancer. He was running for *The Cure*— raising money and awareness for cancer research.

This book represents *my cause.* Healing peoples' hearts, their fears, their pain and their limiting beliefs that have stopped them from living life as the vibrant beings that they really are— which is the source of all *dis-ease*! My cause is to stop the pain and the bleeding that gets passed down from generation to generation. Because it is only hurting people that hurt others. It is only people in great pain who don't know the beauty and the power of who they really are and all that they can be, do, have and achieve!

This is my Marathon for the Cure!

Instead of letting my dream die with my mother, I too, am running it in her honor.

What is your marathon? And are you ready to start preparing for it? Are you ready to start living your soul's life dream, purpose and intention? Are you ready to express this passion before *your* expiration date? Because we never know when that will be.

After my mother's death, I had a tragic accident. I fell 40 feet off a cliff, died, crossed over to the other side and saw my mother. I wanted to stay with her and our animals, but I was told I had a mission and I had to come back and share this message. I was given a second chance to fulfill my soul's dream and intention, and to stop wasting the opportunity in fear, victim consciousness and doubt. After my fall, I was taken on an internal journey to heal my relationships and *transcend* all of the fear and limiting beliefs that have been unconsciously driving my life and keeping me from running my race. I was shown how these obstacles were formed and how to *transcend* these patterns that have shown up in my life, time and time again, that have kept me from achieving my life goals, dreams and living happily.

The work and awareness that came through that journey, which I will be sharing with you in the following chapters, has allowed me to be here with you now, on the other side of the finish line, finally celebrating and truly living my heart and soul's dream and intention! Finally free of the internal pain and continuous obstacles, and now experiencing the life that I asked you if you would want to experience at the beginning of this preface. So would you like to experience all of those things? If so, are you ready to do the work it takes to get there? Because, like a marathon, it does take work and preparation. There is not an easy pill you can take for it.

If you were running a race, what would you do if you fell down? Give up, or get back in the race? **See what this woman did:**

www.HealYourHeartFreeYourMind.com/marathon

See what this man had to do to live his life dream:
www.HealYourHeartFreeYourMind.com/dream

I often think to live a happy and fulfilled life, we should live our lives with the end in mind. Below, a nurse reveals the top 5 regrets people make on their deathbed:

For many years I worked in palliative care. My patients were those who had gone home to die. Some incredibly special times were shared. I was with them for the last remaining weeks of their lives. People grow a lot when they are faced with their own mortality. I learned never to underestimate someone's capacity for growth. Some changes were phenomenal. Each experienced a variety of emotions, as expected: denial, fear, anger, remorse, more denial and eventually acceptance. When questioned about any regrets they had or anything they would do differently, common themes surfaced again and again. Here are the most common five:

1. *I wish I'd had the courage to live a life true to myself, not the life others expected of me.*

This was the most common regret of all. When people realize that their life is almost over and look back clearly upon it, it is easy to see how many dreams have gone unfulfilled. Most people had not honored even a half of their dreams and had to die knowing that it was due to choices they had made, or not made.

It is very important to try and honor as many of your dreams as possible along the way. From the moment that you lose your health, it is too late. Health brings a freedom very few realize, until they no longer have it.

2. *I wish I didn't work so hard.*

This came from every male patient that I nursed. They missed their children's youth and their partner's companionship. All of the men I nursed deeply regretted spending so much of their lives on the treadmill of a work existence.

3. *I wish I'd had the courage to express my feelings.*

Many people suppressed their feelings in order to keep peace with others. As a result, they settled for a mediocre existence and never became who they were truly capable of becoming. Many developed illnesses relating to the bitterness and resentment they carried as a result.

We cannot control the reactions of others. Although people may initially react when you change the way you are by speaking honestly, in the end, it raises the relationship with them to a whole new and healthier level. Either that or it releases the unhealthy relationship from your life. Either way, you win.

4. *I wish I had stayed in touch with my friends.*

Often they would not truly realize the full benefits of old friends until their dying weeks and it was not always possible to track them down. Many had become so caught up in their own lives that they had let golden friendships slip by over the years. There were many deep regrets about not giving friendships the time and effort they deserved. Everyone misses their friends when they are dying.

It is common for anyone in a busy lifestyle to let friendships slip. But when you are faced with your approaching death, the physical details of life fall away. It all comes down to **love and relationships** in the end.

That is all that remains in the final weeks, **love and relationships**.

5. *I wish that I had let myself be happier.*

This is a surprisingly common regret. Many did not realize until the end that **happiness is a choice**. They had stayed stuck in old patterns of victim consciousness. The so-called 'comfort' of familiarity overflowed into their emotions, as well as their physical lives. Fear of change had them pretending to others, and to themselves, that they were content. When you are on your deathbed, what others think of you is a long way from your mind. How wonderful to be able to let go and smile, long before you are dying.

Life is a choice. It is YOUR life. Choose consciously, choose honestly, and choose your happiness. **Run Your Marathon!** Live your life to the fullest and go for your dreams, no matter what the Naysayers think! Remember, what the word impossible is really saying is — **I'm Possible!** Don't be one of those many stories of unfulfilled dreams lying in the cemetery. Don't leave this world without singing *your song*. It's your time! And it is time to **Heal Your Heart** and live the fulfilling, joy-filled, magical life you have always longed for!

Courage does not make a man; it reveals him!

Transcend*Transform*Inspire

Chapter One

Awareness to Freedom

To begin our journey, I would first like to share with you a story about one of my clients, Todd. Todd came to me really concerned about his marriage. Things between him and his wife had become so bad that he was beginning to consider divorce. Now, Todd was a strong Christian and divorce was very much against his values, so these thoughts were very troubling to him. He still loved his wife, but their communication had come to the point of being unbearable.

This is the story he shared with me: "When I first met my wife, I could not believe how lucky I was to have met her first of all, and secondly I could not believe she actually wanted to be with me! She was like a dream come true, and we fit together oh so perfectly. She was my queen and I hung on every word she said. It was the same for her. I'd never felt so seen and so heard before. I mean, I would talk and she would just be present and listen."

"When we got married and as time went on, our relationship changed a bit, and it was more like she would talk all the time, and I would just listen. And that was okay, too."

"But now it's awful and I can't live a day longer with it staying the same! I mean she talks, and I talk ...., **but now, ... the entire neighborhood listens**!"

Laughing out loud! OK, that story was a little tongue-in-cheek. But why is it so true at the same time? Why is it that most of the world can totally relate to this situation? Why do the statistics say that there is a divorce happening every 13 seconds!?

Why is it that all of our relationships that start off being great and wonderful, slowly begin to diminish and demise? Why do we always say, "We feel most hurt by the ones we are the closest to?" or, "We tend to hurt the ones we feel the closest to?" And why do we have the same **patterns** showing up in our lives, over and over again? A similar situation happens to us with just a different face and a different name, time and time again? And because of these repeating **patterns**, we have all said to ourselves, "*Why does this always* — what?....... *happen to me?*" or, "*I knew that was going to* — what? .... *happen!*"

So, why is it that you were able to finish my sentences? Because we have all said these words to ourselves, or have heard others around us say these words, time and time again.

Why do we all have these **patterns** that keep showing up repeatedly in our lives? The same thoughts, the same feelings, very similar experiences, just at different times and involving different people? Now, your pattern might not be about your relationship with a significant other. Your pattern could be different, it could evolve around finances or health or family; or perhaps work, the feeling of being abandoned or rejected, a push-pull pattern, etc. As my best friend says, we all have a cross to bear. So the type of pattern can look different for each person, but we all have a pattern that has caused us to say, "*Why does this always happen to me?*"

So, why does this seem to be such a common human experience for us all?

This phenomenon is caused literally by how human beings are made! It's what naturally and scientifically happens during the development of a human being from the point of conception. None of it being your fault, and mostly none of it being your parents' fault either! I know this is a strong statement, and perhaps it created a supercharged reaction in you, but I will explain further this strong statement later in the book. The repeating patterns are also because of a very powerful Universal Law that governs all of life, just like gravity. We will go into more detail about this later as well. This is a very crucial and vital law to know about and to learn how to work with effectively, so that it will no longer work against you and your life dreams. The comprehension of these two truths is **the key** to understanding how you are creating your life experience right now and *why* your life is the way it is today. And it is also **the key** to learning *how* you can *transform* your life experience into the one of your heart and soul's desire!

So have you been struggling with why your life is the way that it is, and no matter what you try, you just can't seem to break through some invisible barrier that always seems to be keeping you from your goal? You learn something new, you try something new, but no matter what you do, the same type of pattern still somehow shows up in your life, blocking you from your dream and goal? Do you sometimes feel like that fly on a window that sees where it wants to go and keeps trying to get there— but just comes up against some invisible barrier? Like the fly, you work harder, you try harder until the point of exhaustion, but to no avail. Have you ever reached a point where the situation seems hopeless, you don't know what to do, and you feeling like giving up?

If your answer is yes, then I know how you feel, because I have lived it. I have lived it to the point where I wanted to die like that fly and not exist anymore. The feeling of being stuck, having no way out, and not being able to get where I wanted to go no matter how hard I tried was unbearable, like being stuck in the Alcatraz prison. (You know, where you can see all of the beauty and fun others are living through the window of your jail cell, but you just can't get to it? It's more like a form of Chinese torture!)

The great news is, **if you apply** the teachings that you get through this book and you **go through all of the processes**, you **will *break free*** from these **patterns** and the ***obstacles*** that have blocked you from achieving your life's goal. You **will *transform*** your life to one that is more joy-filled and pleasing to both your heart and your soul. And you will live a life that is ***inspiring*** to you, and for others! How do I know all this? Simply because I have lived it personally. I have also witnessed thousands upon thousands of other people do the same.

When I found this work, I was beyond the breaking point of not being able to get past all of the obstacles that I described above— I was at my absolute lowest low. The thought of continually living with the emotions I was feeling had become unbearable. I was at the point we call existential suffering, meaning that at the soul level, I did not want to live or exist. I would just pray for the angel of death to come find me and take me quickly.

You see, as I began to share with you before, my mother died suddenly at the young age of 59. When this happened, my entire family and all of the foundations that I had known and built my vision of life upon, blew up from underneath me. I had loved my mother more than life itself. Spiritually, I always felt like we were soul mates and that I only came to live on this earth, at this time and space, to be with her. She was my best friend, my spiritual teacher and my confidant, and I felt, my one safe place in this world.

After she died, I went through all of her things and found her journals; in one, I found a family secret that shattered my world. It crumbled every belief I ever had about my family! Only my mother knew this secret, and she had kept it locked up in her heart and mind for years, and now it was passed on to me...... No one else knew about this. No one would have believed me if I told them. This is how contrary it was to how my family appeared to other family members, friends and to the world. It tore out my heart and soul at my very core; I felt dejected, confused, fearful and lifeless. I became afraid of the repercussions if I told anyone else about this secret, so I didn't. I, too, just kept it within.

But of course it didn't go away. It just bored deeper into my heart, my soul and into my body. During this time period, I became so stressed and overwhelmed that my body went into a constant state of anxiety. The cortisol would hit me at night so that I wouldn't be able to sleep, and the adrenaline would kick in when morning came. In this constant state of anxiety, I couldn't do much. I would just go in circles, feeling fearful, hopeless and stuck. It was such an awful, dreadful feeling that overtook every cell of my being— and if I couldn't be free of it, then I didn't want to live. Hopeless and helpless and on my knees, I kept praying and looking for anything in the spiritual or personal development world to help me feel better. And it was then, in this total helpless state, that I was led on a journey that helped me discover all that I am about to share with you in this book.

Through this healing journey, I was freed of all the fear, hurt, stories, patterns, obstacles and limiting beliefs that once stopped me. Now, I am excited to be living the life of my dreams from a quiet and peaceful mind, a totally healed heart, and an absolute, limitless soul that knows its mission and is living its intention! Daily, I am excited about all that I can do and experience. Every day is like a blank canvas for me to create any beautiful picture I choose. I am boundless, and my only limitations are the ones that I let my mind put upon me. I am no longer shackled by the generational victim consciousness that I inherited, that once bound me in an emotional prison. But instead, like the words of Martin Luther King, "Free at last! Free at last! Thank God almighty, I am free at last!" Free to live the life of my heart and soul's intention without all of the obstacles and patterns that once limited me!

And so can you, if you go on this journey of *awareness* with me. **Really living it, and applying it.**

Are you ready? If so, grab yourself a journal and dedicate it to this powerful inner journey. And when you have it, turn the page and let's begin.......

Transcend*Transform*Inspire

Chapter Two

The Secret is In Your Heart

Let's try out an experiment a friend of mine does with her audience. Take your index finger and point to yourself. Notice where you are pointing. If you are like the thousands of people she has done this experiment with, you are pointing at your heart. Why is that? Why is it that most people do not point to their heads, their stomachs or their legs? It seems that, instinctively, we know that the heart is the essence of who we are. Imagine looking deeply into the eyes of someone you care about and saying, "*I love you with all of my head.*" It doesn't sound right, does it? Throughout history, people of all cultures around the world have considered the heart space to be the seat of their soul or Being.

But do you know how powerful your heart really is? Do you know that it is **5000 times more powerful electromagnetically than the brain?** That the heart is the strongest electrical and magnetic field generator in the human body? The emotions your heart feels affect both your DNA and outside matter— meaning, your heart affects everything in your body and the things outside of your body as well! It affects both your *internal world* and your *external world* at the subatomic particle level (what everything in the Universe is made of — all of matter, including you and me.)

> *"Concerning matter, we have been all wrong.*
> *What we have called matter is energy, whose vibration has been*
> *so lowered as to be imperceptible to the senses. There is no matter."*
> ~ Albert Einstein

Did you know that the heart is the first organ developed in the body when we are conceived, that it has its own brain (made up of a network of 40,000 neurons) and its own intelligence? Do you know it sends more information to the brain than the brain sends to it, and that the heart is a key driver of what messages the brain sends out to the rest of the body? With every beat, the heart sends out an electromagnetic pulse at the speed of light. (Light travels so fast that it can go around the earth seven times within a single second!) The heart is a powerful process center with a very complex nervous system, second only to the brain. And as the heart changes, the brain activity affecting the body changes as well.

Our hearts broadcasts out to the world what's really going on inside of us, and it also picks up the broadcasts of other hearts around us. When we are connected to another person, either by physical touch or just simply through mutual caring, our hearts begin to communicate electromagnetically, become entangled and entrain with one another. Have you ever experienced just 'knowing' what someone you're close to was thinking or feeling without them ever saying a word to you about it? That is because your hearts were communicating at an electromagnetic level. At my live events, I give the audience a powerful experience of this phenomenon, and the reality of its existence becomes undeniable for them.

In fact, in a related study, the Institute of HeartMath conducted a test where three people, who practice meditation, would get into a meditative state while wearing heart monitors. As they got into this meditative state, all of their heartbeats began to synch up in the same rhythm as pendulums do, and their hearts became coherent with one another. They then were told to focus on a 4th individual who knew nothing about meditation, nor what they were monitoring his heart for. At first, he was just sitting there in a confused state and his heart rate was very erratic; but soon, his heart became in coherence with the other three and synched up into the same peaceful rhythm.[1] Here is an example for you on how our hearts get in coherence with one another.

http://healyourheartfreeyourmind.com/Coherence/

In another study that the Institute of HeartMath conducted to see how both the heart and the brain would respond to random pictures shown to volunteers, proved, beyond a shadow of a doubt, the intuitive intelligence of the heart. Some of the random pictures shown were peaceful and loving (about 66% of them) while others (about 33%) were of violence. When the participant pressed a button, the screen would go blank for at least 10 seconds. The study found that when the screen went blank, the heart would go back to its normal rhythm. Then, 6 seconds before the next picture was shown, the participants' heart would react to the upcoming picture as if they were seeing it in that moment![2] Yet they weren't! They were only seeing a blank screen! Then, one second and a half after the heart reacted to the upcoming picture, the brain reacted to it! Clearly proving the heart's intuitive intelligence, and that it is the heart that is actually sending information to the brain, and the brain then sends out a chemical reaction to the rest of the body. The brain thinks, but ***the heart knows.*** Remember that when you are trying to make difficult decisions!

Further research has shown that when the heart is healed, when it is in coherence, it sends out more life-affirming messages that heal the body, increase the immune system, normalize blood pressure, improve cognitive function and trigger the release of anti-aging chemicals like DHEA. What our hearts are sending out collectively even affects our solar system, the Earth's magnetic field, and its protection from outside forces. It also affects weather patterns and even earth changes. Our energetic frequency is interconnected with one another in a vast web that affects not only life on this planet, but our solar system and beyond. Our hearts are THAT POWERFUL. Thus, it is a very IMPORTANT organ to heal what it is transmitting out into the world, in order to *transform* our lives. Whatever your heart is broadcasting out, internally and externally, **IS DETERMINING YOUR LIFE EXPERIENCE!**

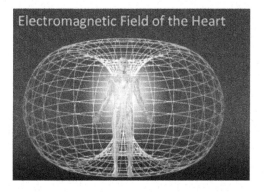

Electromagnetic Field of the Heart

More Powerful Experiments of the Heart

Modern science is confirming what ancient wisdom has been telling us for eons— how powerful our hearts and our emotions are in affecting our lives and the world around us. That our hearts communicate with the stuff, the energy or the subatomic particles, that our world is made of. Many years back, the military did an experiment to see if the emotions of the heart could affect DNA outside of the body. So researchers took some DNA from a volunteer in Los Angeles and put it in a device that could measure changes in the DNA and sent it to Phoenix, Arizona. They then put the volunteer in a room in LA and showed pictures, videos, and did other things to them to provoke various responses and emotions. The volunteer's responses were then measured via an EKG-type of device and compared to the simultaneous readings of the DNA. What they found shocked them. The DNA, located over 400 miles away from its owner, was having the exact same response, at the exact same time as the donor! What this is telling us is this— that our emotions affect our DNA both if it is inside the body or if it is outside the body. This study gave us our first big hint that our emotions **can** and **do** affect matter outside of our physical body!

A Russian biophysicist, Dr. Vladimir Poponin, proved this same principle in a study he conducted in 1990 called the *Phantom DNA Effect*. In this experiment, he discovered that human DNA he added into a test tube affected the photons that were in there. Photons are the energy packets making up matter— everything that our world is made of. The photons exactly replicated the same shape and form as the DNA! The photons even remained in that form after the DNA was removed from the test tube.[3]

In 1999, a Japanese doctor, Masaru Emoto, furthered this awareness by publishing his landmark study in a book titled *Messages from Water*. In this book he displayed how the words and the emotions a person felt towards a sample of water physically affected and transformed it. Meaning, people would write words of love and gratitude on the Petri dish of polluted water and pray over the water with these same emotions, and the water would transform from a nebulous mess into a beautiful, crystalline form!

After this discovery, Dr. Emoto took his experiments to the next level and attempted to transform some of their most polluted dams around his city. This water was very dirty, very tenuous and un-formable. They gathered up a large group of over five hundred people to pray and send love and gratitude to this body of water, and then captured a sample of the water to test. What they found was pleasantly surprising. The water had transformed into a pure, clean, drinkable water that now crystallized into spectacular formations![4] Again, this is how powerful your heart is! The emotions you are transmitting out not only affect your internal well-being, but also the external well-being of the world around you.

BEFORE PRAYER.........AFTER PRAYER

*So, the question is, if over eighty percent of our body is made of water, then what are **our** thoughts doing to our body?*

So, what is your heart transmitting out? Whatever state your life is in right now, is just mirroring what your heart is broadcasting out, internally and externally, into the world.

What determines what your heart is transmitting out?

The state of your relationships. Life is a series of relationships. In this world of duality, we can only define ourselves in relation to something or someone. We are in relationships with people, animals, organizations, and with everything. We define ourselves and our very existence based on our various relationships, and we usually determine our level of happiness based on the state of these relationships.

If I were to ask you, "Who are you?", what would you tell me? Wouldn't you say something like: I am the son or daughter of my parents; I am the mother or father of my child; I am the husband or wife or partner of this person; I am the sister or brother of so and so; I am the friend of that person; I am the employee of this person or company and this is my profession; these are my qualifications and I belong to this organization; and these are my hobbies, etc... Is this not how you would describe yourself?

It is the experiences we have had, since the moment of conception, with all of these various relationships that determine how our hearts feel, what data in our subconscious mind it is processing through, and what it is transmitting out into the world that the world is responding to. **A healed heart that is returned back to its essence is the pathway to transforming your life experience.**

All of our feelings can be divided into two all-encompassing emotions, **Love and Fear**. All of the variations of love, such as joy, gratitude, compassion, excitement and appreciation— expand and create *coherence* in the heart— causing the heart to send out a positive vibration internally and externally. On the other hand, fear-based emotions like anger, worry, sadness, hurt, shame and guilt contract the heart and put it into *incoherence*, causing the heart to send out a negative energy or vibration instead. At any given moment, either the emotion of love or fear is driving your life experience. How much of your time during the day do you spend focusing on all of the things that you are happy and grateful for, and how much of your day do you worry about all of your hurt, anger, problems or fears? Your feelings of love and fear affect each and every cell in your body. It is not so much what you are eating that is affecting your total health and well-being, as it is, *what is emotionally eating you.*

So again, *how is your heart*? Is it filled completely with love or is there some hurt, anger or fear living in there? How are all of your relationships? Do you have some that need some mending? Are there some people in your life that you need to forgive? People you need some forgiveness from? Are there any old friends or family members that you are no longer speaking with? Is there some old hurt or shame that you have been hiding and carrying? What is your heart broadcasting out that the rest of the world is responding to? What is your heart's *electromagnetic signature* in the world?

In the depths of their being, everyone understands that love is the essence of a fulfilling life. This message appears consistently in all of the world's ancient teachings and religions. So why is there so much discord, negativity and pain in human relations? It is so hard to see all of life's wonder when you're wearing glasses tinted by fear, anger and pain.

We could also title this book as, **Heal Your Heart and Transform Your Life.** So this is the journey we are going to take you on...... a journey into your heart— your most powerful and sacred place. Because at the heart of the matter, **it is the heart that matters!** The mind thinks, ***but the heart knows***!

> *"To put the world right in order, we must first put the nation in order;*
> *to put the nation in order, we must first put the family in order;*
> *to put the family in order, we must first cultivate our personal life;*
> *we must first set our hearts right."*
> ~Confucius

So are you ready to ***break free from all of the struggle*** and start living a more joy-filled, magical life? Well let's begin!

Transcend*Transform*Inspire

Chapter Three

So How Was Our Life Created Anyway?

Well, beyond the obvious— that our parents were horny! (Smile.) How does it all work? How are human beings created?

Before we get into the details of *that*, let's talk more about the subconscious mind. The subconscious mind is an astonishingly powerful information processor that will out-compute any supercomputer ever envisioned! It can process over thirty billion pieces of information per second and is over a million times more powerful than our conscious mind. It can record all perceptual experiences and forever play them back at the push of a button. Unfortunately, we normally only become aware that we have these buttons when someone else is pushing them!

The subconscious mind is primarily a recording/playback mechanism. It is like a hard drive that never sleeps, and from the point of conception it is recording everything for later playback. After receiving a repetition of data such as learning a behavior pattern like walking, talking, breathing, running or driving a car, these programs get relegated to the subconscious mind and begin to run automatically. Aren't you glad you don't have to remember how to walk or talk anymore? Luckily, due to its massive processing capability, the subconscious mind can run all of our internal systems and chew gum at the same time, because usually it has to. This is because the conscious mind can process only 2,000 bits of information per second, and it is usually wasting that on either thinking about the past, worrying about the future, or trying to fix some imaginary problem it came up with, so the tasks at present have to be handled by the subconscious mind. Neuroscience has now established that the conscious mind runs the show, at best, only about 5% of the time. Thus, about **95% of our lives**, our actions, decisions, emotions, behaviors and what we draw into our lives **is derived from the playback of the programming of our subconscious mind!**[5] Thus, the outcomes of our lives are predominantly under the control of old, pre-recorded programs that go back in time. And as we will soon discover, **THIS IS THE PROBLEM!**

People often believe that the subconscious mind is just a part of the brain, but that is a false assumption. To better understand how and why the subconscious mind has such a hold on our Being and is predominantly running our lives, is to become aware that as we have developed and grown, the subconscious mind also has become a part of our body. The seat of our subconscious is in the cerebellum part of the brain, but the rest of it has been programmed into the neuro-network and into the cells of our body. Powerful evidence of how these subconscious memories get stored in the cells of our body comes from recipients of donated organs. One conservative, health-conscious transplant patient was astonished when she developed a taste for beer, chicken nuggets and motorcycles after her heart-lung transplant. Her doctor talked to the donor's family and found out she had the heart of an eighteen-year-old motorcycle enthusiast who loved chicken nuggets and beer! Another young girl started having nightmares of being murdered after her heart transplant. Her dreams were so vivid that they actually led to the capture of her donor's killer![6]

With this greater understanding of the integration, vastness and power of the subconscious mind, and the limitations of the conscious mind, let's take a look at how a human being is developed. How each one of us came to be exactly who and where we are in life today.

For the development of a human being, nature increases the subconscious mind's ability to download massive amounts of information, and the fetus is like a sponge picking up and soaking in everything. From 0-2 years of age, our brain activity is mostly in Delta, the lowest EEG frequency range from .5-4Hz. During this time, nutrition is not the only thing a mother provides for the development of her child. The chemistry of the developing fetus is affected by the chemistry of the mother, and from the point of conception, the fetus is also being imprinted with everything the mother thinks, feels, believes and experiences. All of her thoughts, fears, concerns, beliefs, joys, cultural conditioning, ancestral conditioning and excitement get programmed into the neuro-network of her unborn child's body and subconscious mind. So by the time we are born, close to **50% of our personality has already been created**![7]

Let's say a child was not necessarily planned and was instead a product of passion. (Which is actually quite common.) Whatever thoughts, fears and emotions that come up for the mother when she finds out she is pregnant, will just be programmed into the child! So as she thinks about if she wants to be a mom or not, or if she is ready to be a mom or not, all of that gets imprinted into the fetus. When she tells the father, friends and family members about her pregnancy, whatever response she gets from them, and whatever reaction it creates in her will also be programmed into the child. As she thinks about if the father would be a good father or not, or a good husband, and if she wants to marry him or be tied to him forever, all of those thoughts and emotions are impressed upon the infant. And as she begins to consider her options, all of those thoughts, fears and emotions also get imprinted on the child. So, if the mother thinks any thoughts of rejection towards her fetus or about being a mother, the nervous system of the fetus will record those feelings of rejection. **Bruce Lipton**, author of *The Biology of Belief*, shows a video in his programs from the Italian National Association of Pre-natal Education, demonstrating how whatever the mother is experiencing is affecting her unborn child. In this video, you observe what happens to the fetus when the mother and father begin to argue while the mother is hooked up to a sonogram. You can vividly see the fetus jump up and arch its back, as though it is on a trampoline, when the argument is punctuated with the sound of broken glass. This very delicate imprinting time period of the infant includes *whatever happens during the birthing and delivery* process as well, and **how** the child is received once he or she is born. We will go into this some more later, but the key point is that this is such a vital and impressionable time period in the development of a human being!

This gestation time period is where major behaviors and belief systems are created that are **unconsciously driving our lives**, yet we have no conscious awareness of them. For instance, I always had this fear of not wanting to be a burden to anyone, but especially to my father. This fear has driven me for most of my life, and has caused me to be overly independent and very fearful (almost petrified) to ask for any help from anyone. It wasn't until I learned more about how a human is developed and explored a little more about my conception, and my mother's conception, that I discovered where this came from.

You see, I was a product of passion, and when my mother told my father that she was pregnant, she quickly added, "But don't worry, the child and I will be fine on our own and we won't be a burden to you." My father would ask my mother to marry him and she would say, "No, you haven't finished college yet. You need to do that and don't worry about us; we won't be a burden to you." My father proceeded to ask my mother to marry him more than 20 times before she finally believed that he had been in love with her since he was 11 years old and that it was his dream come true to marry her and have a family with her. He grew up telling his little sister that he was going to marry my mom someday! But throughout this process while being in the womb, all my mother's protesting about not being a burden was programmed deeply into my subconscious mind.

And where do you think this big fear got programmed into her? You're exactly right, in the womb! You see, my mother too was a product of passion. My grandfather was a flyboy during World War II, and was taking advantage of the local talent when he got my grandmother pregnant. And in accordance to the culture in 1944, he *'had to do the right thing'* and marry my grandmother, which he did resent and saw as a burden. He was not happy about his new marriage and instant family. He did see my mother as a burden to his life and goals, and this was deeply programmed into her— to the point that my mother chose not to fight for her life because she couldn't be independent, and she couldn't bear the thought of being a burden, of any sort, to her family. This is how deeply programmed this belief was ingrained in her!

Again, gestation is a very critical time of development for a human being, and 98% of the population is not aware of this as they are going through the pregnancy process. It's no-one's fault, this just isn't taught in school, although it really needs to be!

The mother of a friend of mine was born and raised in Vietnam, and through her upbringing and culture, she believed that a man would not want a daughter, only a son; and that he would quite possibly reject her and her child if the baby was a girl. She believed that in order to keep a man, you'd better deliver him a boy. So when my friend was in the womb, her mother was deeply distraught and fearful when she found out she was having a baby girl so she lied to her husband and told him that they were having a son. So, although my friend was very close to her father, she always felt like he was disappointed that she was a girl, so she spent many years of her life rejecting herself as a female and really tried hard to be his little boy!

Can you SEE how things just get passed down from generation to generation, unconsciously? Our basic psychological predispositions are a result of hand-me-down software from our parents who received it from theirs. We **all** have these major beliefs systems that were programmed into us while we were in the womb, and we are not even aware of them because we don't have any cognitive memories associated with them. We are all carrying these invisible garbage bags filled with eons of crap that we are filtering life through, unbeknownst to us! These invisible bags are the toughest to liberate from with the mind and it's a process that really requires Grace.

Again, 50% of our personality is already created by the time we are born. I still remember the moment I had one of the most powerful examples of that for me. A girlfriend of mine was adopted and never knew who her biological parents were until her mother found her at the age of 28. A year later, my girlfriend decided to renew her vows in witness of her biological mother and friends for her 10 year anniversary party. It was a two-day gathering and during this time, we were all shocked to see how much alike she and her biological mother were. I mean, it was like they were matching book ends! They had the same mannerisms and used the same words and gestures, yet they never lived one day of their lives together. They didn't even know each other until a year before. They met once in person and since then had just been getting to know each other over the phone. Wow, so much for our personalities *all* being determined by the environment in which we grew up!!

The birthing/delivery process alone is very traumatic for almost all babies. First, you have the flood of hormones and chemicals that the mother is going through and the fetus then experiences. As the baby grows, it begins to feel crowded, cramped and trapped; no matter what it does it can't escape the enclosing walls. The infant is then turned upside down, and as labor begins, feels all of this contracting and pushing and the mother's fear, pain and screaming. The fetus may experience a feeling of being pushed forward just to then be drawn back; feeling stuck and in oscillation between hope and struggle. An ongoing circle of hope and hopelessness, and a feeling that it is hard to advance and progress.

If there are complications in the delivery, the child could undergo a number of traumatic experiences, such as a sudden tight clamp on their head and being forcefully pulled out; being induced and rapidly being pushed out; or all of a sudden the roof of their once safe and comfortable home being ripped open, only to be confronted suddenly with bright light and strange objects. More trauma awaits after delivery: the baby experiences suddenly being cut off from its life source, strange people with strange masks holding and looking at them, being slapped, suddenly cold and taken away from their mother; and perhaps, if it is a boy, even physically cut.

If there were further complications with the birth, the child could experience not being welcomed into the world by its mother, father and family members but instead, alone and connected to a cold machine. All of these experiences get recorded in our subconscious mind, and later, false belief systems get associated with them. Everything a baby experiences during this birthing process, and during those first few hours in this world, has a huge impact on how accepted, loved and safe the child feels unconsciously, and whether they are programmed with the belief that life is effortless or a struggle.

From the age of 2 through 6, our brain activity primarily operates in Theta (4-8 Hz). These brain frequencies are at a hypnagogic trance state, the same state hypnotists use to directly download new behaviors into the subconscious minds of their clients. So the first 6 years of our development is spent predominantly in a hypnotic trance! These first 6 years are called the **Imprinting Period of Human Development**. The Imprinting Period is the window of development in which children are like sponges, absorbing everything around them, accepting it as true, and recording it in the subconscious mind for later play-back when the data appears to be needed. The conscious mind, the Alpha state, does not engage as a predominant state until after the child is 6 years of age. So our subconscious mind, which is literal in its understanding and just a recording/playback mechanism, is simply being programmed without us having the analytical capability to understand, choose or reject what is being recorded into us! We are simply just being unconsciously programmed like electronic toys.[8]

Perceptions acquired during these imprinting years become the most power-ful, influential and fundamental subconscious programs that shape the charac-ter of an individual's life! Unfortunately, our parents and caregivers are not that conscious or aware that everything they are doing and saying to us, and around us, is being permanently recorded into our *Being,* and having a life-altering impact on us. When a young child is frequently scolded as being *'bad',* or *'can never do anything right',* or *'not deserving'* of something, or *'not good enough',* the child does not comprehend the reprimand as a temporary condition associated with a recent action. Instead, the young, innocent, ego-centric subconscious mind registers these declarations as a permanent condition that defines who and what they are! Such comments are unfortunately recorded into the child's subconscious mind literally, as absolute facts, just like programs that are downloaded onto your hard drive and affect the capabilities of your computer.

Egocentric does not mean selfish; it means that the child takes everything personally. They think that everything that happens around them is because of them. They think "if mom and dad aren't present or are mad, then it must be because of me; I must have done something wrong. I must be bad, something is wrong with me." These misunderstandings get unconsciously programmed into our bodies and mind and express themselves in our lives as limiting and self-sabotaging beliefs. So in a manner of speaking....., parents and care-givers are the family hypnotists and they don't even know it. The things that they say to and around their children, including the messages they send through their own behavior, are like implanting post-hypnotic suggestions into their children's minds. These thoughts will stay with them unconsciously, and affect their potential for life. It is this early lack of discernment from the conscious mind (because it's not yet active and it doesn't have enough data) that creates the mental software that is the foundation of our adult personalities and how we perceive and experience life! If, for any reason, an infant has an experience where they ***don't feel safe***, this fear will be permanently registered into their subconscious mind, and a type of *personality* will start to be created to protect the child. Almost every human being on this planet has had this happen, and we will get into this in more detail throughout the book.

The values and beliefs learned in this imprinting period are deeply ingrained in our subconscious mind and body (in our biology) and are the most difficult to change later in life. For the most part, we have no memories of the beliefs learned during this time period, and they just become a part of our Being, unconsciously driving our lives like the operating system of a computer. They are not even looked at or questioned until some event causes us to do some deeper inner work. For example, take my mother's and my vast unconscious drive *not to be a burden*— this program drove my mother's life, unconsciously, until her death; and it drove me until I fell to my knees helplessly in existential suffering. According to sociologist Morris Massey, 90% of our belief systems are integrated into our body's neuro-network, our subconscious mind, by the time we are ten![9]

Our lives then become just like that of a captive elephant that was once tied up to a stake as a baby and learned that it couldn't move away from the stake when it would try, so it created a wrong belief that it was destined to be tied up and couldn't do anything about it. That it was forever stuck no matter how big and strong it grew. After a long time of trying and not being able to break free, the elephant created a belief system that shaped its life forever, and it never challenged that belief system as it grew and got older! After a certain number of years of this programming, trainers no longer need to tie the elephant up to something; they simply just need to have a rope around its ankle, and the elephant thinks it can't move away from that space.

The same is true for us. We all have these programmed beliefs running our lives, that were programmed into us as an unaware child, that we never examined or challenged with our more mature and evolved mind. Often times, we don't question our beliefs until something happens in our life that guides us to a program like this, that then leads us into deeper introspection. So another way you can think of your subconscious mind is like that of a computer hard drive that has an old, outdated, inefficient Operating System that needs to be erased and replaced with a new, more powerful one, with updated intelligence. So its time to look within and upgrade your OS — you have been running your life from an inefficient, outdated and ancient system!

The Jesuits, from the time of the Bible, were very aware of these impression-able years and would say, "Give me the child until it is seven and I will give you the man." They knew whatever was programmed into the child's subcon-scious mind in these first few years would inevitably influence most of their behavior for the rest of their lives!

So, for the development of a human being to live and operate in the environ-ment in which they are about to be born into, nature prepares the child by downloading massive amounts of information from its parents' genetics and from the society and culture they are living in. All of this coding is loaded into the child's subconscious mind for future playback when the information is needed. The subconscious mind is just storing this information until it can be used or processed by the conscious mind— when the Alpha and Beta waves actually become active in the child. It's just like a cow that quickly swallows its food and stores it in its first stomach until it has time to properly process the food, or its *cud.* After birth, if the biological parents are both present in the child's life, they will typically perpetuate the pre-conditioning received during gestation.

After the age of six, when the Alpha brainwaves become more fully functioning, the conscious mind begins to process its experiences through the programming or *charges* (the *cud*) that were recorded since the point of conception, and it comes up with answers or belief systems based on the input from this innocent, undeveloped child's mind. It can do nothing else, for it cannot operate from a blank slate. It can only analyze information and come up with decisions based on what data is stored in the subconscious mind. The mind *begins* to form these decisions and belief systems once the Alpha state *starts* to become active, normally somewhere around the age of four. That is why most of us don't have any memories until we are about the age of four. The earliest memories you have are indications of when your Alpha state became more active.

So this is the time when many of our belief systems, which are unconsciously driving our lives today, began to form. We made these decisions from experiences we had that created emotional highs and emotional lows through the eyes and the understanding of our naive and undeveloped, childhood minds. If we experienced any form of emotional deprivation or trauma as children, we may have acquired feelings of rejection, abandonment, feeling unloved, unimportant and unworthy, and our emotional growth may have been stunted. This is called *arrested development*, and these childish patterns will remain with us as we grow into adults, until this inner child has been healed.

This *arrested development* and these feelings of rejection and abandonment are quite prevalent in children. They can be due to actual extreme emotional deprivation or abusive behavior of a parent **or from something quite innocent a parent did in the child's development.** For example, I spent most of my life afraid of rejection, or feeling like I was always being rejected, just because a scared 21-year-old woman starting off her life as an adult found herself unexpectedly pregnant with me innocently said, *"that she and I would not be a burden to my father."* My mother was frightened; she loved my father and she was just being loving and thoughtful towards him— but that is not how it got recorded or imprinted into my undeveloped, infantile subconscious mind. The same incorrect feeling of rejection could be felt by a child whose parent was hoping for a little boy and was blessed with a little girl instead. A young man I know felt extremely rejected and abandoned when, at 6 months, his mother abruptly stopped breast feeding him because she learned she had breast cancer and had to immediately go into the hospital to have a double mastectomy. She didn't really reject him, or abandon him at all, but that is how an undeveloped egocentric infant interprets why mommy suddenly is not there with him for a while, and never connectedly feeds him the same way again.

Because everything is made of energy, we call the unconscious generational programming we received, and all of these beliefs we created from the experiences we have had during our *imprinting years* and thereafter, **charges** (our *cud*). A **charge** is *unprocessed energy that has been stored and stuck* in our body and subconscious mind. These *charges* are the data the conscious mind is processing through, and what the heart is broadcasting out to the world! We think we are running our lives, but truly, **these *charges* are determining our life experience**. Kind of like Candida— we think it is *us* having these urges for sugar, but truly it is the Candida that is driving our sweet tooth or making us crave carbohydrates, because it needs the sugar for its own survival.

So how do these charges continuously control us even though we get bigger, stronger and smarter like the elephant?

The subconscious mind is a recording playback/mechanism and it is always recording information that comes to it that *can't* be presently managed by the conscious mind. The subconscious stores it and waits for the opportunity to present it for processing when the conscious mind is able— like a cow does with its *cud*. As we shared earlier, this is automatically happening until the Alpha state is more fully engaged (around the age of 6-7), but it is also happening later in life all the time when the limited conscious mind is busy doing something else or when a situation is too painful for the conscious mind to handle.

The part of the conscious mind that was developed to keep us safe, the *ego/intellect*, does this to protect us, and so it has developed a myriad of ways to avoid pain. In reality, the subconscious mind is a large database of stored programs whose function is strictly concerned with reading both internal and external environmental signals, and engaging the matching stored program to handle them. Whenever something similar to a stored *charge* shows up in our environment, it triggers back up these old memories and emotions from the subconscious mind (*our cud*), to the forefront of our conscious mind to be processed. Just like a juke box that plays a song when the associated button for it is pushed. But because the conscious mind is designed to avoid pain and gain pleasure, it will normally try to use one of its myriad of tricks to distract us and push the *charge* back down immediately, so as to not deal with it. This is how these programmed, unprocessed *charges,* collected by an innocent child's mind, stay stuck inside us for years, unconsciously driving our lives! The conscious mind is not doing this out of maliciousness; it is more like a well-meaning but misguided friend who is just trying to help or protect you.

The good news is that subconscious programs are not fixed or unchangeable. We do have the ability to be liberated from our programming and by doing so, we can take back more control over our life experience and *transform* the way our lives unfold. Our subconscious minds have been allowed to stay in this state of recycled mayhem because of a lack of knowledge. But now that **you** are **more aware**, let's begin to *transcend* this dis-order! We must start by doing a little digging into our family history, and into the depths of our subconscious mind!

Transcend*Transform*Inspire

Inner View

Now that you have a greater understanding of how a human being is developed—how 50% of our personality is already created by the time we are born; how whatever our mother and parents were going through while we were in the womb was just getting programmed into us, passed down from generation to generation— it's time to do a little external investigation of what may have been imprinted on you, and what may be unconsciously driving your life. So pull out your journal you have dedicated to this process and let's do a little mining for what may be lurking in your subconscious mind.

If your parents are alive, go ask them about how they met, how their courtship and relationship was, and how things were going for them when you were conceived. Were they married when you were conceived? Were you planned, or a surprise? How did your mom feel when she found out she was pregnant with you? How did your dad feel? What was his response when she told him? How did your mom feel about being a parent with your dad? How did your mom feel about being a mom in that moment? Did she feel ready or was she feeling afraid? What was her family's response when she told them? What was your father's family's response? What was the culture like then? What was your parents' relationship like while you were in the womb? How was their life at the time—happy and joyful, or fearful and stressful?

How was your mother's childhood? How was her relationship with her parents, grandparents, siblings and other family members? How about your father's child-hood? What are some of the belief systems they grew up with because of their childhoods? Because of their culture at the time? What was your grandparents' childhood like on both sides, and how did that affect how they interacted with your mother or father?

How was it when you were finally born? How did your delivery go; what did your mom experience? Did it go smoothly or were there complications? Was it a natural childbirth or did they have to induce, use forceps, or perform a c-section? Did your mom get to hold you right away– or were you put into some kind of incubator? What were your first few hours like, after delivery?

What was life like for your parents after they brought you home? What was life like for your family during your first three years? I am sure that, like most of us, you don't remember anything from that time. What is your earliest memory, and how old were you? What was life like for you from the time you start to have memories? What was life like with your mother? Your father? With them together? What were some of the things they would say to you? What was life like with your siblings if you had any— or if you didn't, how did you feel about that? How about with your grandparents on both sides? Did you feel loved, appreciated and taken care of? How about with your aunts and uncles? How were things between you and your cousins?

These are all of the questions you are going to want answers to, to better understand what has been programmed into your subconscious mind and what has been unconsciously driving your life. If your parents aren't around, then ask other family members and perhaps family friends who were around during those years. I wish I had asked my mother more about her life and about my conception and birth before she died, but I didn't have this awareness then. I had to ask my father, my aunts and my grandfather to figure it all out. This awareness has freed me from years of inner conflict, pain and confusion. It was so liberating to learn that so many beliefs and feelings I carried were not even real, and not even mine! I learned that these things were just programs downloaded to me, or things that I had learned or picked up from my family or from society around me. Or, they were beliefs and strategies I created, from an unaware child's mind, in response to my family's behavior.

Capture what you discover here, or in your journal.

....

....

....

....

....

....

....

....

....

....

....

....

....

....

Chapter Four

Why Our Life Has Been Unfolding As It Has

So why is your life the way it is today; and why has it unfolded as it has? Why do we all have these *patterns* that keep showing up in our lives, over and over again, with just a different name, a different face and at a different time period? Why do we all have these *obstacles* that we just can't seem to get around to reach one of our life goals, no matter how hard we try?

The answer to this question is a ***universal physical law that*** governs our world, just like the Law of Gravity and the Law of Buoyancy. And that is, the **Law of Reflection**. This is the same law that some of us might have learned from Christianity referred to as *Sowing and Reaping* and it is very tied to the scientific law we know as *Cause and Effect*.

So do you believe in the Law of Gravity? Are you glad you didn't float away when you got out of bed this morning? Yes? Well, we have the Law of Gravity to thank for that. It is a useful law. But does the Law of Gravity care if you know about it and how it works? No. It just keeps doing what it does, whether you understand it or not, right? It is just a physical universal law that drives and affects our world. The ***Law of Reflection*** is one of those same universal laws driving and affecting our lives, whether or not we are aware of it, or if we understand it or not! But as with gravity, it really helps to understand it so that we can work *with it* to more powerfully create our life experience, instead of allowing it to continue to unwarely drive our lives.[10]

So, have you heard about the Law of Attraction? Since the movie **The Secret** came out, many people have become aware of the Law of Attraction. But there has been a lot of misunderstanding about how it really works and thus, a lot of frustration with it.

The Law of Attraction and the *Law of Reflection* are the **same** universal law. But understanding the *Law of Reflection* will help you better understand how the Law of Attraction **really** works, so that you can now apply it appropriately!

The laws of the universe merely describe the way things are. These laws aren't invented; they're discovered. They are not dependent on our knowledge, nor our faith. You don't exactly have faith in the Law of Gravity, as much as you just **know that it is** and you live your life accordingly. Just as we respect the laws of nature for our own good and survival, we live our lives by these laws, not because we have to, but because we are aware of them and *know that it is in our best interest to do so*. The same goes for the *Law of Reflection* once you really understand it.

The Law of Reflection is this: *the outside world is merely a reflection of your inside world.* Mirroring back to you what is inside of you, just like an echo. So when you yell out into a canyon, the canyon just reverberates back to you what you just transmitted out. Everything is made of energy, made of the same subatomic particles, so we are all transmitting out a frequency or a vibration through our very powerful heart based on our subconscious programming, like a radio station that is attracting like vibrations.

The world is just reflecting back to you what you are transmitting out, consciously or unconsciously. But **what you are mostly transmitting out is unconscious**, because of how we are developed as a human being and how our subconscious minds are programmed unknowingly as children in our Imprinting Years. So right now **about 95% of your life is being driven by the programmed subconscious mind** and only 5% of your life is being driven by your conscious mind![11] How scary is that?! And we think we are so in control!

> *The Law Of Attraction is this......*
> *You don't attract what you want.*
> *You attract what You Are!*
>
> ~Dr. Wayne Dyer

So however your life is right now, it is just a reflection of what is inside of your subconscious mind. It is a photocopy. Whatever you are attracting in your life, whatever patterns keep showing up, are just reflections of your hurts, wounds and belief systems (your *charges*) that were programmed into you from the time you were conceived. How you are seeing the world, or perceiving the world, and how you *judge* or perceive others **is just a reflection of what is inside of you**. Always try to remember: when you are pointing a finger at someone else, there are three other fingers pointing back at you! How you react to others, and what you expect and the actions you take, are all just reflections of your hurts and your belief systems. Your experience of life in general, your suffering, your pain and your reality, is just a reflection or a **re-production** of what is stored deep inside of you that needs to be *seen* first, and then *allowed* to express itself so it can be healed.

The mirror is impartial to what is being transmitted out. It doesn't care if it's negative or positive — it doesn't have that human construct. It just reflects back to you whatever you're vibrating or broadcasting out like a radio station.

The truth is, reality is different for each individual. If there are 7 billion people in the world, then there would be 7 billion different perceptions of the same event. This is because each one of us has had our own upbringing with varied genealogy, cultures and experiences that created different *charges* and belief systems within us. The mind then filters through all this data to come up with a meaning about what it is experiencing through the senses. Each one of us perceives the world through this *colored lens*, and then *projects* onto the world whatever story our mind comes up with. Our perceptions then affect us biologically as the mind sends out a flood of hormones and chemicals into our bodies, such as dopamine, serotonin, adrenaline, cortisol, oxytocin, norepinephrine, histamine and cytokines, to name a few. These chemicals affect our cells within milliseconds; and filled with these chemicals, we become biologically even more certain that our story is absolutely true— and the body reacts accordingly.

As the mind is processing stimuli, it brings back memories, feelings and stories that have been stored in the subconscious mind, to now process the *cud*. But instead of processing the *cud*, we see the event through **our lens** and get emotionally caught up in the story and the blame game and react, validating the story and making the *charge* even larger. Now the *charge* has an even greater vibration, and we attract from it all the more. And again, perceiving the world through it, we project it onto others and react from it all the more! All of us have these unwitting, disempowering and untrue belief systems that were created in childhood, stored up in our subconscious mind that are running our life experience and determining **our** version of reality.

We live in a magnetic universe. Perhaps you recall an elementary school experiment that involved a magnet, a piece of paper and some iron fillings. When you placed the magnet beneath the paper with the iron fillings, they would arrange themselves in a defined pattern that reflected how you were moving the magnet around, in accordance with the invisible magnetic field. The same concept applies to your life. When you have internal conflict or a *charge* (as we all do), you attract to yourself the like negative energies out in the world, because your internal state (what you are vibrating out) is like a magnet.

So, if while growing up, you felt hurt, disrespected or rejected, you would very naturally attract people who would further hurt you, disrespect you and reject you. At least you would *perceive* and experience their actions that way. If instead you grew up feeling very loved, pampered, taken care of and respected, you would attract greater prosperity, more nurturing relationships, and people who respect you, who are kind to you and honor you for who you are. *As your state is, what you are vibrating out, so will you attract.* And like the childhood magnet experiments, just because you can't see a magnetic field doesn't mean that it is not working all the same. On the same note, just because you don't see the radio waves passing by you, doesn't mean you can't hear their music when your radio dial is tuned to their frequency!

For instance, my father would get drunk when I was young and would accuse me of doing things I didn't do. When I would tell him I didn't do whatever he was accusing me of, he would say I was lying and hit me. The more I denied it, the more he would hit me. I would then run to my mother to try and get her to protect me, and she would just say, "You know better than to argue with a drunk." So based on this, I created the wrong belief that "*I am not good enough to be loved.*" Because "how could I be good enough to be loved if my father would accuse me of such things, won't believe me and hits me, and if my mother won't even protect me," I thought from a naïve, egocentric child's mind. Around that same time period, I also developed another very disempowering belief system that has driven my *perception* of life for many years. You see, I was the first grandchild of the family, and at first I was the apple of my grandmother's eye. That is until my little cousin Kim was born. After that, my grandmother would say to me, "Why can't you be more like Kim? She's so sweet and you're just a little brat!" Well, from this I created the wrong belief that, "I'm not only not good enough to be loved, but *I am not even good enough to be liked!*" Growing up, I really felt rejected, unliked and unloved. So much so, that I would say it to my mother and she would just tease me and say, "Oh, poor me," and sing me a silly song, "Nobody likes me, nobody loves me, I think I will go out and eat some worms." She sang that song to me so many times, I think it became my childhood mantra! So these two wrong beliefs have driven a lot of my life experience and the *patterns* that would show up in my life. I would always attract men who would validate that *frequency* or story, of *not being good enough to be loved*, over and over again! Or I would at least interpret this as the reason behind their behavior, and I would react from that feeling and of course, always make things worse. Or if someone didn't call or email me back right away, I would deduce that *they didn't like me and that they were rejecting me*. I would think, "Oh it must be me, I must have done something wrong — they're mad at me," and busily try to fix it. And again, I always made it worse by believing my mind's story and reacting to it as if it were true. Oftentimes, I created what we have termed as a *self-fulfilling prophecy.*

Before I would even meet someone, I would have this thought that *'people don't like me'* in my head, so I would act uncomfortable as I was talking with them. They would sense this *vibration,* and it would in turn make them feel uncomfortable around me, and they would move away. Of course, that would validate my wrong conviction (and *charge*) even more so, causing me to project this belief onto my life experience all the more....... causing me to always say what?

Yep, you got it! "*Why does this always happen to me?*" or "*I knew that was going to happen!*"

The biggest example of mirroring back the childhood experience that I referred to above happened after my mother died. At this time, I was brought to my knees, and my conscious mind could no longer fool me into thinking that I'd done all of my work and I had it all figured out. During this time period, the hurt little girl who lost her mommy had taken over, and big Brandy, who thought she had it all figured out, was nowhere to be found. I was in so much pain that I was just trying to distract myself and fill the void, and that is when I attracted the perfect mirror for my childhood wounds.

After the honeymoon period was over, I soon discovered that my boyfriend, whom I attracted after my mother's death, was both controlling and verbally abusive. Quickly, after not standing up for myself, the verbal abuse turned physical. The more I would take the high road and try to talk him out of his perception and anger, the more violent he would become. When I finally hit my breaking point and decided it was time to leave, I knew I would need support because of the weak state I was in, so I turned to my friends. I shared with them what had been happening between my boyfriend and me, and asked for their help and support. The shocking response that I got back from them was their turning their backs on me, saying, "What must you think of yourself to stay in a relationship like that? You should know better." And they refused to help.

Does any of that sound familiar? A perfect mirror to my two biggest childhood wounds! And the perfect opening to heal them. Of course, I didn't have this *awareness* at the time, and I just stayed in the victim consciousness, giving it an opportunity to recycle back into my life, for processing at a later time.

I still remember the day that this understanding became so very clear to me — *that the outside world is just a reflection of the inside world.* By this time I had done a lot of clearing of this programming, and I was in a really great state. I felt so much love inside of myself, that wherever I was, there was love. I felt complete happiness, joy, gratitude and bliss, and the outside world was reflecting this back to me big time. And I was traveling in India, where that is not normally the westerner's experience. I mean, people were going way out of their way to help me, take care of me and protect me. I would just think about needing something and the next thing I knew—someone was right there offering it to me. With each moment and each event, I would feel and experience more and even more gratitude. And of course with each positive broadcast I was transmitting out, the more blessings I would receive. Life in that time period was grand! I only saw beauty all around me. Everything was vibrant and gorgeous. Until one moment...... on one day.... I had an experience in Mumbai....... with the owner of an Internet Cafe.

Now, I don't know the source of what we were mirroring back to each other. All I know is things turned ugly quickly, and we were soon yelling and screaming at one another. I said a few choice words, grabbed my stuff and left his shop steaming. As soon as I walked out the door, a man across the street bee-lined straight for me and started saying the rudest, crudest, unkind things to me I have ever heard! I kept switching directions trying to get away from him, and he would just stick to me like glue, repeating himself over and over again. To escape him, I finally had to return back to my hotel and lock myself in my hotel room. And it was then I saw how quickly the Universe responds and mirrors back our *frequency*, sending us the like vibration as an opportunity to balance it out!

Our relationships in life replicate our relationships from childhood.
Hurt begets more hurt, fear begets more fear
and love begets more love.

Let us say you had a very angry, controlling and authoritative father growing up that put fear into you. As you grew up and got older, you would most likely attract many other people who were angry, authoritative, controlling and who would tend to make you feel fearful. The experience *continually replicates* itself (pattern) in an attempt to process it and heal the *charge*.

For example, there was a client who was very unhappy with the way her life was unfolding because it seemed she could never settle down in a relationship with a man whom she respected. Most of her relationships would last only 3-6 months before they would break up. She was beautiful, successful, and could be very thoughtful and kind. She appeared to be what many men would look for; still she could never keep a sustaining relationship with any man. While working with her, it was discovered that the trouble began in her relationship with her mother. During her childhood, she would watch her mother be very dominating, volatile, and angry towards her father. Observing this for years, she became very angry with her father as well, because he would never stand up for himself. She was also very angry with her mother for always being disruptive and for treating her father the way that she did. She never addressed her feelings though, and carried this upset with her throughout her life. Since she never healed the hurt and anger she had with both of her parents, the Universe kept bringing her opportunities to do so. But instead of utilizing the opportunity to heal, she would very unconsciously repeat her mother's behavior with the men she was attracting in her life. (Men with similar energy traits to her father, being softer and meek, and who wouldn't stand up for themselves against her.) Through this repeated *pattern*, she was unconsciously trying to get her father to stand up to her mother, so she could respect him and trust him to take care of her and protect her.

Another client came to me after the 14th girlfriend in a row dramatically left him. When we dug deeper into his childhood, we discovered the source of this *pattern*. When he was just about a year old, his mother fell madly in love with a sailor, and left him with his grandparents to follow this sailor, never to be seen again until he was an adult! This dramatic wound kept boomeranging back to him, trying to be healed, reflected by each of these women.

A friend of mine was routinely molested as a child by her baby sitter, who was an older man. She never told her family about what happened and she has never tried to heal the *charge*; she just tries to forget about it and shoves it down whenever the memory comes back. Which it often does, because older men are always attracted to her and aggressively hit on her right away, constantly bringing up this childhood *charge* over and over again.

Another friend of mine had a very traumatic experience when he was just four years old. He witnessed his babysitter Betty, whom he snuggled with, spent a lot of time with and who was more like a mother to him, get shot in the head several times by a gunman until she dropped dead right in front of his eyes. They were merely waiting in line to purchase a lotto ticket when Betty's boyfriend walked up to them and asked her for money. When she said no, he persisted in asking her more aggressively. When she finally got fed up and shouted at him "Noooooooooooo!", he pulled out his gun and shot her in the head until there were no more bullets in his gun. The boyfriend then grabbed his hand and calmly walked him home and asked him if he was okay. He was in such shock and in a daze that he just calmly answered that he was fine. His mother would not let him speak about it at all to anyone, and they quickly moved many states away. The incident was just shoved under the carpet, never to be talked about or really thought about again. But without his conscious awareness, the *charges* surrounding it had been driving so many parts of his life, until we did some deep inner mining.

The event drew two *patterns* in his life. The first one started from the time he was seven years old, when someone broke the door down and shot his father in the hip, grabbed the items they wanted and calmly left. From that point on, other people's near death experiences happened all around him, all the time, in which he would calmly manage the situation and not get reactive or fearful at all. The second *pattern* was that he became drawn to, and would attract, women who would remind him of his babysitter Betty— full-figured women who had some self-love and confidence issues. He would tend to feel the same kind of maternal love and affection for them that he had for Betty, and he would find himself always trying to help them feel better about themselves. When he got older, he became a fitness trainer and would attract all kinds of Betty's to his gym. The entire time, he wasn't sure why he had become a fitness coach, because he really didn't have a passion for fitness— it was more about helping the women feel better about themselves and fixing the *cause* for their weight and health challenges, not just the symptoms. As we dug deeper, he realized what he had *really* been doing unconsciously all of this time was trying to save Betty! And in a way, bring her back to him — the woman he loved like a mother as a young boy, who was tragically and suddenly taken away from him because of the man she chose to be with, due to her low self-love and esteem issues.

I'm sure you've had the experience of meeting somebody for the first time and instantly liking them and feeling comfortable with that person. The two of you just 'connected' and you both felt as though you'd known each other forever. You were just attracted to each other's energy for some reason. And as much as you were drawn to those people instantly, you have been equally repelled by others. You can't put your finger on it, but there was just something you didn't like about them. Beyond physical appearances, something else energetically, *vibrationally*, is going on. We are all naturally attracted to some people and repelled by others; and while there's nothing tangible to base our like or dislike on, we resonate with some people, and with others we just don't. A few people put out such a 'bad vibe' for us that we can't get away from them fast enough. But others might think that same person is one of their favorite people in the whole world! The Law of Attraction/Reflection says: *That which is like unto itself is drawn.* We are all just mirroring each other's *charges* or energy. Some we match up well with and with some we just don't— the energies actually repel one another. Yet many times, we actually are matching up with people we don't feel like we match with — they are the perfect mirror to our wound, so that it can be healed. To transform your life, you must begin to **know yourself** and others **as a center of energy** living amidst a much vaster, all-encompassing field of energy. When you do, it means you will be able to purposefully raise your own personal energy field to one that matches the actual life experience you would truly like to have, and free yourself from the energy that doesn't!

> *"The day science begins to study non-physical phenomena,*
> *it will make more progress in one decade than in all the previous centuries*
> *of its existence. To understand the true nature of the universe,*
> *one must think it terms of energy, frequency and vibration."*
>
> ~ Nicola Tesla

Our *patterns* will keep showing up in our lives, over and over again, until we heal the charge. The *charges* will continue to live in us, and through us, like a virus, until we acknowledge them and allow them to be fully processed and expressed. They are just energy, and energy is designed to move. There is nothing wrong with you just because you catch a cold— but you do have to do something to free yourself from the virus, so that it doesn't continue to cause havoc in your life. Programs/charges are just like that: we all catch them, and now we have to take the steps to free ourselves, so they can't take over and cause mayhem in our lives.

The Human Condition

You don't really have a weight problem, a drinking problem or another addiction problem. These are just results of the problem. **What you really have is a story problem,** created by the unconscious programming of a young and undeveloped mind. Many times the story problem is exacerbated by conflicting *messages* we received in our programming. For example, you could have been told how great you are and that you can accomplish anything by your parents, on one side of the coin. Yet on the other side of the coin your catholic school teachers may have told you that "we are nothing but sinners and that money is the root of all evil." These conflicting messages could certainly cause a lot of internal confusion and conflict in your professional and financial success.

After many years of our brains retelling the same stories, creating the same thoughts, like sadness or anger, and releasing the same chemicals or peptides, our cells have become addicted to these emotions. Just like they can get addicted to sugar, alcohol or caffeine, they start calling out for their fix, causing the brain to start having thoughts that would create that emotion and send out those chemicals into the body. Of course, we always think that these thoughts and those emotions are us, but really it is just a patterned chemical addiction your cells now have (similar to the Candida calling out for its sugar fix — and you think it is you having that urge). Have you ever been typing along on your laptop, and all of a sudden your computer starts running automatic programs or updates that you can't stop or have any control over? Yeah, it's kind of like that. We just need to program new stories into our subconscious mind that will give us better chemical addictions in our body like those of self-love, gratitude and joy!

Because of childhood trauma and what has been passed down in society since the beginning of time, we are secretly scared— and this fear (**f**alse **e**vidence **a**ppearing **r**eal) has been unconsciously driving our lives. We have been conditioned to see the world the way our family and others were programmed to see it; and as we learned these things, we began to experience them and took them on as our personal truths. We have been conditioned with thoughts of competition, struggle, sickness, guilt, limitation, being a sinner, being bad, scarcity, the constant fear of loss of our connections and being alone. We were taught that we are separate from others, that we have to compete to get ahead, and that we're not quite good enough just the way we are, so we have to keep on striving to have and be more. Or we have been told that we are too much of something and that we have to tone ourselves down or suffer the loss of approval and connection. We are afraid that it isn't the right relationship, or we're afraid that it is. We are afraid they won't like us, or we're afraid that they will. We are afraid of failure, or we're afraid of success. We are afraid of dying young, or we're afraid of growing old. We have all kinds of various conflicting internal thoughts, and we're just plain afraid!

Listen to the lyrics of this popular song of 1979- The Rose:

www.HealYourHeartFreeYourMind.com/rose

We're always seeking ways out of this fear and pain, either through growth or through escape. Through escape there are many things we might do to sabotage our careers, our relationships and even our life. We might drink, smoke, take some kind of drug, overeat, hide, obsess, get angry, control and manipulate, avoid and attack, co-depend, or take on some other addiction — but somehow, express the fear, we will. All of that emotional energy, that we have just been avoiding, distracting and numbing ourselves from, has to go somewhere. Turned inward, this fear and anger can become addiction, obsession, compulsion, abusive relationships, depression or even illness. But it's ALL just **dis-ease**. It's irrelevant what form the dysfunction manifests itself in. We are just trying to stop the hurt and band-aid the fear. Through growth it's — maybe this degree will do it, or this job, this seminar, this diet, this therapist, this relationship, this project, buying this item or this distraction. But too often the medicine falls short of a cure, and the chains just keep getting thicker, heavier and tighter. And the same soap operas (the *patterns*) continue to unfold, with different people, at different times, playing different roles.

It's kind of like how mice self-volunteer for their own destruction by giving into their temptation for some cheese from a fear of lack. They wrongly think, "These people really like me and want to help me and give me some free food." Or, like fish who are always going after pretty shining objects, just reacting from this place of lack and not really thinking it through, to their own demise. But of course, it's only creatures from the rat and fish family who volunteer for their own destruction, from this not thought out perception of lack!

The Human Condition in Greater Detail

Because of the automatic subconscious programming, the **Human Condition** is a world filled with humans with both a mental virus and a skin disease. Humans are born with wounds all over their bodies, caused by this mental virus they inherited from their ancestors. At first they don't know that they have these wounds, because the virus is just living underneath the skin, dormant. But as each human grows up, these wounds begin to rise and show themselves on the skin's surface, and playing with others and experiencing life becomes more and more painful. The more they interact with the world, the more wounds rise above the skin and the more painful it gets, so they try to figure out ways to protect themselves from people hitting their wounds or from giving them new ones. When, as adults, they go out into the world, they find that these wounds get bumped and infected, and they pick up even more sores. Soon they are afraid to get too close to anyone, and terrified that they will experience greater pain. They put up protective shields, ensuring that no one can get too close to their wounds. Yet they feel so alone, and have such a strong desire to be near others, so they try to figure out safe ways to be connected— but not too close, so as not to infect one of their wounds. Feeling this strong desire for love and connection, yet also this great fear and pain, causes so much internal conflict. People try so many different ways to numb the pain or try to make these sores go away so that they can feel close or connected to others in some way. But each attempt lasts only for so long, and the pain and infection come back, even greater. They keep looking for new solutions and say to themselves, "Maybe this will work— or maybe that." And with each new "solution" they try just leads to another disappointment, another wound, and more pain. Each time they hit someone's wound or someone hits theirs, infection spews out from one to the other. This is the **Human Condition;** it is like a plague, a mental virus that creates sores that just gets passed down from generation to generation without a clear description of the illness or how to cure it. So instead, we just try to manage the symptoms and protect ourselves from further infection— or try to numb ourselves from feeling the pain.

That is, **until now!** This book is *the cure*. It gives you a clear understanding of the illness and how to free yourself from it! My live programs will lovingly take you through it, to the other side where your internal peace resides.

Your life, however it is right now, is just a **printout** of your subconscious mind's programming that you have picked up from the point of conception, and over the years. You have been painfully experiencing the **Human Condition** and life within *The Matrix*.[12] And it's now time to take the *Red Pill* and get out of this program! To liberate ourselves from it, we have to **uninstall** the current Operating System and **re-install a new OS,** a *new awareness*! Because if you put in the same *input*, you will continue to get the same *output.* How could it be any different?

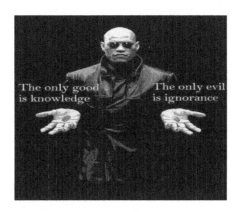

How exciting! You're about to upgrade your Operating System! You're about to free yourself from *The Matrix* and the **Human Condition**! Let's begin the journey to *transcending* all of this *cud* now!

To better understand what we have been talking about, see this clip from the movie, "**What the Bleep Do We Know Anyway**":

www.HealYourHeartFreeYourMind.com/bleep1

Transcend*Transform*Inspire

Inner View

So what are some of the patterns you have in your life that keep showing up with just a different name and a different face? What childhood wound is that mirroring for you that still needs to be acknowledged and healed?

....

....

....

....

....

....

....

....

....

....

....

....

....

....

....

....

....

....

....

....

....

....

Chapter Five

The Power of Your Mind
~*Free it and make it your slave, not your master*~

We've already learned about how powerful our hearts are, and we have been learning how powerful the subconscious mind is in affecting our reality and how it has become our master. Our hearts and minds go hand in hand to create our life experience. The brain is like a bio-computer that manufactures, literally chemically, whatever we feed into it with our thoughts. Think thoughts of success and you will achieve them, expect to fail and you will. Whether you think you can, or if you think you can't, either way you're usually right! Thoughts of fear living in your subconscious mind produce more fear in your body and in your life. Thoughts of love in your subconscious mind produce more feelings of love in your body and in your life. Healing our hearts, our wounds and the limiting beliefs in our subconscious programming will give us a *shift* in how we think, how we feel in our body and thus, what we attract and how we experience life!

The human mind, both the conscious and the subconscious, is a wondrous and powerful tool that will allow you to create and attract to yourself the circumstances and conditions that you most desire to have in your life. With the correct understanding of how each part of the mind functions, and how these two aspects of mind are used purposefully and with *awareness*, you can learn to use them together to produce results that can seem miraculous. Most of us know this power from our conscious mind— as a thinking man. All material things that man has created with his hands first had to exist in his thoughts. And so far, most people have confined the creation of these thought forms to manually making them with their hands and labor. For the most part, man has not yet realized that he can cause the creation of new outcomes and change matter by the way he **consciously** impresses his thoughts and vibration on the invisible— on the energy or subatomic particles that all matter is made of. Just like Dr. Emoto showed us with his landmark study on water. When we fully understand and apply these truths, we will return our mind back to the powerful slave to us that it was designed to be, and it will no longer be our master.

The mind is a powerful force.
It can enslave us Or empower us.
It can plunge us into the depths of misery Or
take us to the heights of ecstasy.
Learn to use the power wisely.

~ David Cuschieri

The Placebo Effect

The *Placebo Effect* is a potent example of how powerful the conscious and subconscious minds really are together in transforming our life experience. Placebos are used in clinical drug trials to prove the effectiveness of a drug for the FDA's approval. In these double-blind studies (neither the patient nor the doctor knows whether it is a real drug or a placebo), a drug must outperform a placebo in two trials before it can be approved. Placebos are not just sugar pills; they can be delivered in a myriad of ways.

The roots of the placebo can be traced back to a lie told by an Army nurse during World War II, as Allied forces stormed the beaches of southern Italy. The nurse was assisting an anesthetist named Henry Beecher, who was tending to US troops under heavy German bombardment. When the morphine supply ran low, the nurse assured a wounded soldier that he was getting a shot of potent painkiller, although her syringe contained only salt water. Amazingly, the bogus injection relieved the soldier's agony and prevented the onset of shock; his conscious mind believed what she had told him, and his subconscious mind responded accordingly. After returning to his post at Harvard after the war, Dr. Beecher became one of the nation's leading medical reformers by publishing a paper titled ***The Powerful Placebo.***

Placebos tend to work on 1 out of every 3 patients, and their effectiveness tends to depend on how much the individual believes and trusts in the doctor, the drug or the procedure. Oftentimes, the placebos actually have better results than the drug/procedure they are tested against. This is definitely the case in the treatment of depression. So much so that psychiatrist Walter Brown, of the Brown University School of Medicine, has proposed placebo pills as the first treatment for patients with mild or moderate depression. The studies show that in **more than half** of the clinical trials for the *six leading* antidepressants, the drugs **did not outperform the placebo**! Mrs. Schonfeld, who took part in a clinical trial to test the efficacy of the antidepressant drug Effexor in 1997, was absolutely shocked when she found out that she had been on a placebo. Not only had the pills relieved her of the depression that had plagued her for over thirty years, but the brain scans she received through out the study found that the activity of her prefrontal cortex was also greatly enhanced![13]

Amazing results occur with the *Placebo Effect* even with supposed surgery. In a clinical test in Houston Texas, people who thought they had knee surgery (they were given anesthesia and doctors made incisions around the knee so that it looked as though they did), reported the same pain relief and increased mobility as the ones who had the actual surgery! In fact, a television news show graphically demonstrated these stunning results by broadcasting footage of the placebo group walking, playing basketball and doing things they reported they couldn't do before the surgery! Two years later, the participants were all shocked when they found out that they never actually had a real surgery.[14]

In a clinical test for Parkinson's disease, patients were told that there was a new antidote for Parkinson's that would free them from shaking. These patients were given saline injections and half of the people's shaking symptoms went away! Researchers found that because of their conscious belief in the medication, the patients' brains actually created 200 times more dopamine than what was found before the study, which made the tremors go away and left them feeling better, clearer and more energetic. In fact, a new gene therapy trial for Parkinson's disease was abruptly withdrawn because it was tanking against the placebos. The fact that nowadays an increasing number of medications are unable to beat placebos has thrown the pharmaceutical industry into a sales crisis. What these results show is that **it is the body that really heals itself**, based on an individual's thoughts and belief systems, and not the drugs or the procedures!

One of the more dramatic examples reported in medical literature about the power of the mind to heal and the *Placebo Effect,* involved a patient of Dr. Bruno Klopfer, a researcher who participated in testing the drug **Krebiozen** in 1950. Krebiozen had received sensational national publicity as a "cure for cancer." These reports caught the eye of a man with advanced cancer — a lymphosarcoma. The patient, Mr. Wright, had huge tumor masses throughout his body and was in such a desperate physical condition that he frequently had to take oxygen by mask, and fluid had to be removed from his chest every two days. When the patient learned that Dr. Klopfer was involved in research on Krebiozen, he begged to be treated with it. Dr. Klopfer agreed, and the patient's recovery was startling— "The tumor masses had melted like snowballs on a hot stove, and in only a few days they were half their original size!" The doctors were so excited and felt so much promise that the injections were continued until Mr. Wright was discharged from the hospital and had resumed a full, normal life. He had a complete reversal of his disease and its grim prognosis!

Unfortunately, within two months of his recovery, a report was leaked out to the press, stating that Krebiozen was not effective. After learning of this report, Mr. Wright immediately began to revert to his former condition. His doctors decided to take advantage of the opportunity to test the dramatic regenerative capabilities of the mind, so the patient was told that a new version of 'Krebiozen' had been developed that overcame the difficulties described in the press. With much ceremony, which increased the patient's expectations to a fever pitch, a saline water placebo was injected into him. Recovery from this second nearly terminal state was even more dramatic than the first. Mr. Wright's tumor masses completely melted, his chest fluid vanished, and he became a picture of health! The saline water injections were continued, since they had worked wonders, and he remained symptom-free for over two months. At this time the final AMA announcement appeared in the press, "Nationwide tests show Krebiozen to be a worthless drug in the treatment of cancer." And within a few days of this report, Mr. Wright was readmitted into the hospital in dire straits. His belief now gone, his last hope vanished, and he died two days later.[15]

This example demonstrates how powerful the mind is on both sides of the equation: how it can positively affect us, and how it can negatively affect us as well! How our negative programming, negative thoughts, negative belief systems— how our fears, can be detrimental to our very lives. How the words from someone in a trusted and respected position can be life-affirming or life-destroying. This is called the *Nocebo Effect*, and that is what happened with my mother when she was given a prognosis of 3 months to live by her doctor. She lived almost exactly to that day. Because of the power the subconscious mind has on our bodies and because of people's total trust in doctors, this is an unfortunate and common story you will hear, over and over again, told by families with loved ones that were given a similar terminal prognosis.

I have a friend who refused to let the doctor tell his mother the prognosis he had for her, that she had only 3 months to live. Instead my friend delivered the news and told his mother, "You have cancer and you can choose to let it beat you or you can choose to beat it instead, and I will be by your side and help you all the way." And the great news is that she did beat it and continued to live another wonderful 11 years! I have a similar story to tell around my fall that I will be sharing later in this book.

That which is living in our subconscious mind **IS** either *Life-Building* or *Life-Destroying*, and **IS** determining how our life is unfolding right now! The subconscious mind is like a hard drive, just playing back what is recorded in it. The thoughts and beliefs of the mind can make us sick **or** they can make us healthy. If a hard drive gets a virus, the computer malfunctions. If you just ignore the virus and pretend it's not there, does it go away and stop causing havoc on your computer? It is time for us to become fully aware of what exactly is recorded in our hard drive and what viruses we have that are limiting our output. It is time to remove the malware, and consciously **reinstall** only positive *Life-Building programming.*

In his book, *Teach Only Love*, Gerald Jampolsky shares a powerful story about one of his students, Colleen Mulvihill, who was 23 years old and legally blind. When she was born, it was standard medical practice to put premature babies into high-pressure oxygen tanks. Later in life, she was told that it was this procedure that had caused her blindness. You can imagine the rage and resentment a person with this condition, resulting from the actions of others, might have against the world. She came to Gerald one day with a very important question, "Is it possible for me to regain my sight?" He answered positively, "Anything is possible. You do not have to be a negative statistic on a probability curve of people with retrolental fibroplasia." She was beginning to understand that the thoughts we put into our minds determine our perceptions and affect our life experience; so she began to work on her thinking and practiced visualizing being able to see clearly and doing some of the things she had always wanted to accomplish. Through this process, she also forgave God and others she had blamed for her blindness.

Soon her bitterness dissolved and was replaced by an increasing sense of internal peace. As this happened, her head and neck pain began to ease. Gradually, a subtle but genuine change began to take place in the way she saw herself. She told Gerald, "It was as though my attitude about myself began to *shift*. Where I had always treated myself as a blind person, I now began to think of myself as normal." Soon her daytime vision began to improve enough that she could now see where she was going. One day her ophthalmologist excitedly informed her that she was now legally sighted during the daytime, although still legally blind at night. But soon enough, she excitedly called Gerald up and said, "I want to take you for a drive. I am now licensed to drive a car in two different states and am legally sighted for both day and night!" Gerald shares, "My drive that day with Colleen was the happiest time I have ever had in a car, even though I cried!" This is the power you have with your conscious beliefs, your healed heart and your rightly directed subconscious mind!

The body is like a robot that is controlled by the subconscious mind. The subconscious mind cannot tell the difference between what is real and what is vividly imagined. Have you ever had a dream that seemed so real, that you were really confused about what just happened when you first woke up? Or have you woken yourself up, or somebody else woke you up, because your body was taking action as if the dream you were having was actually happening in that moment? Well, I have many examples of this on all sides. But one very vivid memory I will share is from when I was a teenager. I had a dream that my family and I were going on a vacation, we had to be at the airport at a certain time and our alarms didn't go off. I suddenly woke up and saw that we needed to leave our house in 5 minutes. By the time I woke up from this dream I was in my parents' room, turning the light on, and yelling, "Get up, get up! We're late, we have to leave in 5 minutes!" My parents groggily asked, "What are you talking about?" I continued to yell, explaining, "We are going to miss our plane and our vacation if we don't get out of here in 10 minutes!" And again, my mother said, "Girl, what are you talking about?" And as the memory of the dream slowly faded away, I stopped to think and said, "I don't know, I think I was having a dream. Sorry." And I went back to bed dazed and confused about what had just transpired.

Can you remember a few moments like this yourself? Can you remember a few times witnessing others doing something similar? This is how powerfully our subconscious mind, our imagination and our beliefs can affect our body.

Here's another example. I want you to imagine that you are going to cut open a lemon. In your mind, pull out your lemon, your knife and your cutting board now. Take a look at your lemon and notice its size, shape and color. Place it down on your cutting board and cut it in half. Notice the juices splash on your hand and onto the board as you do. Lick the juice off of your hand as you set the knife down. Now bring the lemon up to your nose and smell its citric aroma. Wow, don't freshly cut lemons smell so great? Enjoy its fragrance! Now bring it up to your lips and squeeze its juice directly into your mouth. Oooh, how does that taste? How is your mouth and your body responding right now? Are you puckering up? Is your mouth suddenly salivating?...... Yes?....... But it was all imagination, there is really no lemon. You didn't really smell or taste a lemon. Yet, the body still responded as if you had! This is how powerfully our subconscious mind affects the responses and the actions of our physical body!! You have just experienced a taste of how to make your mind your slave and not your master.

One American family, who originated in an eastern bloc country and still had many family members living there, tells this true story. During the period of political and social unrest in Europe during the late 1980's, as the communist regimes were collapsing and reorganizing, the American family received an urgent letter from relatives requesting help in the form of supplies, anything that could make life there a little easier. They gathered various items and sent them off to their relatives in the Ukraine. After 6 months they received another letter from the grateful relatives thanking them for all of the supplies, especially the medicine. They said the medicine had helped many in the family, especially some of the elder members who had seen significant improvements in their health— but now they were running low. Could more be sent? "The **LifeSavers**® have made such a huge difference for all of us!"

So if the power of perception could cause a popular candy to affect the health of people as though it were medicine, what are the possibilities for using the *Placebo/Perception Effect* deliberately to create change in one's life?

Let's take a look at how athletes have used this awareness to positively transform their lives. Let's start with the man who is known to have started it all, Roger Banister. Scientists and experts said for years that the human body was simply not capable of a four minute mile. It was believed to be a physical barrier that no man could break without causing significant damage to his body.

Legends held that people had tried for over a thousand years to break this barrier unsuccessfully. In the 1940's, the mile record was pushed to 4:01, where it stood for nine years, as runners struggled with the idea that, just maybe, the experts were right. Perhaps the human body does reach its limit at 4:01.

But on May 6, 1954, Roger Bannister crossed the finish line with a time of 3 minutes 59.4 seconds and broke through this "four minute mile" psychological barrier. As part of his training, he relentlessly visualized the achievement in order to create a sense of certainty in his mind and body. After doing so, Roger Banister said, "The world record was four minutes, 1.4 seconds, held by Sweden's Gunder Haegg. It had been stuck there for nine years, since 1945. It didn't seem logical to me, as a physiologist/doctor, that if you could run a mile in four minutes, one and a bit seconds, you couldn't break four minutes."

Then 46 days after Roger Banister's breakthrough, John Landy ran the four minute mile in 3 minutes and 57.9 seconds. What made this event so significant is that once the four minute barrier was broken by Roger Bannister, within three years, by the end of 1957, sixteen other runners also broke the four minute mile. Once Roger crashed through this psychological barrier, the rest of the world saw that it was possible. The previous record that had stood for nine years, and a thousand years before that, was now broken routinely. There have been over a thousand people that officially have broken that mark since.

So what happened to the physical barrier that prevented humans from running the four minute mile? Was there a sudden leap in human physical capability?

No. It was the change in *perception* and belief systems that made the difference. By demonstration, Bannister had given people's conscious mind a new belief system of what was physically possible.

Often the barriers we *perceive* are only barriers in our subconscious programming. Previous runners had been held back by their programmed beliefs and mindsets. When the barrier was broken, other runners changed their conscious belief system of what was possible, and then went on to do the same. Their perception had changed. Since then, athletes break world records time and time again. The understanding of the power of the subconscious mind, as a slave to a well directed conscious mind, has become a standard belief system and is routinely utilized amongst the athletic community. Our beliefs and mindsets either limit or expand our world. They can either be our stumbling blocks or our stepping stones!

Witness this historical moment your self here:

www.HealYourHeartFreeYourMind.com/banister

So let's experience this power of the mind and visualization on the performance of the physical body right now. I want you to stand with your feet parallel to each other. Then pull up your right arm and point your index finger straight ahead of you. Now keeping your feet planted and your arm straight in front of you (don't move your arm), turn right as far as you can and notice where on the wall your finger is now pointing. Ok, turn back around to your starting point and close your eyes. I want you to now visualize yourself turning around further this time and pointing to a new spot, further right than you just turned to. See that new spot clearly in your mind's eye. See yourself turning to it easily and effortlessly. Feel how it would feel if you were turning to that spot right now. See and feel yourself easily turning to this new spot three times in your mind's eye. Ok, now open your eyes and point your finger straight ahead of you again and now turn to this new location without moving your arm or feet, meaning just turn at the waist, keeping your finger pointing straight ahead of you.

What did you notice? Did you turn around further this time? Did you turn closer to the location you were visualizing in your mind?....... How did that happen?........

This is the power of a consciously directed subconscious mind! The subconscious mind does not know the difference between what is real and what is vividly imagined. It just records it as if it were so and plays it back! Athletes use this knowledge to their advantage to master their subconscious minds and improve their physical performance. We can use this *Placebo/Perception Effect* to our advantage as well, to improve many areas of our lives!

So our thoughts and our minds don't only affect our internal world and our bodies, but also the external world around us. We've already learned a bit about this when we were talking about the **power of the heart** and Dr. Emoto's work with water. **Dr. Joe Dispenza**, from the movie we introduced to you earlier, *What The Bleep Do We Know Anyway*, conducted an experiment in one of his classes. He took three corn seeds and had the class send love to one of them, feelings of hate to another, and nothing to the third seed. The seed that was sent love grew quickly and began flowering in three days, the seed they did nothing to just sprouted normally, and the third seed that was sent feelings of hate actually rotted and grew maggots! So what are your thoughts and focus doing to the seeds that you have been planting in your life? Your subconscious programming, the state of your heart and what you are focusing on is what is now watering those seeds!

Another friend of mine, Mary A. Hall, performed a similar experiment and videotaped the results. She took two jars of freshly steamed rice and sent daily "I love you" messages to one for a month, and drew a happy face on the jar. Then, she drew an unhappy face on the second jar and sent it daily "I hate you" messages for a month. She then went on vacation to Hawaii for another month and left both jars in the refrigerator while she was gone. When she came back to look at the results of her experiment, the rice she had sent *love* messages to was still healthy and perfect, but the rice she had sent *hate* messages to rotted and molded! See the results of her experiment here:

www.HealYourHeartFreeYourMind.com/experiment

Dr. Joe Dispenza just launched a new powerful book that is very pertinent to the discussion we are having in this chapter called, **You Are the Placebo: Making Your Mind Matter**. To find more information about how to utilize the power of the mind and the Placebo Effect check out his new book at: www.youaretheplacebo.com

Our real power and magic unfolds in our lives **when the collective mind** (our conscious and subconscious minds) **and the heart are in alignment or in coherence**. When they are both transmitting out love, faith and a higher vibration, what we would deem as miracles magically transpire. When your subconscious programming is healed, the heart heals and broadcasts out a higher vibration — love and light — for the world to mirror back to you instead. And then, you become the master of your subconscious mind instead of the slave, and can now easily create a more joy-filled, magical life!

You always have to maintain **HOPE~**
Have Only Positive Expectations!

*Transcend*Transform*Inspire*

Chapter Six

The First Step To Freedom
~Self Empowerment~

So, you have decided to take the Red Pill and get out of the Matrix, and out of the illusion! You have decided to clean up your viruses, upgrade your Operating System and no longer experience life through the limiting filters of your old programming— your current BASIC Operating System. (OK, so you need to be old enough to get that BASIC joke!) You have chosen to stop being a slave to your subconscious mind, and become its master. To learn how to consciously direct and utilize the power of your subconscious mind for your greater good, and no longer unawarely be controlled by this old programming. Great! In the following chapters, we are going to guide you through doing exactly that!

The First Step to upgrading your Operating System is to uninstall the old one. To uninstall the old one, **we actually have to apply this first truth to our life**:

The Outside World is Just a Reflection of Your Inside World!

We have to really **understand** this truth and **REALLY APPLY IT**! It can't just be a concept for us that we have some knowledge of. Just because you hear that broccoli is really good for you and will give you the exact nutrients your body needs, doesn't do your body any good if you don't actually eat any. We have to fully understand this truth, embrace it, and **Fully Apply It** to our lives! If you don't, your output will remain the same.

The pathway to applying this *truth* is to take responsibility for everything! ....Yes, I said — **TAKE RESPONSIBILITY FOR EVERYTHING!**

We have to completely remove ourselves from the *victim consciousness* and get out of the blame game. We have to stop looking for the problems outside of ourselves, and instead, look for them within! We need to let go of the need or the urge **to make someone else wrong, so that we can feel right.** (Read that again. I dare you.)

We have the wrong belief that the outside world is the cause and that we are the effect. But the opposite is true: we are the cause and the outside world is the effect of our inside world. The truth is that over 90% of our problems are self-created— *the outside world is merely a reflection of our inside world*. The problem is not in the other person, it is the *charge* or the wound living inside of you. The other person is only acting as a mirror to you. Life isn't happening to you, **life is responding to you!** You are now the writer of your life story. You determine what your life will be, by what you are vibrating outward, consciously or unconsciously. You are a powerful creator! You just didn't know *how* you have been creating your life all this time.

So, whenever you are feeling hurt, angry, frustrated, rejected or worried about someone or some organization, know that they are just reflecting *charges* you have inside of you. The battles we fight, that appear to be outside of us, are really within. Others are just an *indicator* of your hurts, wounds and limiting beliefs. And you should feel gratitude towards them!

Oh, yes......... I said, **Be Grateful To Them**. They are your *Healing Angels*. They are just playing a role for you, so that you can **SEE** what is living inside of you, driving your life without your awareness. You need them to do this for you, and they are graciously willing to help, for your *transcendence*. Can the eye see the eye? No, it can't— it needs a mirror. And so does the **I**! It needs another *I*, as its mirror. So, you should be thankful that they are willing to participate in your soul's evolvement, and to play this role for you.

Looking at circumstances this way is so freeing and empowering. When you do, you vibrate at a much higher frequency, and you attract oh so much better!

Thoughts and *charges* are like data programmed into a computer, showing up on the screen of your life. If you don't like what you see on the screen, there is no point in going up to the screen and just trying to erase what is showing up on it. You have to go into the program and erase the data to change the screen's output. The screen is just a window into the computer's programming. So are all of these people in your life! You can't get angry with the mirror. You're thankful for it helping you **see** yourself!

So whenever a hurt comes up with someone, it is a great opportunity **not** to get involved in the story or the blame game and continue to stay stuck with the *charge* running your life. **Instead,** utilize the situation as a wonderful opening to *see* within yourself what still needs to be acknowledged and healed that you have been avoiding and shoving out of sight for years. And change that energy from victim consciousness (a very low vibration), to one of *gratitude* (a very high vibration). Know that it is only through the **gift** of our internal suffering that we can truly *see the truth* of what is living within us. This is called the **Art of Seeing**. It is how we can *see* our pain and our true selves behind the mask— the image we have spent so much time and effort to create and protect. This is how we can **see** what vibrations we are *really* broadcasting out and attracting and creating our lives from!

Most of us are reflecting life and not affecting it.
Your inner speech mirrors your mind.
If you do not change your thoughts, you haven't changed their activity.
If you do not change their activity, the conditions of your life cannot change,
for they are only bearing witness to the inner action of your mind.
~Neville Goddard

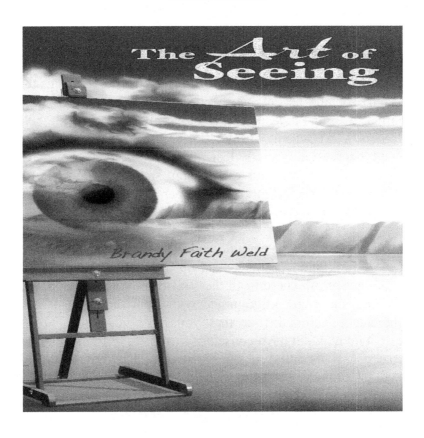

Looking Behind the Mask

Each of us is like an iceberg. We have this beautiful, perfect image above the water that we want everyone to see, and then we have all of this other stuff, *charges*, hiding underneath the waterline that we don't want anyone to see—including ourselves. And we spend so much time and struggle building up and protecting that image, according to our family and societal values, and hiding underneath the waterline anything that our culture does not approve of.

We work so very hard trying to control others' perceptions of us so that we can get their approval, achieve our goals and dreams, and look and feel successful to the outside world; but the **truth is, *we are really creating our lives from everything we are hiding underneath the waterline!*** We are just tricking ourselves into thinking that we are making progress with all of the images we are spinning; but instead, we are just limiting ourselves by ignoring all of the stuff that we're hiding. We are keeping our lives stuck in a status quo by ignoring the *charges* hidden underneath the waterline, participating in the blame game, and working so very hard to try and always *be right*!

Now tell me, what are some of the things we tend to hide under the waterline and pretend aren't there?

Perhaps, feelings of hurt, anger, guilt or shame. Various forms of abuse that happened to us in our childhood. Mistakes that we made, or things that we've done that aren't socially acceptable. Feeling not good enough, feeling like a failure and that we don't measure up to others. Perhaps we hide beliefs that we think others won't accept; or addictions, fears, bigotry, judgments, lies, grief, sadness, depression, secrets, fear of rejection, not feeling worthy, our vulnerabilities, our mistakes, our relationship status, our money or success status, our health and our weight, or things our family did that aren't socially acceptable. The list can go on and on.

There are so many things that we hide under the waterline consciously, and a whole lot more programmed and locked up in our subconscious minds that we aren't even aware of! There is all the stuff from your heritage, everything you experienced and were programmed with from the point of conception through the age of around four that you have absolutely no cognitive memories of. **You** may not have conscious memories of things that happened, but your subconscious mind never sleeps and has recorded and stored EVERYTHING. The image we work so hard to create and protect is often to cover up that pain, the sores that we are hiding underneath our layers of clothes, and to fill up those feelings of fear and emptiness.

74

Now, looking at the total iceberg — where is the majority of it?

Underneath the waterline, right? Just like the largest and most powerful part of the human mind, the subconscious mind– or, we should call it the super-duper mind. The part that can process over 30 billion pieces of information per second and play back recordings at the push of a button; our "undercover boss"– the part of us that is secretly running 95% of our lives!

You can see this super-duper mind makes up over 90% of the iceberg, and that the conscious mind is less than 10%. Clearly, the truth is that it doesn't matter what image we have created and put out there. It doesn't matter how much we are thinking about what we want or what we *'hope for'* with our conscious minds. What matters is the vibration that we are unconsciously broadcasting out to the world from our super-duper, powerful subconscious mind– and all that stuff hiding underneath the waterline! The size, the power and the integration of the subconscious mind throughout our bodies will supersede anything the conscious mind is trying to put out there on its own. The subconscious mind is the man behind the curtain controlling it all– the Wizard of Oz, controlling what the heart is broadcasting out. That is why we **need to see** what *cud* is programmed in there and **assist it** in by-passing the ego/intellect's defenses, so that all this stuff can **be processed and moved out** of our physical beings!

Not acknowledging it, continuing to blame others, distracting yourself and not taking a look at what is underneath the waterline, and focusing all of your attention on keeping the image and the illusion alive, **is keeping you stuck** and unable to *transcend* your patterns and obstacles! And, this is **why** most people's concept of the Law of Attraction is not working for them!

It's like you have a television that only gets channel 2– but you don't like all of the programming on channel 2, only some of it. Can you set up your TV so it only receives the programs that you like on channel 2, the ones above the waterline? If you pretend the programs you don't like on channel 2 are not there, will they stop broadcasting to your television?...... No; your TV will receive ALL the programs that the channel 2 network has– both above the waterline and below. To change what your TV receives you have to first **see** the network's entire program list and **then** go through the process to have the programs that don't work for you, that are under the waterline, **removed** from their network broadcast. This is the one option that will enable you to receive *only* the beneficial programming that you would like for your life. You need to **apply** the *Law of Reflection* and the *Art of Seeing* so that you can determine what your programming actually is, and what you're broadcasting out that televisions (hearts) all around you are picking up and playing back for you. Isn't it time for you to finally get rid of those old shows that you have been playing, over and over again, of someone from your past telling you that you're not good enough?

Transcending Victim Consciousness

Don't feel bad about having *victim consciousness*. It is not your fault. Almost everyone in the world was born that way. It is just the **human condition** that gets passed down from generation to generation, because of *how* human beings are created and because of the lack of the world's understanding of this truth. Unfortunately, this isn't anything they teach us in school— in fact, they practically teach us victim consciousness.

Indeed, the victim archetype is deeply engrained in all of us, and it exerts great power in the mass consciousness. From generation to generation, we have been playing out victimhood in every aspect of our lives, convincing ourselves that this is just the way of the world. Sometimes we are even competing with each other to see who's the bigger victim –"Well, you think that's bad, try my situation......" The time has come to ask ourselves **how do we get off of this un-merry go round**? How do we *transcend* this victim consciousness and experience something better?

The answer is, we have to do something radically different than what we have been conditioned to do for so many years. The definition of insanity is doing the same thing over and over again and thinking you're going to get a different result- yet that is exactly what we have been doing as a species for eons! Luckily for us, our **undercover boss** is adaptable and will let go of old programs and record new, more beneficial ones, when consciously directed to do so. So the **First Step to transforming your life** is to *transcend* your limiting subconscious programming and the victim consciousness. The pathway to doing so is **APPLYING** the *Law of Reflection* and the awareness that *the outside world is just a reflection of your inside world* to your life, and to really **see** what the world is mirroring back to you.

So whenever an emotion comes up, instead of getting caught up in the story, instead of feeling like a victim and getting involved in the blame game, ask your higher self, "Where is this story, this feeling, really coming from? What is this person or situation reflecting in me that needs to be acknowledged and healed? What do I have the opportunity to heal in my subconscious mind right now, so that I no longer have to keep experiencing this?" And **see** what comes up for you. **See** what you're shown!

Also, always remember this *other important truth:* **your suffering is not in the fact, it is in your perceptions of the fact.** The pain, hurt or anger that you are feeling really has nothing to do with what actually happened; instead it has everything to do with the story your mind has told you about it. The pain is a *gift* and just an *indicator* that there is a *charge* that still needs to be acknowledged and healed. The story that your mind comes up with has every-thing to do with the programs and *charges* that it filtered through to come up with the tale. After this, the brain sends signals to flood your body with chemicals aligned with that story, which then affects how you feel. It changes your body's entire physiology- and you then react as if the story in your head is absolutely true! Metaphorically, we run a movie called "reality" through our minds (the projector), and we *project* all of our past programming, since conception, onto the screen of the world. And like any other great movie we watch on television or on the big screen, we get caught up in the story and our bodies react *as if* it were real. Have you ever found yourself startled and surprisingly screaming in the movies or while watching TV?..... Yeah, you too? I have startled many people around me by doing so! In traditional psychology, this is called *transference* or *projection*.

Can you ever remember a time in your life when you got all worked up about something– you were really certain that what you were thinking **was** happening, spent a lot of time worrying about and preparing for it, then later found out that none of it was true? Weren't you shocked and surprised when you discovered that the entire story you were so certain about wasn't even true? Didn't you feel a little silly and kick yourself a bit for some of your actions, or for wasting so much of your time and emotion fretting about it? That is how powerful the mind is in determining our perceptions and life experience! It is actually the scriptwriter, producer, director, film editor, cast, audience, projectionist and critic of our various life movies, all in one!

I remember a time when I was speaking to an audience of about 300 people and there was this man sitting right in front of me slumped down in his chair, legs and arms crossed, looking down the entire time and never responding to any of my stories, questions or jokes. My eyes couldn't seem to turn away from him. The more I looked at him, the more nervous and self-conscious I became. I was certain that I was bombing, and that he was not only not interested in what I had to say, he definitely wasn't even a smidgen impressed. My stomach was turning, and I was so relieved when the whole talk was over. That is, until he started walking directly my way. I felt my heart sink immediately into my stomach as he began to speak to me. He said, "Thank you so very much for that powerful talk. It was very profound for me, and really got me thinking and taking a closer look at some key areas of my life. I am very glad that I came. Your talk really impacted me in a big way. Thank you!"

"Umm... thank you," I said, dumbfounded as he walked away. Wow! It was the complete opposite of everything I was thinking in my mind and feeling in my body. All of the stories in my head had just been a massive lie. All of that fear, nervousness and suffering was for nothing, and only added a little more wear and tear on my heart and body. It was at that moment I learned to not believe all of the stories in my head! This was the day I really understood and learned to always remember that *my suffering is not in the fact, it is in my perception of the fact*, and to not react to the stories in my head before I do the research and talk to the other person. Try to always remember that, and save yourself a whole lot of wasted pain and miles!

To fully comprehend this, it is important to better understand the relationship our thoughts have with our emotions and the sensations we feel in our body. Our brains put out some very powerful chemicals, stronger than heroin or any other drug a person might take. In fact, there are no drugs more powerful than the ones produced by your brain and body. When you have a thought, within milliseconds there is a bio-chemical reaction in your brain that sends ligands (neurotransmitters, neuropeptides and hormones) that match the thought out into the body. When the body gets these chemical messages from the brain, it complies immediately by initiating a matching set of reactions directly aligned with the thoughts. This is why when someone pushes one of your buttons, your reaction can be so intense and extreme. Have you ever completely lost it and later said to yourself, "Who was that person? That wasn't me, that's not who I am. I don't even recognize that person?" Well, this is exactly why. Your brain is like a regular pharmacopoeia with more than 100,000 chemical reactions going off in your mind all the time.

Through the years, the Universe has had to remind me of this *truth* time and time again, because it is so automatic to buy into the stories we have in our mind and the flood of feelings we are experiencing in our body. I most often remember it when somebody else is telling me about a story they have in their head about me. I am normally so shocked and surprised at the story that they have in their mind about me, that it's almost amusing! I mean, oftentimes there is not an ounce of truth in what they are thinking. I don't have the same references or experiences they have had in their life, so I couldn't begin to think in the same way that they do. How I am seeing the world is a reflection of what is inside of me. How they are seeing the world is a reflection of what is inside of them. It's also very helpful to understand that each person's *projections* will tell you a lot about them! Which will help you know how to better interact with them in the future.

As you get these stories in your head that your body reacts to automatically, it is good to remember that the same thing is happening to others as well. So if they react oddly, instead of reacting too, perhaps you should ask them to share what their perception is so that you both can have the opportunity to clear up any misunderstandings. If someone's reaction is hysterical, it is probably historical!

The lack of **understanding** of this *truth* and the *Law of Reflection* is the root of the problems in all of our relationships! And why we are always cross-reacting and cross-firing at each other. The lack of **applying** these two *truths* to our life, is the root of our *patterns* and limitations in life.

The Drama Triangle

Another way we stay in the victim consciousness is by participating in the **Drama Triangle**.[16] An illustration of the *Drama Triangle* is an inverted triangle, with a *Rescuer* in one corner at the top and a *Persecutor* in the other corner at the top. Now, what do both a Rescuer and a Persecutor need?

Correct, a *Victim*. So, all three of these figures are different versions of the *victim consciousness*, and they are just sourced from different primary wounding and programming. They are all derived from pain, cause pain, perpetuate guilt and a sick sense of love, and keep everyone involved caught up in dysfunctional behavior. They are also just different pathways of trying to control our environment in order to protect ourselves. Placing the three positions on a straight line with Victim in the middle is a way of demonstrating that Persecutor and Rescuer are simply the two extremes of victim consciousness.

Persecutor ——— VICTIM ——— Rescuer

Now the title that feels the most comfortable for someone to claim is the *Rescuer,* because it makes us both feel and look good to be 'helping others'. But the truth is, if we get out of our own illusions about it, the act is not sourced from an unselfish, altruistic place. Oftentimes, Rescuers need someone to rescue in order to feel vital and needed. At a young age, they learned that the only way that they felt loved and important to their parents or other family members was when they were helping or pleasing others (the comedian falls under this title as well). Also, focusing on others becomes a great distraction and excuse from having to take a look at themselves and their own problems. It gives them a false sense of feeling loved, needed and superior. Rescuers are the classic co-dependents; and when we really look under the covers, we will find that their actions are just another form of trying to control, wrapped up in a pretty bow.

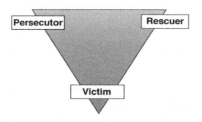

The title of *Persecutor* does not have such a pretty wrapping and is not a title we normally want to claim. The Persecutor is normally developed by someone who was badly hurt as a child, and who has created a mask of power, control and anger to protect themselves and cover up that pain. They have a need to feel dominant and will tend to use psychological, verbal and physical force over someone to do so. Some will also use various forms of retaliation, and passive, or not so passive, aggression. They often have a sense of entitlement and a need to be right. Persecutors tend to be judgmental and blame, criticize, vent and attack when others do not do what they *tell* them to do. They act as if **they** are the victim.

The *Victim* is sourced from great pain and fear, and often times, had a very dominant and abusive parent. Often, they learned the behavior of being helpless as a way to get attention, love and approval, or to stop the abuse. They may even have learned how to feel important and get people's time and attention by having a very significant problem that they can't solve on their own. They feel unable to stand up for themselves and hate confrontation, so they tend to comply, or pretend to comply, and lie and manipulate to cover up their deception.

This is how the *Drama Triangle* tends to play out– you may notice that both the Persecutor and Rescuer are on the upper end of the Triangle, assuming a 'one-up' position over the Victim. Meaning, they relate to the Victim as though they are better, stronger, smarter, or more together than the Victim. Sooner or later, the Victim, who is in the one-down position at the bottom of the Triangle, develops a metaphorical *'crick in the neck'* from always looking up. Feeling *'looked down upon'* or *'worth less than others'*, the Victim builds resentment, and sooner or later retaliates. A natural progression around the Triangle **from** *Victim* **to** *Persecutor* follows and **moves** the *Persecutor* or *Rescuer* **into the** *Victim* position. The now new victim says things like, "How can you do this to me after all that I have done for you?" The once *Victim* **then moves** to *Rescuer* mode, trying to get love and approval back from the now victim through people pleasing. And round and round they go around the Triangle. All players sooner or later rotate positions, reminiscent of a not-so-pleasant version of the game musical chairs.

Although we all go around the Triangle, we all have a **primary starting gate** we use to enter into the Triangle. It is the role through which we actually define ourselves and is a strong part of our identity, and it was created in response to our childhood experiences. Each role has its own particular way of seeing and reacting to the world based on unconscious core beliefs and strategies acquired in childhood. These become 'life themes' that predispose us towards certain patterns of behavior. Each starting gate position has a bit of a script for its *story* and a particular dance around the Triangle. These *script stories* consist of a particular set of beliefs through which we see the world and ourselves.

The Rescuer Story

Rescuers believe that their needs are unimportant and irrelevant. This means that the only way they can legitimately connect with and feel valued by others, and get some kind of love and approval, is through the back door of care-taking or entertaining. Their starting gate story is, "If I take care of others well enough and long enough, then I will be loved." Unfortunately, Rescuers are involved with lifetime victims who have no idea how to be there for them. This reinforces the Rescuers' story that says they shouldn't need anything (they shouldn't be a burden to anyone, so that they can be loved), which then produces more shame and deeper denial surrounding their own pain and needs. They tussle to make it look as if they are self-sufficient and have it all figured out.

The Rescuers' greatest fear is that they will end up alone. They believe that their total value comes from how much they do for others. It's difficult for them to see their worth beyond what they have to offer in the way of 'stuff' or 'service'. Rescuers unconsciously encourage dependency because they believe, "If you need me, you won't leave me." They scramble to make themselves indispensable in order to avoid abandonment. It is just another form of control, topped with a fake, pretty bow. It is designed to make the Rescuer feel that they have a reason to be, that they are worthy of someone's time and attention, and that they are not totally alone. The Rescuer often has an orphan's heart and is always looking for surrogate family— mother, father, brothers and sisters– to feel like they belong, and to fill the void of love they felt lacking in their childhood home. Oftentimes they will get married and have kids for the same very reason. The same can be said for the other two roles, but they just go about filling this void in different ways.

Betrayal, feeling used and taken for granted are trademark feelings of the *victim* phase of a Rescuer's dance around the Triangle. Common phrases for the martyred Rescuer are, "After all I've done for you, this is the thanks I get?" or "No matter how much I do, it's never enough!" A Rescuer may move into the role of persecutor by withdrawing their care-taking, saying, "That's it— I'm not doing anything else for you! You're cut off!"

The Victim Story

The *Victim's* story says they can't make it on their own, and they prove it to themselves over and over again. They believe that they are innately defective and incapable, and spend their lives on the lookout for someone to 'save' them. Though they feel they must have a savior, they are simultaneously angry at their rescuers because, being below the rescuer, they feel put down and looked down upon. Guilt is often used by Victims in an effort to manipulate their rescuers into taking care of them— "If you don't do this, what will happen to me? And it will be all your fault," they might say.

A Victim has accepted a definition of themselves that says they are intrinsically damaged and incapable, which often leads to self abuse. Victims project an attitude of being weak, fragile or not smart enough; basically, "I can't do it by myself." Their greatest fear is that they won't make it.

The very thing a rescuer seeks (validation and appreciation) is the one thing Victims most resent giving, because it is a reminder to them of their own deficiencies. Instead, they resent the help that is given, get tired of being in the one-down position and begin to find ways to feel equal. Unfortunately, this usually involves some form of *'getting even'*. A **move to** the *Persecutor* position on the Triangle usually means sabotaging the efforts made to rescue them, often through lying, bad mouthing, and passive-aggressive behavior. For example, they are skilled at playing the game called, "Yes, but .... ."

The Persecutor Story

Like the other roles, the starting gate for the *Persecutor* is shame-based. This role is most often taken on by someone who received overt mental and/or physical abuse during childhood. As a result, they are often secretly seething inside from a shame-based wrath that ends up running their lives. Persecutors, for survival's sake, repress deep-seated feelings of worthlessness; they hide their pain behind a façade of indignant wrath and uncaring detachment. They tend to compensate for inner feelings of worthlessness by putting on grandiose airs. They may choose to emulate their primary childhood abuser(s), preferring to identify with those they see as having power and strength, to feel more like a bully rather than the *'picked on one'* at the bottom of life's pile. Persecutors tend to adopt an attitude that says, "The world is hard and mean and only the strong survive..... I'll be the strong one."

They protect themselves using authoritarian and controlling methods, and it is very difficult for someone in the Persecutor role to take responsibility for the way they hurt others. In their minds, "Others deserve what they get." These warring individuals tend to feel a need to constantly protect themselves and fight for their survival.

Just like the Rescuer needs someone to fix, the Persecutor needs someone to blame. Persecutors deny their vulnerability in the same way Rescuers deny their needs. Their greatest fear is powerlessness. Because they judge and deny their own inadequacy and fear vulnerability, they need to be right and a place to project their own disowned feelings. The Persecutor's cycle looks something like this: "I was just trying to help (Rescuer), and then they turned on me (Victim), so I had to defend myself by striking back (Persecutor)."

It is easy to think that Persecutors are '*bad*' people, but they are not. They are simply wounded individuals who see the world as dangerous. This requires that they are always ready to strike back, and they live in a constant state of defensiveness and reaction.

Getting Off The Un-Merry Go Round

Living on the Victim Drama Triangle creates misery and struggle, no matter what your primary starting gate position is. The cost is tremendous for all three roles, and leads to emotional, mental and perhaps even physical pain. Efforts to avoid pain, by blaming or looking for someone to take care of us or distract us from our own problems, only end up generating greater pain in the end. Everyone involved in the Triangle dynamic ends up hurt and angry at some point.

For example, you may think you're being a good friend by listening to some-one's story, or that they are being a good friend by listening to yours— but the truth is that when you parrot negative thoughts and feelings, *you are literally jailing yourself,* like a parrot in a cage. Every time you talk about what you don't like or want, you are adding another bar to that cage, and *you are locking yourself away from all of the good vibration that you could create instead.* You are further, expanding and broadcasting that victim feeling (or vibration) so that you will attract even more of it!

Not taking responsibility is a key identifying factor in recognizing when we are on the Drama Triangle. As long as we chase ourselves and others around the Triangle, we relegate ourselves to living **in reaction**. Rather than living freely through self-responsibility and personal choice, we settle into painful lives ruled by fear, manipulation and victim consciousness.

Experiencing a fulfilling life requires a conscious willingness to get off the Triangle, and extend grace to those still encumbered by their drama. Getting honest with ourselves is the most basic requirement for getting off the Triangle. Like any other addiction, it is impossible without self-honesty. Seeing and telling ourselves the truth is the key way of taking responsibility. We then must be willing to take the necessary actions for whatever that truth reveals.

For instance, Rescuers have to be willing to confess their previously unconscious need to keep others dependent on them. This means acknowledging that being a Rescuer is what they do to have their own need for self-worth met. Persecutors need to admit that they are really angry for all of the hurt they have encountered, and that really they are just afraid of being hurt again. For Victims to get off the Triangle, they must see and confess the investment they had in staying 'little', dependent and needy. This means getting honest about how they have manipulated others, using self-deprecating stories of ineptness, in order to be taken care of.

We can't get off the Triangle until we recognize that we're on it; we need to identify what our start gate tends to be, and be honest with ourselves about *why*. What hooks us? What happened to us during childhood that has caused us to pick up this pattern? What payoff are we getting by playing this role?

Ironically, the exit off the Triangle is through the *Persecutor* position. This does not mean we become persecutors. It does mean, however, that once we decide to get off the Triangle, most likely, there will be those who see us as persecutors and will say such things like, "How can you do this to me?" When we decide to take self-responsibility, those still on the Triangle are likely to get angry and accuse us of victimizing them. "How dare you refuse to take care of me?" a Victim might cry. Or, "What do you mean you don't need my help?" a Rescuer might storm when their victim decides to become accountable. In other words, to escape the victim grid, we must be willing to be perceived as the *'bad guy'*.

My starting gate was *The Rescuer* because I didn't think I was good enough to be loved. I kept thinking if I just kept doing things for others, then maybe I would prove my value to them and earn their love and appreciation, and then they would be loyal to me too, and wouldn't leave me. And of course I would always get angry when that wasn't the case, and would either play the victim or the persecutor. I took a lot of personal development courses and thought that, just maybe, I would finally be good enough to be loved. Then, I used those skills that I learned to *'help others'* so I didn't have to take a look at myself and the pain in my life. And I would secretly hope, "Perhaps this next person I help with my new skills and awareness will love and approve of me," and around and around I went!

Being a well conditioned *'people pleaser'*, it was really tough getting off of the Triangle, but it is the best thing I've ever done for myself. Going underneath the waterline and being honest with myself about why I was really always trying to help others. By s*eeing* my wounds and fears, and *seeing* my parents' wounds and fears that I picked up; by applying the *Law of Reflection* and taking **full responsibility** for everything in my life, and discontinuing the drama sharing about how somebody hurt me with others, I liberated myself from the victim's cage that I had jailed myself in. These choices began to change the vibration that I was broadcasting out into the world, and began to *transform* what life was reflecting back to me!

So, are you ready to get off of this un-merry go round and victim band-wagon? Are you prepared to be honest with yourself and *look* at your own patterns? Are you geared up to go under the waterline and look at your child-hood and past to *see* where it all comes from? Are you willing to let go of your past and all of the lies that got programmed into you? Are you eager to take new action for a different result? You may have lived a few dark chapters, but it doesn't have to be your whole book! Now is the time to *transcend* this victim consciousness so you can ***transform* the trajectory of your life story**!

The First Step to Freedom is:

1. **Completely Uninstall and Free Yourself from the Victim Consciousness** by:

   - Taking responsibility for everything! Get out of the Blame Game.

   - Always remember, **your suffering is not in the fact, it is in your perceptions of the fact.**

   - **Apply** the *Law of Reflection* to your life — always remembering that *the outside world is just a reflection of your inside world*!

   - **Apply** the *Art of Seeing*. Be honest with yourself and open your eyes and *see* what your life is reflecting back to you. Dig under the water-line to *see* what you are truly vibrating, out so that you can now change the broadcast. Remember that *awareness* is the beginning to **All** healing! **To see is to be free!**

   - Look at your childhood and become *aware* of your patterns with others and get out of the cycle of the Drama Triangle!

Transcend*Transform*Inspire

Inner View

What is your starting gate on the Drama Triangle? ....

What childhood wounds and belief systems does that come from?

....

....

....

....

....

....

....

....

....

....

....

....

....

....

....

....

What are some of the major things you have been hiding under the waterline?

....

....

....

....

....

....
....
....
....
....
....
....
....
....
....
....
....

As your state is, so is your reality. Whatever your vibration is, so will be your outer experience. So let's take a look at how our life looks right now in these different areas to see what you have been broadcasting out:

    a. Health and Fitness?

....
....
....
....

    b. Career?

....
....
....
....

c. Finances and Life Style?

....
....
....
....
....

d. Relationship with Significant Other?

....
....
....
....

e. Relationship with Family?

....
....
....
....

f. Relationships with Friends?

....
....
....
....
....

g. Relationship with Source (however you define that)?

....

....

....

....

What do you intend to do to get off the *victim consciousness* wagon?

....

....

....

....

....

....

....

....

....

....

....

....

....

....

....

....

....

Chapter Seven

The Second Step To Freedom
~Removing the Obstacles~

Congratulations for deciding to take back some control over your life by stepping out of the victim consciousness, and stepping off of the Drama Triangle! Hopefully, you are actively **Applying** the *Law of Reflection* to your life, and have chosen to get honest with yourself and **see** what is really hiding underneath the waterline that has been unconsciously driving your life.

These are all very big steps that most people in the world are not even aware that they need to do. So, you're way ahead of most! You're already beginning to have a new *awareness* and to **see** life differently. You're already beginning to *think differently*, which is key. Because as long as your mind remains the same, your life will remain at *'status quo'*.

To create something different than what you have grown accustomed to in your personal world, you have to change the way you routinely think and feel each day. By repeatedly doing the same things, you repeatedly think and feel the same way you did the day before, and the day before that. Thus, you continue to create the same circumstances in your life and have many of the same thoughts— and consequently, your brain creates some of the same emotions and chemical reactions in your body, causing you to think some of the same thoughts even more intensely. And round and round it goes! Just like a hamster wheel — the ongoing cycle of the same types of thoughts and feelings. Are you noticing all of the circular analogies? The regurgitation of the *cud*? And you wondered why the same *patterns* kept showing up in your life, time and time again!

Our next change of thinking needs to be — **to stop looking for the problem, or the solution, outside of ourselves** and **Apply** this next *awareness* to our life:

The only way to change the outside world, is to change or heal the inside world!

There is no other way! Any attempt to try and change the other person is both futile and damaging to the relationship. Yet we try and try again, don't we? We always think, "Well if you would just do **this**, then everything would be perfect," and then we attempt to get them to do so. Sometimes over and over again. We always think the problem is *'out there'*, caused by *that* person or *that* organization. "If they would just do what *'I do'* or *'what I want them to do'*, then everything would be ok," we tend to tell ourselves.

So, I want to give you a visual and visceral example of how *futile* it is to try to change the outside world by trying to change others. I would like for you to imagine that you are in Brazil, and you are about to attempt to empty the Amazon River with a bucket. Yes, a bucket. Imagine yourself moving faster and faster, trying to empty that river with a bucket. Faster and faster, faster and faster. Does it look any emptier yet? No? Ok, so I want you to imagine that you've invited all of your friends to come help you with their buckets. Envision them by your side, going faster and faster, faster and faster, faster and faster, in a team effort to try to empty that river. Does it look any emptier? No? How do you guys feel?...... Exhausted? That's how *futile* and tiring it is to try and change your world by trying to change others!

I am going to share with you a little story: There was a man walking in the forest, and he sat on a log. He accidentally sat on a caterpillar, which soiled his pants. So, he took the pants to a local drycleaner and there he met the dry-cleaner's daughter, and they started to date. They shared a lot of interesting experiences that brought them closer together, and they eventually got married and had a child. This child grew up to be President Nixon. So who/what was responsible for Nixon becoming President?

Was it the forest, the log, the caterpillar, the man with the cleaning business, the daughter, the mother of the daughter, the man who sat on the caterpillar, the grandparents of the daughter, the grandparents of the man who sat on the log, or all of the interesting experiences they had that drew them closer? A whole series of events led to Nixon becoming President, and if one of them were to change, then who knows what the outcome would have been? A whole universe is involved in everything that happens, so there is nothing to give credit to and nothing to blame.

In the same manner, it is *futile* to try to change something or someone. Are you going to go back in time and change all the events that led to that moment, or that have contributed to a person or a situation being the way that it is right now? You can't. There is an entire universe involved; a galaxy, and generations upon generations of beings. To try is pointless, and is causing you to suffer, and others around you to suffer as well, just like trying to drain the Amazon River with a bucket!

To control and change a conflict between two people, you would have to change his upbringing, her upbringing, his diet, her diet, the things that happened in her life and in his life, all the generations upon generations of family members and other beings connected to them as well—and just the entire universe. And if you can do all of that, then you can control and change that conflict. If not, you can't. It's more like trying to empty out the ocean with a bucket! Causing you struggle, worry and keeping you stuck; going in circles upon circles of wasted time and energy. Causing you conflict within and causing you conflict with others, which makes you feel even more conflict within. Wow, no wonder you have felt so exhausted, trying to control and fix everything by trying to change others!

When your mind starts telling you what you have to get others to do in order to make everything inside of you okay, don't buy into what it is telling you. That attempt has broken the mind and disturbed its entire psyche for all that have tried. It has created fear, anxiety and neurosis. Your conscious mind has very little control over this world. It is neither omniscient nor omnipotent. It can not control the weather or other natural forces; nor can it control people, places or things around you. Attempting to manipulate the world in order to fix your problems is an impossible task. Just like you can't change the music a Jukebox plays by kicking it. You can only change the music by going into the Jukebox, taking out the old records, and putting in new ones. Relieve your mind of the job of making sure that everyone and everything will be the way you need them to be, so that you can feel better inside. The truth is, everything will be okay as soon as you are okay with everything inside of you!

The paradox is, the moment you totally understand that you're not in control– that is the moment you begin to have more control. It is only when you focus on just healing yourself that you begin to have more control in your life. All the tools to heal your life and change your outer experience are within you, right in front of your nose. There is nothing outside of you to change and fix. There are only mirrors all around you helping you to **see yourself**, and to see what old records are stored in your Jukebox (your subconscious mind) that you need to take a look at and move on out, so that you can experience a new tune!

<u>Changing the Outside World</u>

So again, the next *awareness* you have to apply to your life is – ***the only way to change the outside world is to change or heal the inside world!*** And the Second Step you take to do so, is to *suffer*! Yes, you heard me right — to be able to **uninstall** your old Operating System and to change your experience with the outside world, you have to *suffer*!

Ok, ok– I know that doesn't sound very good, so what do I mean? What I mean is that the only way out of suffering is ***through*** suffering. Meaning, we have to let the *cud* process! We have to let the stuff hidden underneath the waterline rise up and show itself to us, so that we can process it out of our being. So that we can **break free** from experiencing life through it and stop attracting and projecting onto life from it. We have to outsmart the mischievous ego/intellect which is always trying to distract us from doing so, and keeping us stuck! It's like we have been chased by a tiger for years upon years, and we have just kept running instead of turning around and facing it. It is the running that is exhausting us. If we just turned around and faced it, the *charge* would be devoured quickly, and it would be gone— no longer keeping us stuck in this circle of insanity!

To make the process easier to embrace, let's not call it suffering; let's call it what is really is, **energy**. Stored energy, we call a ***charge.*** Energy is designed to move and not stay stagnant, but it is the conscious/ego mind that distracts us and shoves it back down, which has been keeping it dormant. The *charge* tries to move out all the time; every time an intense emotion comes up, and every time a story is told to us by our mind. It wants to be processed, it wants to move out! Lightening ourselves up, freeing ourselves and manifesting what we want, is all about moving stuck energy. Are you finally ready to let it go? Are you ready to take out the trash? Or do you want to wait another 10 years, living the same experiences over and over again— not growing, thriving or shining your bright light?

Whenever a *charge* comes up– a strong emotion tied to a story— we have a choice to make. We can allow it to be our *stumbling block* as we have many times before, getting caught up in the story; or we can use it as our **stepping stone**. It is a ***choice point***, a crossroad. If we make the choice we always have, to be right, get involved in the blame game and believe in the story, we will continue down the same painful path we always have. But if instead, we choose to practice the *Law of Refection* and *The Art of Seeing* and make it our **stepping stone** to a better path, then beautiful new opportunities can unfold! Real transformation **begins** when you embrace your challenges as agents for growth.

Imagine that you have a thorn in one of your wounds in your forearm that is directly poking a sensitive nerve; and when it is touched, it is very painful and really a serious problem for you. It's hard for you to sleep because you roll over onto it. It's hard to get near people because they might hit it. You can't even go for a stroll in nature, because you might brush the thorn up against the foliage. This thorn is a constant source of disturbance in your life, and to solve the problem, you only have two choices.

The first choice is to evaluate your situation and decide that since it's so disturbing when things touch the thorn, you need to avoid everything and everyone to make sure that nothing ever touches it. The second choice is to decide that since it's so disturbing when anything touches the thorn, you need to **remove it.** The truth is the effects of your choice will determine the structural foundation of your future and the course of your life! I mean, if you had a house full of termites that could, if left unmanaged, take the entire house down, you would want to do the work required to get rid of the termites, and not just try to avoid the problem, right?

So, which road do you choose? Are you going to take the same path from the *worm's eye view* that you always have? Stay in victim consciousness, get in the blame game, make the *charge* even larger, and continue to have the same patterns in your life over and over again — basically staying in a negative downward spiral? Or are you going to take the higher path from the ***bird's eye view*** instead, and choose to **see** the problem as a *charge* that is trying to be healed, so that you can expand and thrive? Are you going to be grateful for it showing itself to you, and take full advantage of healing it, then and there, so you don't have to experience that thorn as your reality of the world anymore? What do you choose? The *stumbling block* or the ***stepping stone***?

You must go into the dark in order to bring forth your light.
~ Debbie Ford

The Art of Suffering — The Healing Process

Yes, there is an art to it! And it is not the long, drawn out, miserable, depressed kind of suffering you are used to; the kind your mind definitely wants to avoid and will do anything possible to run away from. Ok, so we will call it something else to make the mind feel more comfortable with it, and resist it less. How about we call it, ***The Art of Moving Blocked Energy*** instead, or, **The Healing Process**?

The Healing Process is one of the most important teachings and practices I have ever come across that has translated my everyday life into a freedom that is beyond belief. Every emotion that you feel, whether positive or negative, translates to a physical sensation in the body. Like how, when you first fall in love, you physically feel butterflies in your stomach and a feeling of euphoria, as if you are on top of the world. If you are scared or angry, you feel a tightening in your chest or a lump in your throat. These are very physical sensations.

We have no problem fully experiencing the positive emotions such as love, happiness, peace etc.. We naturally experience these emotions fully, all the time, and it does feel very good. However, when we start to feel any negative emotions, we do anything we can to escape feeling them, because it is too painful. We are afraid to let ourselves go and really feel it, and the ego/intellect is naturally designed to avoid pain, in protection of *'the self'*. In addition, we have always been told to stay positive and to avoid the stigma of expressing negativity; thus, at any hint of negativity, we are likely to use several methods to escape from feeling the emotion and pain:

> ➤ We justify and tell ourselves it's OK, even when we know that it's not.
> ➤ We use philosophical sayings like, "it's just the way it is", "life isn't easy", "it was meant to be that way", "it will go away", "no pain, no gain", etc....
> ➤ We blame others, or we blame ourselves, and get caught up in the drama of the story.
> ➤ Finally, when none of these methods help us to feel better, we go to McDonald's, eat a tub of ice cream (my personal favorite) or some other kind of comfort food practice; smoke, drink, do drugs or use some other kind of numbing, distracting behavior as a crutch. These are the ultimate escapes because they actually change the chemical physiology of the body, and make us feel temporarily better.

We have all done these types of things; it's very human, so no one is alone. It is great to feel better; however, if we never fully experience these painful emotions, they get physically stored in our bodies and enlarge the original *charge* that they represent. It's like putting band-aids on tumors, thinking that this will make them go away. Eventually these *charges* can cause blockages in our bodies that lead to sickness or disease. These stored negative emotions are actually much more potent attractor factors than any thought you could ever consciously produce. Having these negative *charges* still living within your subconscious mind actually attracts people and situations into your life that will once again give you the opportunity to fully feel a particular emotion, over and over again, until you experience it completely, and finally release it.

Each time you feel the emotion and fail to release it, the *charge* gets stronger and stronger— and the events you draw to yourself become greater. Have you ever wondered why the same basic patterns happen over and over again in your life? This is why! Knowing this information and **applying** it is vital to liberating yourself from these patterns, and to *transforming* your life experience.

Holding onto things and failing to release *charges* reminds me of an example that a psychology teacher used, while teaching stress management to her class. As she raised a glass of water to them, everyone expected they'd be asked the "half empty or half full" question. But instead, with a smile on her face, she inquired: "How heavy is this glass of water?" The answers called out from the audience ranged from 8 oz. to 20 oz. Amused, she replied, "The absolute weight doesn't matter. It depends on how long I hold it. If I hold it for a minute, it's not a problem. If I hold it for an hour, I'll have an ache in my arm. If I hold it for a day, my arm will feel numb and paralyzed. In each case, the weight of the glass doesn't change, but the longer I hold on to it, the heavier and the bigger burden it becomes." She continued, "The worries in life are like this glass of water. The longer we hold onto them, the heavier they get and the harder it is to move about in life. Remember to always put the glass down."

This **Healing Process** is the tool that is going to help you let go of all of these stored *charges* that have been weighing you down, and holding you back from living your ideal life. It's like a *colonic* that forces you to let go of all of the debris that you have been storing and holding onto. As soon as you activate the cleansing process, you let go of everything that has been hindering your life and your well-being without your awareness. The cleansing process may not be so comfortable or pleasant while you are doing it, but after it's complete, you feel so much lighter, freer and happy!

The Healing Process-The Art of Moving Blocked Energy looks like this:

1. Whenever a *charge* comes up, don't get caught up in the story of "what happened and what it means" that your mind will try to tell you. Instead, observe, "Wow, this is bringing up some kind of *charge* in me."

2. Then ask the Divine, Angels, the Universe, your Higher Power— whatever you resonate best with, "What is great about this that I'm not understanding yet?" Change the energy to being curious and excited about the opportunity to grow. Because anytime something happens that brings up a negative emotion in you, it is just life telling you, "Here is a place where your energy is blocked and limiting your life flow, and here is an opportunity to open it up!"

3. When time allows, take some time to yourself in a private room and ask this Higher Power (however you define it), "What *charge* is this reaction (or feeling) reflecting in me that needs to be acknowledged or healed? Please show me, and let me fully feel it and experience it." To get this started, sometimes journaling with this Higher Power is a very effective way for It to bypass your conscious mind and communicate to you through your subconscious mind (dialoging). So you can begin by writing down the above question to this Higher Power.

4. Then allow whatever comes up, to come up. An old memory may arise or an emotion. Whatever comes up is perfect for you! The key is to let the *charge* express itself any way it wants to, **fully**! Don't push it back down and don't contain it. If you feel anger, **express it**. If you feel deep hurt and sadness, **express it**. If you need to scream and yell, scream and yell. If you want to beat a pillow, beat a pillow. In fact, if you have a Wiffle bat around, get it out and beat a pillow with it! Just allow the *charge* to be fully expressed. **Remember it is just** *energy* **that wants to move**. It needs to move. And you want it to move, so you no longer have to live your life through it anymore!

5. When you start to feel the negative emotion, notice **where** in your body you feel the physical discomfort.... normally in the throat, chest or stomach.

6. Focus your full attention on that area of your body.

7. Your mind will try to take your focus off of experiencing the pain, by distracting you with blame, stories, redirecting your thoughts to something else and more. Here is the good news— you can't stop the mind from doing that, so don't waste energy trying. Just let it be.

8. What you can do is be aware that the mind is trying to *'help you'* escape from the feeling. Becoming aware of what is really going on will stop the mind in its tracks. So instead of going into drama, blame or self-pity, you simply say internally, "Mind, I know you're trying to escape, but it's ok, we'll be alright, stay with

me in this moment." This, in effect, is like putting up a roadblock to your mind. Once you have this awareness, you will want to bring your full focus back to the physical sensation in the body. (Just like you have to bring your awareness back to your breath every time you find your mind wandering during meditation.)

9. This is a process that you might have to repeat over and over until all escape routes the mind can take are blocked off by your awareness. You might have to say, "My mind is escaping" every 10 seconds, if that's what it takes. Any distraction, either internally or externally, the mind will grab onto, and try to run away with your attention. (Squirrel!) Blame is the easiest distraction. "It's his fault or her fault, the company's fault or the Government's fault." Be keenly aware that this is a *trick of the mind,* and if you follow it, it will keep you in suffering.

10. You will eventually get to a point in which you feel the physical discomfort in the body, but there is no mind activity or very little. At this point, simply focus all of your attention on it, fully experiencing the sensation. You could simply ask whoever or whatever you consider the Higher Power to be for you, to help you release this emotional *charge* from your body. **You can even imagine a little door right in front of that physical pain, and simply just open the door and breathe it right out the door!**

11. Then just relax and fully experience the physical sensations that occur. Remember, feelings are energy and designed to move, not to last. If you and your mind allow it, it will move!

12. You might experience a range of things at this point, and they are all perfect for you. You may experience a deep peace, laughter and joyful tears. If the emotions are really deep and painful, your body may shake and jolt around, or you may even experience toxins leaving the body in some projectile fashion. And this is great! This is just the *charge* being physically released out of the body, and it is a huge blessing. It is just as if you were going through a food or substance detox. Remember, many of these programmed beliefs and experiences are toxins that have been polluting your psyche and life experience for eons! It could be something passed down from generation to generation. Some could be deeply rooted and require a lot of Divine energy for expulsion. If you simply face it and experience it in this moment, you will be free of it forever in a few hours, and it will save you countless years of continued suffering in the future.

13. As you stick with the feelings and sensations, the negative *charge* will dissolve and will turn into a higher vibration, and you will instead experience a feeling of deep internal peace, joy and lightness.

As you use this process, it will give you a freedom that is indescribable. You can then face any situation, any feeling, and any emotion in life, knowing that it will turn into a feeling of joy or peace. When you experience this release one time, you will have the faith that it works, and magic will start to unfold in your life. Know that as long as you don't resist, **you will be Free**. It is the fear and the *resistance to feeling* that causes the real suffering– the long-term agony. This process is like going into a safe cocoon, and metamorphosing into a beautiful butterfly that is no longer limited to walking on the ground with a worm's eye view. You now have the freedom to fly to new heights and have different experiences, with a new perspective!

Looking over this Healing Process, you may find yourself resistant to scream- ing and yelling, beating pillows and expressing your anger, and that is natural; but it is also a part of the problem. We have been conditioned since childhood that anger is bad and that we shouldn't show it; and if we did show it, we were severely reprimanded. Before we learned this, when we were two years old or so, whenever we got mad we would just throw ourselves down wherever we were; no matter who was around, we'd have our tantrum. Then, when we felt relieved, we would just get up and say, "Do you want to play?" to whoever was around at the time. We would express the anger quickly, and when it was over, we would run off to our next exciting adventure – not to be thought about again! But as we grew, soon we were scolded for showing our anger; we were spanked, sent to our rooms, had our mouths washed out with soap, had to sit with our noses in the corner, or were hit with a belt or some other object. We were told that we were '*bad*' and that "Children are to be seen and not heard," or, "Do not talk back to an adult," or even, "How dare you raise your voice to me?!" So we learned to repress the anger, pouting and brooding instead, and perhaps even berating ourselves for being '*so bad*'. And ever since we learned to repress the anger this way, it has built up inside of us and expressed itself inside of us as hurt, sadness, depression, "poor me", rebellion, some other kind of internal abuse or perhaps some kind of sickness. But *conscious* use of anger **is a very healthy tool** for releasing pent up emotion and energy. Many indigenous cultures have used it to purify themselves and move forward from the past. In the Old Testament, God says, "*Be ye angry, and sin not. Let not the sun go down upon your wrath.*"

It is time for you to let go all of the heavy bags you have been carrying for all of these years, that have been dragging you down as you tried to be the '*good girl or boy*' so as not to lose the love and approval of others. It's time to be free of that pain in the neck, that headache, that backache, that ulcer, that anxiety or that heartburn. The body expresses what the mind represses, and you don't want all of that *dis-ease* you're carrying to turn into disease! It's time to stop covering up the symptoms of your anger with aspirin, anti-depressants and antacid, and to finally treat the cause. Allowing all of the pain, hurt, anger and confusion from childhood to express itself, so we can soon be free from all of this internal suffering that gets mirrored back to us from the world!

Once you get comfortable with this process, and it becomes an **Art** for you, the world won't control you anymore. Because the worst thing the world can do is hit your thorns; but if they are no longer there, or you know how to take them out easily, the pain is very short-lived. You will finally be free from the binds of the psyche. A memory without a charge is just called *wisdom*. Fear of emotion will no longer limit you, and you will be able to walk strong through this world, more vibrant and alive than ever before! Obviously, there is a time and a place to go through this process; you will want to be alone in a quiet place with as little distraction as possible. When you are in the heat of an argument, or at work, for example, you have to do what you have to do in the moment to get through it, and then find some quiet time later to go through this process.

Heal your *charges* and throw away your victim badge! This is the pathway **out** of victim consciousness. This is the road to removing the *obstacles* that have kept you from truly living the joy-filled, magical life of your heart and soul's intention. This is the internal journey I took to remove my thorns, heal my wounds, and to liberate myself from the constant pain and the cycle I had lived for so long; living and re-living the victim consciousness, over and over again. The pathway I took to *transcend* the victim consciousness that got passed down to me from all sides of my family.

Taking responsibility for everything, practicing the *Law of Reflection* and the *Art of Seeing*, and using *The Healing Process* cleaned up my garbage, so that I no longer attracted all of the rats. Life is so much better, the air is so much sweeter, and the world just keeps mirroring back to me more and more love, acceptance and unending possibilities! Before, it always seemed to me like the world was just pushing me around and turning me down. I felt as if I lived in an asteroid game, always ducking and dodging asteroids flying my way. Now it feels like the Universe is embracing me with arms wide open, and always answering my quest with an outstanding YES! **The only way out is through** — and it is very beautiful and peaceful on the other side of that healing bridge! Take the journey of healing your wounds, taking out the thorns and freeing your home from those termites, and find out for yourself how great the view of life is on the other side of that bridge. Our struggles and problems dissolve as we evolve!

The Second Step to Freedom is:

2. Take out the garbage by **applying *The Healing Process-The Art of Moving Blocked Energy***:

    - **Apply** the understanding that **the only way to change the outside world is to change or heal the inside world.**

    - **Give up** the *Control Illusion,* and **know** that trying to change others is futile and damaging to your psyche and your relationships.

    - Be like a two-year-old again and allow your emotions to be fully expressed, in a safe environment, so they no longer plague you. Then you can move quickly on to your next exciting adventure, just like you once did as a kid!

So, let's practice using this **Healing Process**, this **Art of Moving Blocked Energy**, and go from always struggling to look good, to actually feeling good within. Take one of your wounds or belief systems, or one of the major things you found hiding underneath the waterline in the last chapter, and let's move it out now! Find a quiet and private place, get comfortable, have plenty of pillows around you – and perhaps a Wiffle bat in case you feel like hitting them. Grab your Smartphone or Tablet and go to track #1; or click on the link below to listen to it through your speakers directly from our website, or download it if you haven't already– and let me guide you through this powerful healing journey.

Track # 1: www.HealYourHeartFreeYourMind.com/Healing

Then track #2: www.HealYourHeartFreeYourMind.com/Healing2

Again, only listen to track #2 or any of the other audio's through headphones if you are certain you are not pregnant, wearing a pace-maker or prone to seizures of any kind. Do not listen to any of the audios on this program while you are driving.

For extra tools to help you with the Healing Process, learn more about the Sedona Method or Releasing.[17]

This being human is a guest house.
Every morning a new arrival.
A joy, a depression, a meanness,
Some momentary awareness comes
As an unexpected visitor.
Welcome and entertain them all!
Even if they're a crowd of sorrows,
who violently sweep your house
empty of its furniture,
still, treat each guest honorably.
He may be clearing you
out for some new delight.
The dark thought, the shame, the malice,
meet them at the door laughing,
and invite them in.
Be grateful for whoever comes,
because each has been sent
as a guide from beyond.

~ Rumi

Transcend*Transform*Inspire

Chapter Eight

The Third Step To Freedom
~By Passing The Conscious Mind~

Congratulations on taking the next steps to **uninstall** the victim consciousness and being a slave to your subconscious mind; and for taking the brave steps to **take back your power** by facing up to what you have been hiding from, and avoiding, for so very long. You're now getting a better grasp of what a powerful creator you actually are, and how much you have been creating your life unawarely thus far. You are realizing that you've been living life in the *effect* of your subconscious mind's programming (much of which you weren't even aware that you had), and by the *Law of Reflection.* In short, your life thus far has been run by the Wizard of Oz.

Now that you have looked underneath the waterline, are more aware of what you have been broadcasting out, and why the world has been responding to you as it has; and, now that you have a greater awareness of why your life has unfolded as it has, we can begin to move you from living life '*in the effect*' of all of this programming, to living life '*at cause*'. Actually living life **at cause** from the right state, rather than from the illusion of control that you once *thought* your power came from. We can do that as you begin to **apply** all of this new *awareness* **as your new Operating System**. Also, as you methodically **complete** the process that I am guiding you through in this book, to clear out your old limiting programs. It is important that you go through **all of the steps in order** to stop living your life at *the effect*. Don't fall prey to your mind's pattern to skip, avoid and justify that you don't need to take a particular step. This is the exact *pattern* that has kept you stuck where you are at right now. So do all of the exercises, all of the Inner Views, watch all of the videos and listen to all of the audios when guided to. Now is the time to no longer allow your fearful mind to run the show, leaving you to live a life merely as its slave, and in its *effect*! It is time for you to finally be free of all of the struggle, and now live the life of your heart and soul's intention!

To create our lives from **cause** instead of from the *effect*, we need to enroll a **higher level of consciousness**. Because, as Albert Einstein said, "No problem can be solved with the same level of consciousness that created it." And since the *effect* is being created by the *Law of Reflection* of our subconscious programming, we have to *bypass* the guard of it, the egoic intellectual mind, to start creating **at cause!** We have to circumvent the limitations of our conscious minds to *transcend* the obstacles and patterns of our past.

I once heard a wealthy man ask a wise sage, "What do I need to give up to experience true happiness and inner peace?" The sage replied, "Well, I have good news and bad news for you. The good news is that you don't have to give up any of your money or things. Poverty is not the way to happiness. The bad news is that you have to do something that may be even harder for you than giving up your wealth. You have to give up the way you think."

So, how many times have you tried to create something with your thoughts and your intentions, and in your conscious mind you were really excited about it and thought it was really going to happen, but deep down, under many layers in the back of your mind there was doubt— you weren't sure if you could pull it off or if it would actually happen for you? Old stories of failure started raising their ugly little heads. What usually happens when you send these jumbled, incoherent signals out to the world? Your intentions never seem to materialize then, do they?

The messages we send out to the world need to be clear and consistent. There needs to be *coherence* between what the *conscious mind* is sending out through thoughts and intentions, and what the *heart* and *subconscious mind* are sending out in vibration. Right now your heart and subconscious mind are **not** coherent, so whichever one is putting out the most vibration will win the response. Currently, all the stuff hiding underneath the waterline, that has been recorded and conditioned in us, is leading the way.

According to neurologists, we have about 60,000 thoughts a day. That is about one thought per second during every waking hour. The startling fact about that is 95% of them are the same thoughts you had the day before, and the day before that! Your mind is like a broken record skipping and playing the same tune over and over again. (There's that cycle analogy again.) But the real problem is that out of those 60,000 thoughts, about 80% of them are negative. Meaning, most people have more than 45,000 negative thoughts a day!

Neuroscience theory tells us that the subconscious mind is organized to reflect everything we know in our environment, since the moment we were conceived. All of the information we have been exposed to throughout our lives is in the form of knowledge and experiences. So if you are trying to solve a dilemma with a mind that is equal to the problem, then you are just moving around the furniture and you will just get more of the same reflected back to you. If the input remains the same, so does the output! Until we can move out all of the *cud* living in our subconscious mind, we will continue to have this vicious cycle of negative thoughts and their mirrored attraction.

To **free ourselves** from this *cud*, and to really **move out** the current furniture, we have to move from operating in the world from the *worm's eye view* to operating from the *bird's eye view*. We can do this by using the **Growth and Success Formula**. This formula is a pathway for us to access **Higher Consciousness**– the *bird's eye view* and a greater *awareness*. It is the conduit to the **infinite possibilities** that are beyond the constructs of our limited mind.

The formula goes like this:

Clear & Specific Intention + Right Action + Divine Intervention = Success/Growth

This formula is for both your *internal world* and your *external world*. It is the formula we use for your personal growth and healing of limiting subconscious programs, and it is the same formula we use to reach your personal success goals. But as you may have surmised by now, the two aren't mutually exclusive!

Now, the *Clear & Specific Intention* is not much different than the other goal setting models we have learned in the past. But we do have to be **very clear** and **very specific** about what we want. We can't just say that we want more money; we need to give a certain amount and add, "Or more than this" to that request. If we just ask for more money, then the Universe will just lead you to finding a quarter lying on the floor: and there you go, you now have more money! If you just ask for abundance or prosperity, the Universe can give you abundance in a lot of non-monetary ways. Maybe in areas you don't want abundance in! Like say, ants, mail and perhaps even too much attention from others. If you're uncertain as to what you want and you keep changing your mind, for example thinking, "I want a new car, but I can't decide if I want the convertible sports car, or if I want the sport utility vehicle," you're sending out mixed signals and the Universe is uncertain how to respond. So you can find yourself being led in a multitude of confusing directions. So when you set your intention, make sure you don't have any conflicting beliefs and counter intentions— **Get Clear** and **Be Specific**!

Right Action has two meanings. One meaning is that the *action* needs to be aligned with your intention. So if you want to get married to your right life partner, well then you should probably at least go out on a date or two with a like-minded person. It is very important that the action be in alignment with the intention and not in conflict with it. Pay attention to any *inspiration* you get to take a specific action. Meaning, if all of a sudden you get a hunch you should contact a certain person, then you should follow that gut feeling immediately (which we learned is really the heart's intuitive intelligence). We will often find that these emotional nudges are really the Divine Intervention in motion!

The other meaning is that the *action* needs to have **right intention**; *it needs to be good for you* **and** *good for others*. This creates a higher and positive vibration. You can't have ill-intent and be praying and taking actions that you know will be harmful to someone else. Right action puts you in alignment and agreement with the intention, and sends out a congruent high vibration signal to the *Field*.

The **Divine Intervention** is the most crucial piece of this formula! This is how we get *access* to the Higher Consciousness and the *bird's eye view*! We have to **ask** and **turn the answers over to the Divine;** the Presence will not intercede if we don't **ask,** because it honors our free will.

The Divine is like the Internet: everywhere, yet nowhere, and it is Know ware. It is the Divine Matrix, the Quantum Field, the Universal Intelligence and whatever you want to call it. This power is the same Consciousness that animates every aspect of the material universe. It is a part of, and connected to everything and the ALL! This Divine Consciousness can find the right resources and bring them all together in a greater way than you could even begin to imagine with your limited left-brained mind. It has the ultimate *bird's eye view*, whereas our conscious mind only has the *worm's eye view*. When you connect yourself and tune yourself into this Higher Consciousness, you will find yourself accessing infinite guidance and help. You will find yourself in the flow of a tremendous power and a greater wisdom. Life suddenly feels as though it were a rigged game, because like the Internet, the Higher Consciousness is everywhere and knows where all the required pieces are and how to bring them together in perfect timing to win the end game — your intention.

It's like Google™. You give it a clear and specific intention of what you are looking for, and it has the right intelligence to quickly search the world and bring you the right resource for your quest. When you make an intent and connect to the Higher Consciousness, it can move people across the world as though the planet were a large chess board and people merely pawns on it. With all the right people getting linked up with each other in perfect timing, feeling as though it were an amazing coincidence and an intriguing synchronicity.

When you set an intention, you need to **not** be attached to what it will look like and how it will show up. For instance, if you want a certain amount of money, don't be limited to thinking it can only come from the mediums you know, like your company, the lottery or through a loan. The Universal Intelligence that animates the existence of all things will both surprise you and delight you in how it answers your quest. With its Divine Intelligence, it will make your desire even bigger and better than you could begin to imagine with your limited mind.

For example, Oprah once shared that she was visiting a television set for a meeting she had there, and for some reason she felt drawn to go and start talking with one of the female camera operators. In their conversation, Oprah asked her if she liked what she did, and if it was a life goal. The camera operator told Oprah that this was just a job she found herself in and shared what her dream had always really been. Oprah asked what has been stopping her in making her vision come true, and as the camera operator answered her, she suddenly felt compelled to help make this woman's dream come to reality! Oprah said, "I can't explain it, but this energy just overtook me, and I felt so driven to help her out!"

This is an example of the much bigger ways the Divine can answer our call, if we just believe and we are open to how it shows up. When this woman was dreaming about her vision, she never imagined that Oprah was just going to walk up to her someday and offer to help her out! We are *All* vehicles of the Divine Presence and *It* can use any representation of *Itself* to answer the request! We are just responsible for the *what*, and a greater consciousness will handle all of the *how*. We are responsible for the order, and the Divine will handle all the details of the delivery!

Another powerful example comes from my own life. I was working at Cisco Systems as a Sales Representative, and I was attending Tony Robbins' events for my own personal development. During this time period, I started really getting focused on what my life passion and life purpose was, and I was asking God to guide me to it. It became clear that I loved personal development, I loved to help people, and I really loved to travel; but at the time I just couldn't see how I could make a living and a job out of all of that. I also learned to love Cisco as a company and the financial security I received from it, so I couldn't imagine leaving the company. At the same time, I started to notice changes in our marketplace and some holes in our company's ability to answer them, so I wrote up a solution and sent the suggestions to our Executive Vice President of World Wide Operations– the second in command of our company.

The answer I received back from him both shocked me and exhilarated me! He said, "Great idea! Why don't you join the new group we just started and make this happen!" I was the second employee of this new division, and had all of top management's support to make my vision come true! It was my dream job! The Universal Intelligence took all of my passions and put them together in a job that I couldn't even begin to believe was possible, at the time of my awareness. It was bigger and better than I could have even imagined at the time. I was managing Sales Skills and New Hire Training and Development for all of Cisco's Sales Force, worldwide. This meant I had to travel the world to work with my internal customers, create personal development programs for our global sales force, and attend them to make sure they were meeting our company needs— all on Cisco's dime. **That's the power of turning things over to the Divine Intelligence and its Omnipresent Bird's Eye View!**

I want to share with you a very amusing, yet visceral example I experienced in India that gave me a greater understanding and awareness of how our limited perspective, our drive for control, and *doership* hinders the great success we could have if we just surrendered to the power of this Higher Consciousness and its *bird's eye view*. I was sitting on a rock watching this little bug roll this piece of shit (literally) up the hill. He would bump into an obstacle and the piece of shit would roll over him, down the hill, and took him along with it because he would not let go! (Sound's like a lot of people, doesn't it?) He would then push it up the same path, hit the same obstacle, and roll down the hill holding onto his piece of shit all over again! It was quite amusing to watch, and I videotaped the whole thing. I decided I wanted to help this little guy get past his obstacle, so he could successfully get this piece of shit up the hill. So, from my grander perspective, my *bird's eye view*, I took a stick and was trying to redirect him around this upcoming obstacle that he could not see from his perspective. But he would not be guided away from his committed direction. He was determined to stay on his course, no matter how much someone with a better vantage point and a greater awareness was trying to guide him and redirect him. He would just try to roll this piece of shit over my guiding stick, and would end up rolling right back down the hill with it again! Wow, this was such an eye-opening experience. Seeing how we humans do the same with our fixed point of view, and our need for control and being the *'doer'*. Stubbornly hitting obstacle after obstacle and continually ignoring the guidance that something with a greater perspective has been attempting to give us!!

There is a true story, published in a book called **Small Miracles**, that powerfully demonstrates how intelligent this Divine Presence is, and how it can bring the right people to the right places at the right time, without boundaries of geography or dimensions:

This is a story of a Jewish boy named Joey living in the states, who rebels against the Jewish faith and tells his father that he is denouncing Judaism and is following his own religion. Adam, his father, who was the lone survivor of the Holocaust in his family, was very passionate about honoring the Jewish religion that so many in his heritage died for, became very angry and disowned his son. Joey, becoming hurt and angry himself, leaves home and moves to India, following Guru after Guru to find his own way.

Six years later, he runs into a childhood friend in Bombay who tells him that his father has died of a heart attack. Feeling a profound sense of guilt for his father's heart attack, and with deep anguish, he goes to Jerusalem to the Wailing Wall. With endless tears, he writes a letter to his father saying:

"Dear Father, I beg you to forgive me for the pain I caused you. I loved you very much and I will never forget you. Please know that nothing that you taught me was in vain. I will not betray your family's deaths. I promise."

He rolls the paper and tries to insert it in the crevices of the wall, as is the culture and custom. He finds that every crevice is filled with too many papers, so he walks a long way and finally finds one particular crevice where there is space for him to lodge his note. He pushes his paper into the crevice and notices another paper is dislodged. He bends down to pick up the paper so he can reinsert it and notices the handwriting on the front looks a lot like his father's writing. Driven by curiosity, he opens the paper and there in his father's handwriting is a letter to him saying:

"My Dear Son Joey, If you should ever happen to come to Israel and some how miraculously find this note, this is what I want you to know: I have always loved you, even when you hurt me, and I will never stop loving you. You are, and always will be, my beloved son. And Joey, please know that I forgive you for everything, and I only hope that you in turn will forgive a foolish old man.
~Adam Riklis, Cleveland Ohio"

I can go on and on about magical experiences of **Divine Intervention** just from my own life alone, but the key message is this: if you trust and turn things over to the *Divine Intelligence*, miracles upon miracles that defy human logic can unfold. It is time for us to start living by the words of the almighty US dollar, "In God We Trust." But first, you have to **ask**– and oftentimes this can be the most difficult part for us control freaks and human doers. For help with this, read **Jack Canfield's** book *The Aladdin Factor*, where you'll learn not only how to ask for what you want, but you'll discover the five barriers we all face in asking for what we want, and how to overcome them. For more information, please go to: http://jackcanfield.com/products/aladdin-factor

It's a simple formula, **just dig a hole, plant a seed, fill the soil and water it,** and the Divine grows it for us bigger and more beautiful than we can begin to conceive.

A Tool to Access Higher Consciousness & Divine Intervention

A powerful tool to access Higher Consciousness and the Divine Grace, or Intervention, is meditation. Meditation is an easy way to drop down from the conscious mind and access the subconscious mind. To purposely put yourself into that same hypnogogic trance state in which your subconscious mind was originally, inadvertently programmed in. So that we can get to the *cud* and move it out! So that we can bypass the analytical, conscious mind that is always trying to *'not deal with it'* and shove it all back down. So that we can connect back to our own Spirit and Source. This is how you open the doors to true personal change. ***Transcending obstacles and permanently transforming your life!***

In fact, if you did a little investigation, you would find that many thought leaders and many people in entertainment, from Oprah to Clint Eastwood, are avid meditators! They will all tell you that the practice has changed their lives. It has opened up the channels of creativity, and it has freed them from prior illnesses and destructive addictions. You will find many of our most influential speakers and authors have a dedicated meditation practice.

www.HealYourHeartFreeYourMind.com/meditation1

The Sanskrit definition of meditation is *'to cultivate self'*, which is a great description of what we are doing. We are churning up the old dirt to remove the weeds, old roots and rocks that have been limiting and blocking us from truly flowering and living the life of our desires. Through the cultivation, we are creating new soil in which the new seeds we'll plant can grow in unhindered earth, to foster an inspiring garden! Many people will spend a lot of time and effort on their physical body, yet the other parts, their Spirit and Mind, get almost completely ignored. Meditation cultivates and heals all three, watering and providing the nourishment new seeds need to grow and flourish in the soil of the Mind, Body and Spirit!

To make the right the choices in life,
you have to get in touch with your soul.
To do this, you need to experience solitude....
because in the silence you hear the truth and know the solutions.
~Deepak Chopra, MD

So, we are returning to our childhood and going back the way we came in. We are moving our brain waves from Beta, down to Alpha, down into Theta and perhaps even Delta, for the practiced yogis. While your conscious mind is processing information, you will be predominantly in Beta, but you will go in and out between Beta and Alpha during your waking state. When you close your eyes and shut out 80% of your sensory input, your mind instantly drops down to Alpha, begins to relax and bring its focus internally, and you move into a light meditative state. Close your eyes right now for a few minutes and experience that instant quieting of the mind. Put both hands on the center of your chest, one on top of the other; take three slow inhales and exhales as you do this, and notice what you feel. Does your mind feel a little quieter? Do you feel a little calmer?

Later in the evening as we are getting sleepy, or as we awake in the morning, Theta waves emerge. It is a state in which you feel half awake and half asleep. It is a highly programmable state that hypnotherapists take you to, to access and reprogram your subconscious mind. For most of us, Delta represents deep sleep, and the time in which our bodies are regenerating.

As a result of normal daily changes in the brain chemistry, there are two times a day that the door to the subconscious mind naturally opens— when you are waking up in the morning, and when you are going to sleep. These are the times you are just moving in between Theta and a low-range Alpha, and thus, the easiest and best times to meditate and create change in the subconscious mind. During meditation, the object is to fall slowly, like a feather, down from the top of a building, as your body completely relaxes and your mind slows down and gets quieter, yet is still awake and aware. Here is some step by step guidance.

1. Find a quiet place to sit up comfortably with your spine erect.
2. Close your eyes and bring your awareness to your chest and your breath.
3. Take three deeps breaths, holding each breath in for a count of 5, and then slowly letting it out for a count to 10.
4. As your mind relaxes, gently bring your awareness to your normal breath, and visualize a bright light shining down on the crown of your head.
5. Feel the white light flowing from your head down your neck and into your chest, lighting up your heart. Feel the vibration and expansion of your heart area.
6. Continue to see the light flow down your arms, down your spine, into your torso, down into your hips, filling all of these areas with white light all the way down to the bottom of your feet.
7. Continue to focus on your breath, and feel the vibration of this energy charge up your entire body.
8. Just observe and experience whatever sensations, emotions or memories that come up. If your mind wanders off on a tangent, gently bring your awareness back to your breath.
9. When you feel ready to finish your meditation, just begin to move your hands and feet, and gently open your eyes.

Not only is meditation a powerful tool to access our subconscious minds and to move out the dis-serving *cud*, but it also has a powerful effect on our entire well-being! Hundreds of studies have been done over the past 40 years, demonstrating the powerful effects of meditation on our minds, bodies and emotions, and it now has become medically accepted as a good practice for stress management and overall good health.

The Mayo Clinic says that research has shown that meditation may help such conditions as allergies, anxiety disorders, asthma, binge eating, cancer, depression, fatigue, heart disease, high blood pressure, pain, sleep problems, substance abuse and overall improvement of immune functioning. They also say it is not a replacement for traditional medical treatment, but that it may be a useful addition to your other treatments.

Studies have also shown that a consistent practice of meditation will positively rewire your brain, due to the brain's neuro-plasticity. It will enhance activity in the areas of your brain associated with happiness, compassion and other positive emotions, while the areas responsible for anxiety and other negative emotions will begin to wither. Check out these reports on the effects meditation is having in various areas of health and well-being.

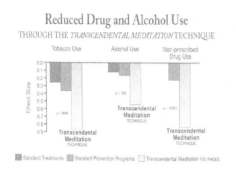

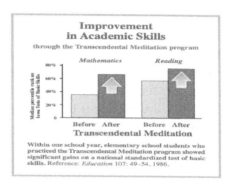

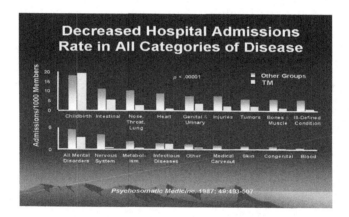

The intention of meditation is to fully develop the potential capability of the brain, since right now we are only using about 10 percent of it. As you can see from the reports above, meditation can improve your mind, your focus, your health, your emotional state and stress levels– but it's not a good method for birth control!

So let's experience this powerful tool right now. In this meditation, we are going to wake up and shake up all of the energy centers of your body. This is where all of the charges, the *cud*, is living. When we wake up these centers, the blocked energy will begin to show itself and move out. It will make the

Art of Moving Blocked Energy— The Healing Process – much easier and quicker!

As I lead you through the meditation, I will have you bring your awareness to each center and sing a Sanskrit chant that creates a vibration that causes the energy center to activate and move. The first energy center (the Sanskrit name is Chakra) is at the base of your spine, at your perineum, and the sound that we will chant for it out loud is *lang* (sounds like long). We will elongate the sound, as you do when you chant OM, and we will say each mantra three times. In between each energy center (Chakra), I will sing another Sanskrit chant to help Prana (life force energy) rise up the spinal cord. As I do this, just visualize golden energy rising from the base of your spine up to the center we are focusing on, filling it up, and turning into a beautiful golden color. You will then begin to feel that energy center move and vibrate more and more.

The second energy center is in the bladder region, and the mantra is *vang* (pronounced vong). The third energy center is in the upper abdominal area, above the belly button, and the mantra is *rang* (sounds like wrong). The fourth center is in the heart region, in the center of the chest, and the mantra is *yang* (sounds like yong). The fifth center is at the throat, and the mantra is *hang* (sounds like hong). The sixth center is right above the eyebrows in the center of the forehead, and the mantra is *OM*. The 7th center is at the top of the head, and the mantra is *ogum satyam OM* (sounds like o goom, sat e um, OM).

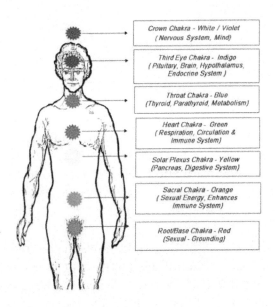

Crown Chakra - White / Violet
(Nervous System, Mind)

Third Eye Chakra - Indigo
(Pituitary, Brain, Hypothalamus,
Endocrine System)

Throat Chakra - Blue
(Thyroid, Parathyroid, Metabolism)

Heart Chakra - Green
(Respiration, Circulation &
Immune System)

Solar Plexus Chakra - Yellow
(Pancreas, Digestive System)

Sacral Chakra - Orange
(Sexual Energy, Enhances
Immune System)

Root/Base Chakra - Red
(Sexual - Grounding)

So let's try it! Find a quiet place and when you do this meditation, please *sit up* in a comfortable position with your back erect. Grab your MP3 playing device and your ear buds, and play track #3 or download this meditation here:

www.HealYourHeartFreeYourMind.com/WakingUp

The **Third Step** to Freedom:

3. Use the **Growth and Success Formula** in all areas of your life to live life **at cause**!

   - For your *internal world*: to heal and move out the *cud*. **The Healing Process — The Art of Moving Blocked Energy** is basically this formula for the internal world. You just get clear on what *charge* you want to heal, and move yourself into private space to let the Divine Intervention take over.

   - For your *external world*: to achieve any personal goal that you have in all areas of your life.

   - **Be Aware**: that these two things are not necessarily mutually exclusive. The *Divine Intelligence* might take you through an *internal process* to move blocked energy, to help you achieve your *external world* intention! As we evolve, our issues naturally resolve!

   - Use meditation to activate the *Divine Grace and Intervention*. Also use it as a part of **The Healing Process.**

For more information about meditation and how it is improving the lives of many people you know, watch these videos from ABC's Good Morning America and David Lynch:

www.HealYourHeartFreeYourMind.com/meditation2

www.HealYourHeartFreeYourMind.com/meditation3

Transcend*Transform*Inspire

Inner View

So let's start putting this formula to practice right away:

Clear Intention + Right Action + Divine Intervention = Growth/Success

What is a personal goal that you have? Get very clear and be very specific on your intention.

....

....

....

....

....

....

....

What are some right actions you can take right away towards it? Do these actions have right intent? Are they in alignment with your intention? Are they good for you & good for others?

....

....

....

....

....

....

....

Ok, so you just dug a hole, you planted a seed, you're going to take the right action and fill the soil and water it, and now watch the Divine grow it. Pay attention to all of the Divine Guidance and all of the synchronicities that begin to flow into your life and follow them. Follow the white rabbit! (wink, wink)

Chapter Nine

Fourth Step To Freedom
~You Gotta Have Faith~

So, you have decided that you are tired of living life in *the effect* and now want to start creating and experiencing life *from cause*— but **to do so** you know **you need to be free from the programming** that was passed down to you, and that has been unconsciously driving your life. You understand that to be free from this *cud*, you need to *bypass your conscious mind* and **tap into a higher consciousness.** And, you just learned a **powerful formula** to do so, both for your *internal world* and also to manifest the things you want in your life (in your *external world*). The **most important** part of that formula is to **turn things over to the Divine Intervention.** And that can be the toughest part for us Humanoids — us Human Doers, as I pointed out in my cute little story about the bug and how he held onto his piece of shit!

We have been so conditioned to be the doer! "If it's gonna be, it's up to me," is our doer's mindset. We have been conditioned by Darwinisms– like *'survival of the fittest'*, *'every man for himself'*, and *'it's a dog-eat-dog world'*. In addition, most of us unfortunately learned at a very early age that we couldn't always count on or trust the people that we were dependent on. As we grew up and had many more experiences of the same, we learned to not trust others, and to only depend on ourselves. To overcome this pain and negativity in our world, we have armored ourselves with 'self-empowerment', 'not needing anyone', 'independence', 'taking the bull by the horns', and beating our chests and saying, "Now I am the voice" (wink, wink to a few of you who get that joke). I'm not saying all of that is bad. What I am saying is, this has been a source of our lack of trust in the **Divine Intervention** and why we **avoid asking for help**; and perhaps, why we are not too sure about how we are feeling about this part of *The Success Formula* right now....

The other big reason is that we aren't sure how we feel about the Divine or God. We aren't sure if we totally believe in *It*, or if we can totally trust *It*. For some people, because of their life experiences, God can be a frightening and confusing concept. Asking God for help doesn't seem very comforting if we think of Him as something that is capricious and judgmental, and outside ourselves. Because of the Human Condition, there are a number of reasons why you might feel very hesitant about God or Divine Intervention right now, even if you were raised with a devout religion!

It could also be the opposite: it could be that you were raised more in a scientific, atheist or agnostic type of home, and those are the beliefs that you adopted. Perhaps, just so you could feel more like your family and get their love and approval. Because these unconscious decisions are made so long ago, when we are very young, we tend to not remember even making them; and they just unawarely become a part of our identity.

Or, it could be that the religious beliefs we had a hard time believing in were so heavily pushed on us, that we rejected God altogether! Maybe it was fear and damnation you were rejecting; or, that you were told that you couldn't talk to God directly, and that you had to go through a middle-man. Maybe you had a hard time believing in an angry God, a judgmental God, a jealous God, or a God that would allow you to stay in limbo or burn in hell for eternity if you didn't believe in what you were being told to believe. Perhaps you just didn't feel loved and safe with a God like that, and felt the need to protect yourself. Or, maybe it didn't feel so great to be told that you were nothing but a sinner. That if you were a woman, you were less than the male and needed his permission and leadership to do anything, and that you were an evil temptress and the cause of man's fall from Grace. Ouch! If those were some of the beliefs you were raised with, they can all be some very good reasons why one might experience incongruence when thinking about God, and decide to keep an arm's length distance instead.

Another reason for your hesitance could be that you've seen or experienced so much separation in the name of God, even within the same religion. How many different denominations are there of just Christianity? Around 41,000?..... Really?... Perhaps you have been uncomfortable with feeling like you are *'less than'* because your beliefs or your lifestyle are different than someone else's, and you have felt rejected and judged.

> *I like your Christ, I do not like your Christians.*
> *Your Christians are so unlike your Christ.*
> ~Mahatma Gandhi

Maybe you experienced peer pressure to feel superior to someone because of the religion you were raised with, and that didn't feel comfortable either. Possibly, at the soul level, you really knew that we all come from the same Source. Just like how all bodies of water originally came from the same substance that falls from the sky, no matter how different they look and where in the world they are located. Perhaps, you don't want to be a part of the ego's need to make someone wrong in order to feel better and right. Maybe you just want to feel peace and happiness with your brother, so it has been easier to just not deal with all of the uneasiness and separateness experienced in the name of God.

Or, it could be the cruel things you've seen people do in the name of God. Throughout history, religion has been used as an excuse, or a driving force, for some of the worst human atrocities imaginable. How many wars have been fought in the name of one religion or another? How many people have been enslaved, gassed, burned alive, decapitated, tortured, starved to death, martyred, shot, blown apart, or hacked into pieces, in the name of God? As far back as we can look, in the ancient writings of all Deity-based religions, we see death, torture, and destruction in the name of a Deity.

Be it the abuse of innocent children and women or just mere fraud and greed, throughout history, religion has been used as an excuse to take advantage of people or kill them, in order to fill a void in one's soul, and to gain control, money and power. Some devout people have followed religious authority without a thought or question. The revealed word from a person who represents or says that they hear directly from God is enough, and they just believe and follow. With this kind of driving philosophy, a good person is defined as one who adheres to religious dictates without deviation, and where questioning the word is a sign of ignorance at best, and dangerous at worst.

Or, it may be that something bad happened to you in your personal life, or that you have seen horrific things happen in other people's lives around you. Because of this, you might have a lot of anger with God, and say to yourself, "How could there be a God who lets things like that happen?" I know there was a time period I felt like that, when my mother died. I would tell God very angrily, "Fuck off! I can't believe in a God who would take my mother from me at such a young age."

Another reason could be the relationship we have or the experiences we have had with our parents, who are God to us when we are small children. They are our source for everything, and we completely depend on them for all of our wants and needs. Whatever experience we had with our parents as a dependent and innocent child, we project onto God. Especially, whatever we experienced with our father, because most of us have been programmed with the concept of 'Father God'. So, if you had a father who would hurt you in any way while you were growing up, then you probably created a belief that you couldn't trust 'father' to take care of you or protect you. If your father often said "no" and wouldn't give you things that you would ask for, then you probably don't trust that God will give you what you ask for. If you had a very dominant and controlling father who made you afraid to ask him for anything, then you have probably learned not to ask "Father God" for things, either. If you felt like a burden, or didn't want to be a burden to one of your parents, then you probably learned not to ask for help from anybody, so as not to be a burden to them. So, as your relationship is to either one of your parents, and/or anyone who raised you as if they were your parents, most likely, so will be your relationship to the Divine.

As we reflect on the many reasons why we may have some separation and discomfort with God, let's remember that most of those reasons come from issues with man or humans, and not the Divine. People have mistakenly transferred human qualities onto God, and we have all bought into them because the humans before us who raised us did, and it was just unconsciously programmed, or *'passed down'* to us. Because we are fearful, angry and judgmental, we have projected those characteristics onto the Divine. We have made up a God in our image, instead of remembering that **we were created in the Divine's image**, which is a pure, unconditional love.

Humans have been using the *'Fear of God'* and *'Eternal Damnation'*, and the carrot to be in *'God's Favor and sit by his "right" side'*, to try and control people and get them to do whatever the *human powers to be at the time* wanted them to do. When thinking about the Divine we have to remember to **separate the baby from the bath water**, and not throw them both out! We can just throw out the dirty water instead, and keep the precious baby. Just like how, oftentimes, we have to separate the message from the messenger. Just because a human being is unable to live congruently with their message, doesn't make the message bad or wrong. You can throw out the messenger and just keep the message, and apply it to your life with congruency.

There have been a lot of misinterpretations of the Bible, by people we have believed and put our trust in, that have really negatively impacted our belief systems and have added to our fear. For instance, how the word 'sin' has been defined for us. In Aramaic, *'sin'* simply means to **miss the mark**. Like an archer missing the target when shooting an arrow. So, God is not saying that we're 'bad', just that we have a wrong perception and that we are **missing the** *mark*. We are not being punished **for** our '*sins*'; we are being punished *by* them — **by our totally missing the mark**!

I remember how this misinterpretation by ministers became so apparent to me when I went to Israel and actually walked the lay of the land described in the Bible. Doing so made the truth of the Bible come alive for me. Seeing the actual locations and having a greater understanding of the culture and the historical time period made my vision clearer, no longer just being filtered through and colored by my culture, conditioning, knowledge and experiences. For instance, I learned that the '*eye of the needle*' is a small, little door that is a part of the very large church doors. Parishioners were made to go through the eye of the needle, when entering the church, to ensure that they didn't try to bring their camels into church out of fear that they might be stolen. So it's not as impossible for a rich man to get into Heaven as for a camel to go through the eye of a sewing needle, as it was taught to me in Bible study. And while we are on the subject, '*repent*' is really an invitation to '***think again***' or '***think differently***'! So, I think we should all *repent* about our beliefs around God. ☺

Transcending the Cud

Now, all of these experiences or belief systems are just more *cud*! And to *transcend* this cud, the first relationship we have to heal in almost everyone is their relationship with the Divine. When I use the word Divine, please substitute it with whatever name you are most comfortable with; be it God, Jesus, Buddha, Krishna, Mohammed, The Universe, Source, The Field, The Creator, The Presence, Energy, The Light, Gaia, Mother Nature, Life Force, Universal Intelligence or whatever term best resonates for you. It does not matter; it is your path, however you know it. I am just choosing to use a universal term that is comfortable for me to share, and you will see me change it up in this book quite often. The truth is, there is only one God, and *It* doesn't care what you call **It**. Giving it a name, an identity with human emotions, is just a human construct. In most spiritual teachings across the globe, the universal answer to the question has just been, "**I Am!**"

We have to heal our relationship with the Divine first, so we can start using **The Formula** to move out the *cud,* so that we will no longer be driven by it – or at *the effect* of it! So that we can access the **Higher Consciousness** and start letting the **Divine Intervention** move out this blocked, limiting energy. So we can start doing a little *let go and let God* do the heavy lifting for us. So we can stop living life like the worm (and from the worm's eye view), and start soaring high like an eagle (with a bird's eye perspective)!

To get out of the minutia of the worm's eye view as described above, we need to fly above to a higher perspective to better understand these two statements:

1. God is everything, thus God can be anything.

2. Through religions led by humans, we have tried to limit and define God with negative and controlling human emotions.

Now, to take this out of just theology and look at it from a scientific perspective, let's take a look at Einstein's famous equation he presented to the world in 1905. The equation $E=mc^2$ demonstrated that energy and matter are so fundamentally related that they are one and the same. This directly contradicted previous beliefs, and a whole new field of science was born: **quantum physics**, which ushered in a new understanding of how the universe functions. Through this, a **Quantum Model** was discovered— that all physical reality is primarily energy (99.99999 percent) existing in a vast web that is interconnected across space and time, which holds all probabilities, and which is **affected by our observation**. (Our consciousness — *our thoughts, feelings and state of being* (our vibration)). Like clay, the energy of infinite possibilities is shaped by consciousness. As we saw with several examples in Chapter 2, *The Secret is In Your Heart*, but most specifically with Dr. Emoto's studies about how our emotions affected and transformed bodies of water. Also in Chapter 5 on the *Placebo Effect*. Your consciousness has effects on energy (matter) because your consciousness *is energy* — with a consciousness!

One of the key principles of **quantum physics** is that our thoughts determine reality. Early in the 1900's, researchers proved this beyond a shadow of a doubt with an experiment called the *Double Slit Experiment*. They found that the awareness of the observer is the determining factor affecting the behavior of energy (particles) at the quantum level. For example, electrons under the same conditions would sometimes act like particles, and at other times they would switch to acting like waves (formless energy); this change was completely dependent on what the observer expected to happen. Whatever the observer *believed* would occur, is what the **quantum field did**! And it would keep changing as the observer's expectation changed. Clearly demonstrating that the human energy field is interacting and influencing the quantum field around us, all the time.

Thus, the quantum world is waiting for us to make a decision, so that it knows how to behave. Demonstrating that we are truly co-creators with the Divine; because what we believe and expect, from an energetic, vibrational perspective, decides how the energy responds in the moment, and what manifests into form, out of the field of infinite possibilities.

Now let's relate this understanding of energy to Sanskrit definitions of the Divine — **Yathokthakari,** "*One who does as is bidden,*" and **Bhakti Paradina,** "*One who is at the beck and call of the devotee.*" Wow, what a great belief! One that aligns with Einstein's theory and quantum physics — that the Divine actually does what we ask, and behaves according to **our expectations**! Kind of like Jesus's, "*Ask and it will be given to you; seek and you will find; knock and the door will be opened to you,*" and, "*If you have faith as small as a mustard seed, you can say to this mountain, 'Move from here to there,' and it will move. Nothing will be impossible for you.*"

So, from this *awareness*, let's look at these statements once again. **God is everything, thus God can be anything**; and, **through religions led by humans, we have tried to limit and define God with negative and controlling human emotions.** If you believe in a jealous, angry, vengeful or judgmental God, then God will be that for you. If you believe in the *'Wrath of God'* as some religions suggest, then you may have experienced that. But if you want a loving and nurturing God, with characteristics of a loving, caring mother or friend, God will be that to you instead. If you want to have a God that is playful and has a sense of humor, God will be that for you as well. Take God out of the judgmental, vengeful, authority figure role and put God in the nurturing role if you want a more open, loving relationship. **You define your relationship with God; you set the expectations; and God just answers, "Ask and believe and you shall receive."** So, be very careful and astute in what you believe about the Divine! And, take a good look at what your current beliefs are, and where they came from.

Let me ask you a question. Do you think you could have a better relationship with the Divine if you could give Him/Her characteristics that you are more comfortable with, that you can identify with and more easily relate to?

To answer that question, let's take a look and see how you relate to various types of people in your life now. So tell me, how do you relate to a stranger? Do you feel really comfortable around this person? Are you asking them for help, trusting that they will help you and that they have your best interests in mind? How about a neighbor? Or an acquaintance? Are you really able to tell them your worries, and trust that they won't use them against you at some time? Do you feel that you can really ask them for help with big, important things in your life, and have the confidence that they will be there for you? How about with somebody you feel judged by? Now, how about with a distant relative you rarely see? You know that you '*should*' love them, but you don't even know them very well and you're not even sure what to talk to them about. How safe do you feel sharing your biggest struggles with them, and asking them for help?

What about with your best friend, the one who really knows you — the good, the bad, and loves you anyway? The one who sees all of your great qualities, even when you don't. The one you know is different than you, but doesn't judge you for that. That one great friend who you know will forever protect what you confide in them, and will always be there for you when you ask for help.

Which kind of relationship do you feel the most comfortable and confident with? Where you could let down some of your walls, let go some of your fear, and trust that they will be there to help you whenever you call? Looking at your life, *which kind of relationship has your connection with the Divine been more like, thus far?*

What if we had a relationship with the Divine where we accept It as our best friend that we *know* loves us unconditionally, doesn't judge us and always has our best interest in mind? As a friend that always has our back, and is there to support us whenever we call for help? What if we could really see the working force of that relationship in our daily lives and grew to know that we could really trust and depend on it? How different would your life be if you had this wise, powerful and trusted best friend, who had a greater perspective and more connections to help you out? **We define our relationship with the Divine**; and, we have to create and develop our relationship with the Divine just as we would with any other great relationship we have in our life.

Ask, Believe and You Shall Receive

To take a further look at this proclamation from Jesus, "***Therefore I tell you, all things whatever you pray and ask for, believe that you receive them, and you shall have them***," I want to share with you a fun story I heard while traveling in India:

There was a man who was a passionate devotee to Krishna, who would travel from town to town in India and preach to his fellow man, in the town square, about how much Krishna loved them and that He would help them and answer all of their prayers. In one particular town, people were just not paying attention to him at all, so he knew he had to do something big to get their attention. So he did the unheard of. In the middle of a town festival, he got up on a platform with a cow and a loudspeaker and announced, "Hear me, hear me, my fellow brothers — Krishna loves you and is devoted to your happiness and wellbeing, and will answer any of your prayers within 3 days— and I will prove it to you!" And at that moment, he took out a sword and killed the untouchable Holy Cow!

There was an instant uproar of anger from the crowd, and he announced back to the crowd, "Calm down my brothers! As I told you, Krishna loves us and will answer all of our prayers within 3 days. He will bring this cow back to life for us, to show you the power of faith in Him." They shouted back, "Well he'd better, or you're a dead man!"

The first day came and left, the cow remained lifeless, and the townsmen were yelling and swearing at the devotee, "Where is your Krishna now, you lunatic?" He calmly replied, "Have faith my fellow man! Krishna always provides; and He will answer our prayers and bring this cow back to life!" The second day came and went, the cow remained dead, and there was no sign of Krishna. The townspeople began to get furious; their slurs got harsher, and some showed up with weapons. The devotee tried to remain calm as he announced to the people again, "Put down your weapons my friends, and believe; Krishna is faithful, and he will hear our prayers and bring this cow back to life." The townspeople yelled back, "Your Krishna had better do so by tonight, because if he doesn't, you're a dead man- and we're going to take an eye for an eye." And, as the day got later, and as more and more people showed up with additional weapons, growing in their numbers and their anger, the devotee got on his hands and knees, desperately praying and crying out to Krishna. As it turned dusk, the townsmen started up the stairs onto the platform, saying, "Your time is up, you crazy, fanatical old man, you'd better start praying for Krishna to save you, because now you're a dead man!" And right as the townsmen were about to trounce on the devotee, Krishna appeared between them and held out his hand towards the cow, who quickly rose to his feet. The townsmen stopped in their tracks and gasped in surprise as the devotee turned to Krishna's feet, crying and profusely thanking him, "Thank you, thank you Krishna, for answering my prayers and saving this cow's life. Thank you for saving mine- but what took you so long?" And Krishna answered, "Well, you gave me 3 days!"

So that is a little tongue-in-cheek story of a powerful message for us to **get**, and *incorporate* in our belief in the Divine, and how quickly **It** can answer our prayers. Because, again, the Divine responds to ***our beliefs and expectations***. So if you are still believing in human terms that *'things take time'*, then that is exactly what your experience will be. If you're still believing in some of the Church's teaching, "*that it is all in God's timing*," well, you might be waiting for a very long time, because God is following ***your direction*** and just responding to ***your belief*** about '*waiting*'.

Oftentimes, it can *seem* as if God actually does wait until the last minute to intercede and perform a miracle in our lives. This is because we tend to have to be down on our knees, after trying everything we can to fix things on our own, before we feel desperate and helpless enough to ask God for help. When it comes to spiritual surrender, a certain amount of desperation is usually necessary, before the ego is ready to let go of control. Until we hit that breaking point, we attempt all of our old tricks, the ones that never worked before; but we think — just maybe it will work this time. Once we can no longer handle all of the struggle, we begin to consider the possibility that perhaps there really is a God who could help us out. That moment of surrender is not when life is over, **it's when it really begins**. Life would be much better for all involved, if we could just learn to ask for help right away! Know that it's God's great pleasure to respond to your request immediately.

A more practical and tangible example of this is the true story of a woman who had a large tumor in her stomach, and was a part of a study researchers were doing of some faith healers in Beijing. In this study, the scientists were observing, via a sonogram, the effect the faith healers were having on tumors in the bodies of patients, while the session was in progress. They simultaneously videotaped the healing session along with the monitor of the sonogram. In this video, right in front of your eyes, you watch the faith healers pray and chant over the patient, and at the same time you watch the tumor on the monitor get smaller and smaller until it **completely disappears within three minutes!!!**

It didn't take months; it didn't take weeks or even days, and it certainly didn't take chemo or radiation! It took only 3 minutes for the Divine to completely make the tumor disappear, right in front of your eyes! That is the power of your belief in the Divine and how **quickly It** will respond! You have heard this term many times from other authors, "***Change your mind, change your life***." You have to trust that the same Source that made you, can also heal you instantly. If you would like to see this video for yourself, you will find it here on my web site. www.HealYourHeartFreeYourMind.com/Gregg

Miracles defy the supposedly immutable laws of physics. We need to start paying more attention to them as they show up in our life, so as to give our mind new references to begin *transforming* the limiting beliefs we have been programmed with. The fact that I am here with you today, to write this book, is one of those examples. My survival of a 40 foot fall off a cliff in Fiji, dying and coming back, and my total physical healing, is one of those miracles that defy science.

When I first came to, the doctors told me that I didn't know who I was, where I was, or who my family was. They had taken an x-ray of my head, found a fracture, and were about to drill my skull open to release the pressure of the blood. But before they did so, some monks from a spiritual center where I was volunteering, which was located on a completely different island, just 'happened' to show up at the hotel where I was staying (out of many hotels on that island) the afternoon of my accident and heard the news of my fall. They asked to be taken to me in the clinic, and all I remember is waking up to them praying over me.

When I woke up, I knew exactly who they were and began to introduce them to everyone else in the room!! Before they prayed over me, I didn't even know my own name, I didn't know the name of my father, and I didn't even remember talking to anyone before that moment. But after they prayed over me, I knew everyone in that room and my entire family. Seeing that miraculous transition, the neurosurgeon had a last minute intuition to not do the surgery. Literally, **thank God**, because the clinic was filled with typhoid disease and dirty needles; and three weeks later I got a CT Scan back at home, and the doctors could not find a sign of that fracture in my skull at all! Yet, they could clearly see it in the x-ray I showed them, taken right after my fall. There is a long list of miracles that transpired around this fall that defy logic and baffle the mind. But let's just say that the Presence was really showing me, in a big way, that I didn't need to worry, and that I was being Divinely taken care of!

So, let's do an **inner view** of where your relationship with the Divine is right now, and why. Only by searching and mining are gold and diamonds obtained, and one can only find the truth, connected to his soul, if one will dig deep into the mine of his Being! Before we write down our answers below, let's do some internal digging into our subconscious mind with the following meditation and discover what transpired in our development that has caused us to have the belief systems and relationship, or the lack thereof, with the Divine that we have today. So, get into a private and comfortable meditation position and play track #4, the **Divine Meditation**; or click on the link below to download it now for some Divine support, as you go on this internal exploration.

www.HealYourHeartFreeYourMind.com/Divine

What is your relationship with the Divine like right now?

....

....

....

....

....

....

....

....

....

....

....

....

....

....

....

What are some negative experiences that you have had in association with the Divine? Because of those and because of your upbringing, what are some of your limiting beliefs you have had about the Divine?

....

....

....

....

....

....

....

....

....

....

....

....

....

....

....

....

....

....

....

....

....

....

....

What have you believed in the past about how quickly the Divine will respond?

....
....
....
....
....
....
....
....

So from this new awareness, how have some of the beliefs you picked up, around trusting the Divine, limited you in your life? How better could your life be if you allowed yourself to have a little more Divine guidance and help?

....
....
....
....
....
....
....
....
....
....
....
....
....
....

Now shake off that past conditioning, and let's start envisioning your life moving forward. So how would you like your relationship to be with the Divine instead? Would you like God to feel more like a trusted friend? One who is always looking after your best interests, guiding you, taking care of you and protecting you? One who is always helping you with the things that you want and need? Would you like to be more taken care of like a baby lion, versus fending for yourself like the baby monkey — always holding onto your mother's neck for dear life, as she busily swings from tree to tree without a worry about your well-being? Would you like to feel listened to and supported by the Divine, and have your requests responded to instantly?

My life and my relationship with the Divine forever changed when I learned the meaning of these powerful Sanskrit names for God, **Yathokthakari**, and, **Bhakti Paradina**. That *God depends on the belief of the devotee and actually behaves according to our expectations*! This helped me believe in, and develop a concept of a God that I could actually walk and talk with, like a friend. As a child, I had seen evidence of this before, in my best friend's devout grandparents, who indeed always got what they asked God for. No matter how strange their evangelical hell and brimstone beliefs seemed to me, they had a close and personal relationship with God that really worked for them. I could not relate to this judgmental God that they always preached about, so unfortunately I disconnected from God and became *'the doer'*.

As I grew, I thought I had ditched unhelpful concepts of God I learned from childhood and that I had embraced a more progressive, inclusive God. But soon, I realized the vast, formless God I had created was too nebulous and impersonal for me to really relate to in any heartfelt way, so the relationship remained distant. I realized I needed my God to be more like someone I could relate to on a day-to-day basis, like my best friend who I felt close and comfortable with, and who I could trust to help me with all of life's little challenges.

When we are children, it is very easy for our image of our parents or caregivers to get mapped over onto our image of God. It's understandable since our parents or caregivers were like God to us, the conduit through whom all things seem to depend on and flow through during our most impressionable years. If your parents were like the average parents, you may need to weed out those less-than-positive unconscious perceptions of God, and replace them with qualities you want in your Divine instead. Because God will behave the way you expect, and life will bring you the consequences of that thinking. And since all of this gets conditioned in us before we learn to form sentences, it can be an invisible driving force for us, and very hard to identify. It's so deeply ingrained in our Being that we don't even notice it. I mean, how could fish notice they are in water? No other reality is imaginable to them.

So I began to create a persona of God that I could really talk and relate to. Giving Him/Her all the qualities my heart desired, all the qualities my earthly parents didn't have, and all that I had wanted from life but hadn't received. This became uplifting, hopeful and fun! I asked that my God relate to me with humor, playfulness, thoughtfulness, and caring, on top of all the expected Godly qualities like all-knowingness, love and power (without being authoritative, of course). A God that really cared about my every need, and my every concern in every aspect of my life. One who would guide me and give me messages I could understand, and who loves to co-create with me as a partner in life. A God that would delight in participating in all my adventures, and even my everyday tasks.

As I did this, God became a tangible reality to me, *an experience* instead of a concept. The Divine even performed a humorous miracle for me to give me evidence of our new-found relationship. I had a small flashlight that I used to keep by my bedside in case I had to get up in the middle of the night. One evening, in the beginning of our new relationship, it fell and its small handle broke off— no matter how hard I looked for it, I could not find the handle. Frustrated, I finally gave up looking, sat the flashlight back on my nightstand and went back to sleep. The next morning, the handle on the flashlight reappeared and was perfectly fixed! The missing piece had reappeared, and there was no crack or a sign of where the break in the handle had been. I was shocked and ecstatic. My thoughtful and playful Divine had sent me a life-changing message— "No matter how small it may seem, what is important to you is important to me. I hear you and I am here for you." And I keep that flashlight close to me as a powerful reminder of that truth!

Minute by minute, day by day, my relationship with the Divine vastly grows. God finally feels like an inner best friend who really listens and communicates back to me in signs, events and sometimes in a clear voice or knowing. This is quite different from the old, one-way pleas to an angry, judgmental God that my friend's grandfather used to preach about. Many of us now have the kind of relationship with the Presence that allows us to simply think of something we would like, show gratitude for it being presently so, and it shows up.

You can have that type of relationship with the Divine too. When God is that friendly to you, that intimately involved in your daily life, everything you ask for, no matter how mundane, is delivered. People who have this type of relationship with God don't have to pray, or write it down, or set a goal. They just simply ask and the Divine delivers their request, just like a doting parent or grandparent would. You can have such a relationship when you begin to regularly talk to the Divine like your friend and confidant, and stop thinking of God as some judgmental, vengeful authority figure in the sky, separate and distant from you, who is too busy and uninterested in your everyday desires.

I have what I call an *'A Team'*, that consists of the Divine, my Angels, Guides, and deceased loved ones — like my mother. Every morning before I get up, I plan my day with them. I tell them what I am working on and what I need help with, fully expecting that it will get done and thanking them for it. I tell you, things get done so much more quickly and easily, and a hundred times better, when I turn it over to them!!! And I experience a lot less stress and internal conflict. It really brings me closer and closer to the Divine and my *A Team* — there becomes a real trust and a real bond. I thank them every night when I am going to sleep, for all of the things that they helped me with that day; seeing all of the blessings they bestowed on me and really feeling grateful for them. I see the Divine and my *A Team* as my true *Life Partner*. The ones I know I can truly trust and turn to for help and support in my life.

You see, together God and man make the best creative team. God is like electricity and we are the lamps. A house can be wired with electricity, but if there aren't any light fixtures, any physical forms to express it, what good does it do? And without a Source, what good are the lamps? Together, however, they cast out all of the darkness, and light the way.

So, as you create your own personal relationship with the Divine, let go of and replace any concept you might have *that you have to earn things*, because if you have that belief, you will have to earn everything. Decide that God wants to grace you with all that you want, with ease.

Also, let go of and replace any wrong notion you may have of being *unworthy to receive something*. Decide to agree with God that your worth is already a given, and that your very existence proves it. Remember, worthiness is not a concept of God. Unworthiness is a mind-construct based on wrong, unhealthy human programming. You are more than worthy, just as the birds and flowers are worthy of their sustenance.

Let go of the theory that *life is about lessons*, because if you believe that, you will get lots of them! Whereas, if you believe life is about enjoyment, you will have a lot more of joy instead. Life will make you evolve, you will learn and grow naturally— but lessons? This isn't school. Decide that God wants you to joyfully evolve instead! You can actually do a lot more for the Divine when you are happy. A struggling, unhappy person does not make a good steward!

Let go of and replace any wrong perception you may have that *your worldly desires are not important to God*. If you think God has no interest in your daily needs, then you won't ask; and that makes it less likely for Grace to come and respond to your needs. The Divine wants to give you what you ask for; so the more you can get out of the way and let that in, the easier it can be delivered. People who have their material needs met are freer to share their spiritual gifts with others, don't you think? One who is constantly struggling to make ends meet makes neither a good model for others nor has much time or money to contribute to the whole.

Make your communication with God a *two-way conversation*. Be still and let God talk more. Meditation is a powerful tool for this. The answer may not be a voice; it could be more like a feeling, a knowing, a simple thought, an event or even a person that solves the problem for you. Listen, watch and feel what comes up; and say thank you for it already being done now!

So now, it's your turn to create your perfect relationship with the Divine! How do you want to relate to God and how do you want God to relate to you? How do you want to interact? How involved in your life do you want the Divine to be? How quickly do you want **It** to respond to your requests? Do you want God to be serious or light-hearted, playful and fun? Listen to track #5 and design your perfect relationship with the Divine below. Remember the **Divine responds to the requests of the devotee**. *Ask, Believe and you shall Receive*!

www.HealYourHeartFreeYourMind.com/Divine2

What characteristics or personality traits would you like for the Divine to have with you?

....

....

....

....

....

....

....

....

....

....

....

....

....

....

Based on these characteristics, create your new relationship with the Divine, including how He/She interacts with you and how quickly *It* responds.

....

....

....

....

....

....

....

....

....

....

....

....

....

Divine Grace is a gift for ALL. All you need to do is **Ask** for it, and it is given freely. The stronger your relationship is with the Divine, and *the more you trust the Divine* and become more like the baby lion, the more Divine Grace you will experience, along with all of the miracles that it has to offer. Only Divine Grace can override the *Law of Reflection.*

It's why so much doctrine tells us to be like an innocent child again. Little children don't think they know what everything means. In fact, they know they don't know. They ask someone older and wiser to explain things or help them out. Often, we are like children who don't know, but think we do, and try to figure it out all on our own. The wise person doesn't pretend to understand what he or she doesn't know, and instead, steps back to let someone with more awareness step forward and lead the way.

When we surrender like the baby lion, we surrender to something bigger than ourselves — to a Universe that knows what it is doing. We relax while a power much greater than our own takes over, and it does a much better job than we could have ever begun to imagine. We learn to trust that the power that holds galaxies together can handle the circumstances of our relatively simple lives. Surrender means, by definition, giving up attachment to how and when things happen. That includes not trying to take back control and continuing to open the oven door to see if the bread is done yet — which only ensures that it never gets a real chance to bake.

I experienced this truth the most when I was traveling. The times I didn't know the language, the rules, or the lay of the land and I couldn't figure it all out with my mind. The times where I was in the situation where I could do nothing else but ask the Divine for help, and turn things over to my *A Team.* I can't tell you how many *'miracles'* happened for me when I did. The things that would just show up for me defy logic. When I was in this total state of helplessness, I would just think I needed something, and someone would just come up to me and say, "By the way, do you need help with this? Let me help you."

I remember one day when I was in a small town in Argentina, and I was trying to figure out how to get to my accommodations, but no one could tell me how to get there. I felt scared and confused, and I didn't know what I was going to do; so I just sat at a bus stop with my head down, crying, asking my angels for help. All of a sudden I heard a bus pull up, and as I looked up, the bus driver asked me in broken English, "Are you going to the Albuquerque Chino?" "Yes," I answered. He said, "Get in, I'll take you." He proceeded to go far out of his way, off of his bus route, and drove me directly to my accommodation. When I tried to pay him, he refused to take any money from me. These were the kinds of experiences I would have all the time as I traveled and turned things over to my *A Team*– being totally cared for, like a baby lion.

When I would come home, it was a completely different story. When I was back to having it all figured out and taking care of everything, nothing good would unfold for me. Nothing would flow and everything felt like a struggle. I felt as if I was all of a sudden left to fend for myself, much like a baby monkey. Everything was easier and much better when I got out of the way and the Divine took over. **Our only job is to Initiate Grace, Ask for what we want, Let Go of control, Follow the guidance and Let Go and Let God!** We are not making it happen; we are just setting our clear intention, asking for help, and getting out of the way and letting the Grace come through us and to us!

Prayers, meditation, the *Blessing¹⁸*, centering yourself by closing your eyes and putting your hands on your heart, and a chant that I am going to share with you, are a few ways to invoke the Divine Grace. This chant is called the **Moola Mantra,** and it is an ancient Sanskrit chant to invoke the Divine that is Omnipresent in All. Below, I will give a little definition to each word and an association to Christianity so you know what you are singing. (If you so choose to.)

Om: Behind Creation, immanent to all existence, you find hiding the sound and vibration "Om" or "Aum." This Divine sound has the power to create, sustain and destroy, giving life and movement to all that exists.

Sat: Pure Existence

Chit: Pure Consciousness

Ananda: Supreme Bliss

Parabrahma: The Universal Conscious in the Absolute aspect. The One who is beyond space and time. (*The Father*)

Purushottama: Even though the nature of the Universal Conscious is formless, **It** decides to take a form in order to closely relate to creation. **It** is the energy which has incarnated in a body to guide us. *Like Jesus (The Son)*

Paramatma: At the same time, the Universal Conscious is immanent in the Soul of all living beings. (*The Holy Spirit*) The Divinity present in every living being. The Inner Dweller.

Sri Bhagavati: In Creation there is a feminine aspect and a masculine aspect. "Bhagavati" is the female aspect of the Universal Conscious.

Sameta: "Together with", "In communion with."

Sri Bhagavate: The male aspect of the Universal Conscious

Namaha: Salutations to the Divine in you.

So you sing the below mantra three times in whole. Then you sing the last two lines twice, and then the last line twice before you end the entire chant with a long OM. Please go to track #6 or go to the link below to download a sample of the song to hear, and that you can play and listen to instead, anytime you want to invoke the Divine for some help.

www.HealYourHeartFreeYourMind.com/Mantra

OM
SAT CHIT ANANDA PARABRAHMA
PURUSHOTTAMA PARAMATMA
SRI BHAGAVATI SAMETA
SRI BHAGAVATE NAMAHA

If you have a challenge that you have questions about and that you really need answers to, a great way to connect with the Divine or your *A Team* is to *dialog* with them through Automatic Writing. **Automatic Writing** is a process of shutting your conscious mind off to allow your subconscious mind to take over your writing, allowing Spirit to communicate to you, through you. So, for example, first invoke the Divine Grace any way that best suits you; then pull out your journal, put your name or initial down and write down your question. Then, perhaps use a different colored pen, write the name or initial down of whom you would like the answer from, be it the Divine, your Angels, your Spirit Guides, a deceased loved one or in general your *A Team*, and start writing. Let the answer just flow through you *automatically* without any interpretation from the mind. And just continue to dialog with Spirit until you feel clearer and complete. This is a great tool to use anytime you feel confused about anything.

The **F**ourth **S**tep to Freedom is:

4. Heal & develop a very close, trusting and strong relationship with Source, so that you can get Divine help in all areas of your life, making it bigger and better than you can begin to imagine!

   - Dig deep into the mine of your Being and see what unhealthy beliefs and wounding you have around God that have been limiting your trust and your relationship. Where did they come from, and are they really true? Which ones are just projections onto God, based on your experiences with your parents and family?
   - Use **The Healing Process** to heal these charges
   - Recreate and redefine your relationship with the Divine. Create a new relationship that has all of the characteristics that you can really relate to, trust and engage with.
   - Practice and engage in this new relationship daily.
   - Start with the 30 Day Challenge and the Prayer Journal described below.
   - Use Automatic Writing as a way to connect with the Divine to help you with any difficult questions and decisions you need to make.

Transcend*Transform*Inspire

A Thirty Day Challenge

It takes 30 days to recondition a new behavior; so I have a 30 day challenge to assist you in building up your relationship with the Divine, so that you can strengthen your use of the *Growth and Success Formula*. For the next thirty days I want you to consistently practice your new relationship with the Divine, from the time you get up, to the time you go to bed. Interact with God like a best friend, a nurturing parent, a trusted confidant, a close business or life partner, or however you defined your relationship, every day, for the next thirty days. Perhaps utilize the practice of **Automatic Writing** daily to *dialog* with your Divine. So this means if you miss a day, that is ok; just start your thirty days all over again the very next day! Wear a rubber band on your wrist, or one of those rubber positive affirmation bands you can find anywhere to remind you, and if you accidentally miss a day, just switch it to the other wrist and start your thirty days all over again.

Another good way to do this, and also apply **The Formula** at the same time, is to create a **Prayer Journal**. Every morning ask for help with something from the Divine and write it down in your prayer journal. Every night, open it up again and capture **when** and **how** your prayers or requests were answered, expressing gratitude. It will help you strengthen your trust and relationship with the Divine as you see the responses documented, and how quickly they are responded to. Make sure to capture all of this information so you can see, with your own eyes, all of the results that are unfolding. For example, the heading of your journal entries could look something like this:

Date/Time	Prayer	Date/Time Received	Acknowledgement

So go find a brand new notepad or journal to dedicate to this, and let's get started right now! And remember you're not praying to God, you're praying **with** God!

Chapter Ten

Trinity
~The Power of Three Will Set You Free~

Now that you have the formula to start living life *at cause* and not just at the effect, and now that we have opened up and strengthened your relationship with Source, let me ask you a deep and profound question. Who are you?

The true understanding of the answer to that question will forever set you free, and ignite something far grander and greater than you have ever experienced today. You are not your body. You are not your identity and the name you have been given, or any of the labels that have been given to you. You are not your intellect or your conscious or subconscious mind. You are that which has never been born and that which will never die. What you really are is pure, and it has never been tarnished by programming!

You are a soul, you are Spirit. You are an Infinite Being, and not the finite body in which you are living in. You are a Spirit that has a vehicle ~ a body, in which to live in this material world. You are a soul that has a mind to help you run the body, and to figure out how to function in this realm. But you are not this body, nor this mind. They are just your tools, your soul's tools in which to live on this Earth.

Through all of the subconscious and societal programming that has happened from the time you were conceived, through the process of how this gets integrated into the neuro-network and the cells of your body; through the development of the intellect to protect the body from the hurt and fear that it has experienced or was programmed with, this truth has gotten lost in the shuffle. It has been covered up by layers upon layers of fear-based decisions and programming. Your *Essence* has always been there; it has just lain there quietly waiting for you to wake up from all of this illusion and **from the control of your fear-based mind**, so that it can get on with the intention it came here for. It is like a diamond, pure and radiant at its core, that has been buried under many layers of dirt that have kept it from radiating out its brilliance – but it has always been there — present and eternal.

You are a Trinity~ Mind, Body & Spirit. You are primarily a Spiritual Being who existed before birth and who will continue to exist after the body's death. You really have no beginning nor an end. You live in a body that was given a name by your parents, and you have a mind whose job has been to take care of you and your body. ALL parts of you are *very important,* and ALL parts of you need to be acknowledged, loved, appreciated and taken care of. This is where your power lies. Disowning any part of you is what has weakened you. Owning your **Trinity** will liberate and empower you. Only bringing them all together in unity will conquer all of the internal demons, with fear being the toughest one to overcome. You have all been separated because of this fear. We need to do some healing and mending to align these parts together because right now they are in conflict; this is another reason why you feel so much internal conflict. Trinity in itself means the unity of three— and **the Power of Three Will Set You Free!**

For most, this would mean you need to wake up to your *Spiritual Essence* and allow it to now take over as lead from your mind. For others, like myself, it may be that you need to actually acknowledge, love and appreciate your body and stop treating it as if it's not who you are, so it's not important. And for others, again myself included, it may be that you need to also acknowledge, love and appreciate your mind as well, for the same reasons. Not one of the three can live fully in this life if either of the others is cut short of full life and expression. It isn't noble to live only for the soul and try to deny the mind or body; and it is wrong to live for the body and try to deny the soul and the mind. **ALL** parts of your *Trinity* need to be acknowledged, appreciated, listened to and supported. When a part goes unacknowledged and unattended, it will become like a toddler throwing a tantrum!

Your mind is made up of two parts: the **emotional body** and the **intellect**. The **emotional body** is basically all of your *cud—* your *charges*. It is all of the stuff you have been programmed with from your parents, family and society from the time you were conceived. And because of the childhood traumas and the *Arrested Development,* your *emotional body* is usually stuck at a very young age. Until you heal all of the *cud* your *emotional body* represents, and **is,** your hurt and afraid little girl or boy. As your **intellect** was being developed around the age of 6-7, it started creating belief systems and strategies to protect the *emotional self* from further pain or danger. And this is the part of you that has since developed the most, and has taken over control of your total Being. It has become so dominant and integrated into your body that it has fooled you into thinking that you are it and it is you. And as a part

146

of its modus operandi of protection, it does all that it can to keep you from figuring out that you're not it — the mind. Which is easily done, with both the hurt little kid and the protective, scolding adult (intellect) integrated into the neuro-network of the body and leading the way.

But it is time for your **Spiritual Essence** to wake up out of the fog and take back control of its vessel. It is time for it to sprout out of its acorn and be the Oak that it truly is. These parts of you have been running amuck, out of control and without direction, because they didn't have a captain listening to them, taking care of them and reassuring them that they would be ok. They have been hurt; they have been afraid. They have been in conflict; fighting, disputing and blaming the other parts for their problems; vying to be heard, helped, and wanting some kind of relief or control. And all of their internal conflict is being mirrored back to you as conflict with your external world.

Your **Spiritual Self** is ready; it is probably the part of you that has secretly brought you on this journey, so it can liberate itself from its confinement. Because your *intellect* would've said, "Don't worry, I've got this all figured out and under control," and your *body* would've said, "I am too tired," and your *emotional little kid* would have said, "I am too afraid." But your **Essence** knew this was the way to free ALL parts of you from this Matrix, and finally truly live as it intended.

So close your eyes, and put your hands on the center of your chest and connect to your **Essence** now. Take three deep breaths, hold each one for five seconds and slowly exhale. Keeping your focus on your heart center, take a deep breath and do three *Yangs* (sounds like yong). Now, keep your awareness here in your heart center and feel the quiet and calm. Connect to that feeling. That is really you. The quieted mind and the internal peace you felt when you did the meditations, that is who you really are. That energy, that prana, you felt rising up in your body and filling up your energy centers, that is who you really are. That vibration you felt in your centers and that you began to feel in every cell of your body— that is you, that is your **Essence**. That light you felt coming into your crown, that is where you came from and are a part of. You are this light and this energy. And it is time for you to now wake up from your slumber and know this, and take responsibility for your vessel.

And from this place, **Spiritual Self**, you are going to listen to the complaints of each part of you, giving them a safe place to express their frustrations and their truth; and promise each one of them that you are going to help and support them with the other parts of your vessel. A safe place where the other parts will hear them but will not be able to interject. For this exercise, I want you to grab a pillow and imagine that the pillow is the part of you that is expressing itself to you in the moment.

Now providing a safe place for these parts is key, because *not feeling safe* is the foundational problem driving the challenges in people's lives. It is the cornerstone for the development of the *emotional child* and the *intellect*. It is the foundation of the **Human Condition**. It started with the trauma of the birthing process; it continued with ancestral and cultural downloading; it expanded with childhood experiences; and it grew further with each blow to its love and trust from society. Safety and security is a primary *charge* that almost all of society needs to heal. It is why our ***intellect*** has become so developed and prevalent, and why it ineffectively tries to control everyone and everything.

The first part of ourselves that we are going to listen to is the part of us that rarely gets to express itself unless it has been abused for so long that it starts to rebel and express itself in discomfort and dis-ease — and that is the body. Your body is your life partner. You can't experience life without it; thus it is critical that you listen to it and pay attention to all that it has to say. The two of you are in a deeply committed, lifelong relationship. And like a relationship with a spouse or a significant other, it has the potential to either offer you tremendous joy, pleasure and freedom; or, if not properly cultivated and nurtured, it can create a great deal of pain, anxiety and frustration instead. The best relationships are ones in which the partners appreciate and acknowledge each other consistently, and refrain from harsh criticisms. But how often do we really treat our bodies with such loving respect, and without disparaging thoughts, words or deeds from our other parts? How often do we thank our body for all of the miraculous things that it does for us on a daily basis? If we did to a romantic partner what our other parts do to our body, would that romantic partner still be committed and around? If we had a fight with our loved one and we knew that we were in the wrong — being neglectful, critical and abusive— would we most likely want to make it up to them by apologizing and being extra grateful for all that they do?

So, *intellect* and *emotional kid*, we don't want our body to have any dis-ease; that wouldn't be any fun for us. We need to listen to the body now and make amends with it. Let's reverse the impact that the body has faced, living in a society where we tend to take for granted the one we will be spending the rest of our lives with. Let's do our part to make this lifelong relationship as joyful, peaceful and pain-free as possible, ok?

So *Spiritual Self*, with your eyes closed I want you to imagine the pillow is your body, and I want you to look it in the eyes and ask, "*Body*, how are you? What do you need to tell me? What do you need? I want you to vent out all of your frustrations to me about all parts of this vessel. They can hear you, but you're *safe*; I am here to help you, all of you, as a safe guide. Now is your time to express to all of us what your frustrations are and what you need from us." And then, *Spiritual Self*, I want you to just listen to all that it has to say. Let it vent to you how everyone is always taking it for granted, never appreciating it and always rejecting it.

"You guys are always badmouthing me, giving me bad food, too much food, too much sugar, lots of alcohol or other substances; and then you expect me to run properly. What would happen to a car if you continuously put bad gas in it? I run every single part of the body while processing all of this crap, desperately trying to keep up with all of the shit you put into me, just trying to keep you alive, and you never even say "thank you." You don't even do things to take care of my exterior, like exfoliating or moisturizing my skin. You just look at me and tell me all the things you don't like about me, and complain! You're always comparing me to others – to models and celebrities — then criticizing me, making me feel like I don't measure up. You're always putting all of this stress on me with all of your out-of-control emotions, day after day, year upon year— like fear, anger, worry, sadness, anxiety and ongoing depression. You flood me with all of these chemicals and stress out all of my organs; then you eat, drink or take something to numb yourself from it all. And you wonder why I gain weight and don't feel very good! What do you expect!? Then when you don't like how I look, you are cutting me, injecting me, or sucking something out of me, lasering me, or putting chemicals on me or in me. You are always putting me in physical danger and when something happens, I have to work triple-time to fix and repair it, all while running everything else in the body at the same time! And again, all you do is complain, never loving or appreciating all that I do and the marvel that I am! Hell, you've spent most of your life treating me as if I were something evil, rejecting me and not wanting to live inside me. I should've just shut down right then and there, you ingrate! That way I wouldn't have spent all these years just being abused and working so hard just trying to get a little of your love and appreciation that you never, ever give!! If you would just listen to me, I could expertly guide you to excellent health. My instincts for food, exercise, sleep and what I need for my wellbeing are infallible— not the *emotional little kid* or the *intellect*! Why don't you two complaining ingrates take a moment to contemplate what life would be like for you if I had a chronic or terminal illness!"

Just close your eyes now and let the *body* rant and rave about all of its frustrations and pain until it has exhausted itself.

Once it has worn itself out, I want you to hold the *body* in your arms. Hug it lovingly close to you and tell it how sorry you are that you all have been mistreating it. Tell it that **you are here now, captaining the vessel**, honoring the temple for you that it is, and that what has transpired won't be the case moving forward. Tell your *body* how much you love it, and how appreciative you are for all that it does and has done, for you and the team. Go through and list all of the things that it does and your deep gratitude for it. I will help you out, with this little **Body Appreciation Meditation**. So go into a quiet place, grab your MP3 player and headset, and go to track #7 or to this link to listen to it or download it now.

www.HealYourHeartFreeYourMind.com/Body

Now feel how much the *body* is enjoying this love and appreciation. Feel it awaken and enliven up. Feel all the cells in your body begin to vibrate and dance. Your *body* now feels heard, appreciated and loved. Healing and peace has begun. Let's now do the same for our *emotional body* — for our inner child or our little kid within.

Self care is never a selfish act, it is simply good stewardship of
the only gift I have, the gift I was put on earth to offer to others.
Anytime we can listen to true self, and give it the care it requires, we do so
not only for ourselves, but for the many others whose lives we touch.

~ Parker Palmer

For this one, find a picture of yourself when you were a little kid. A picture you really identify with, where you are around 7-8 years old. Look into your *emotional child's* eyes, and what do you see in their eyes and face? Is there fear, pain or confusion? What are they feeling, what are they going through, and what do they have to say to you and the rest of your Being? Let them vent and tell you all they need to express now!

"Thank you ***Spiritual Self,*** for finally letting me express myself!! I am very sick of the *intellect* always shutting me down! Every time I try to express myself, the *intellect* is always telling me to shut up, stop whining, grow up; you're such a baby, get a grip, stop being so pathetic, you're always messing things up, you can't do anything right, you're always throwing a tantrum, stop being so dramatic, stop being so needy, you're so lazy, you're irresponsible, stop being so emotional, you're fat, you're going to get fatter, no one's going to love you, you're going to be alone your whole life, you're going to die alone, it's your fault that we're alone, and it's your fault that we don't have any money, you're such a disgrace. I am so fricken tired of it! Stop criticizing me, stop putting me down, stop just abusing me more! I am tired of being a doormat! I'm also tired of you always being so serious and never letting me play, joke around, be funny or express myself! You don't listen to me at all; you just immediately shut me down and distract me with something else! I am tired of it! I need to express myself; I need to get it out; I need to be heard and acknowledged, and my feelings cared about. My needs and desires cared about! I need to matter — to matter to somebody! Do you hear me? My thoughts, my feelings, my needs, my desires — they need to matter! You have to listen to me and try to help me, not just try to shut me down and ignore me and pretend I'm not there! I am, and I need to be heard now!"

Just close your eyes now **Spiritual Self,** and listen to your own *inner child* and all that it needs to say; and when it's done, grab your pillow and just love and hug your *inner child*. Tell it you're sorry for all that it has gone through, and that it hasn't felt heard or supported for all these years. Tell your *emotional child* that you love them, that you are here for them now and that everything is going to be different from now on. Tell them you know how much they went through as a child and continue to go through now that they are older, and that you appreciate how brave and strong they have been through it all. Tell them that they have a beautiful, sensitive heart, and that you so appreciate how they keep you young and their playful nature. Tell them all the many things you love and appreciate about them, as you love and hold them tight! Let the tears fall, and feel all the love and appreciation pour through you that you have for your little *innocent child* who has gone through so much without a safe place to express itself. And as you do, feel how grateful they become for this love, attention and appreciation. Feel them begin to enliven and energize. They feel heard, supported and lighter because they were able to release all of this pent-up hurt and resentment. They are feeling joy, happiness and peace! They are finally feeling safe in your arms and under your care and guidance......... And now it is time to hear from your *intellect*.

"*Intellect*, you have heard all of the complaints of our *emotional kid* and our *body*. What do you have to say to everyone? What have you been struggling with and what do you need to communicate to us all? I know you have felt as if you have been on your own, taking care of everything, and nobody under-stands the stress that you're always under trying to manage it all; but I am here now to support you as **the captain of this vessel**, and as a safe place for you as well. Please tell me about all of your frustrations, and don't hold back at all."

"Well thank you for your understanding *Spiritual Self*, and thank you for hearing me out. That *emotional little kid* always gets on my last nerve and wears me out! I am here to take care of them, protect them, guide them and keep them on track. I'm here to make sure they are not taken advantage of again, or abused or hurt; and they just run amuck. They don't listen to me, they don't mind; and they're always causing trouble, making me have to work triple-time to undo all of their mistakes. I get tired of the emotional rollercoaster going on all over the place; it is exhausting. They always just want to play or cry about something, and keep me from my work and from getting anything done. They have wasted years of my life feeling sorry for themselves, crying to others and eating their woes away that I have not been able to get anything I wanted to get done, finished. They are the reason why we are not as successful as we should be; they are the reason why we don't have the money we need; they are the reason we are fat and out of shape; they are the reason why we are single and alone; and they are the reason we don't have all the things that we want. It is their fault, because they waste all our time crying over the past and what this person did to them; and having me waste time trying to fix it all, instead of being focused on our goals. They are always procrastinating and trying to distract me from my work with, "I'm cold," "I'm hungry," "I wonder who is doing what on Facebook," with TV, or with, "What fun event is going on that I might miss." OMG, we have wasted so much time over the years, focusing on what is going on because of their fear of missing out! You know how much money and success I would have by now, if I weren't wasting so many hours trying to keep them happy, feeling approved of, and entertained? That *emotional kid* is always trying to fill a void they feel, all the frickin time! It is amazing I have been able to get anything done with all of their emotional acrobatics! It's a miracle I am not a blimp! That child is exhausting; trying to keep it happy, and get it focused and back on track! They hijack my work all of the time! And they are never grateful for all I do for them; taking care of them, protecting them and guiding them. Always just complaining about how I don't acknowledge and listen to them, how mean I am, and how I never let them express themselves or play! Ugh! How about some gratitude for all that I do instead— all that I have done over the years, you ingrates! I am tired of your whining and non-appreciation!"

Close your eyes and continue to listen to all that your *intellect* has to tell you, and all of its complaints. When it is done and has exhausted itself, grab your pillow and hug your *intellect* tightly to your chest, telling it how much you love it, and how appreciative you are of everything it has managed and taken care of while you have been away. Tell it **how grateful you are for all of its hard work to try and protect the *body* and the *emotional child* for all of these years.** That it has done an amazing job, **but now it can rest, because you are here to love and support and take care of everyone.** And that you are directly connected to a Divine team, that has a greater perspective and more connections and influence, to help them with anything that they need. Let your *intellect* know all the many things that you appreciate about it; and all that it has done, in your absence, that you are so grateful for. "I am sorry I have been hidden for so long under all of the layers of programming, but **I am here now as your captain**, the captain of this vessel, supporting you and all of our team members. You no longer have to take care of everything. You can now take the weight of the world off your shoulders, and just play the normal role of capturing and analyzing data that you were meant to play. I've got you covered."

Feel the *intellect* begin to relax in your arms, beginning to unwind. It has been so stressed, so tight and wound up, trying to control and hold everything together. Feel more energy flow within its Being. Feel it begin to feel calmer, lighter and more joyful. Hear its words, that it trusts you and knows that you will be there to take care of them all. It knows it can now relax and not be on guard all of time; that you and your *A Team* have its back and will handle things.

"Now that we have heard each other's challenges and have a greater understanding; and now that we know that we will always be heard and supported by me and our *A Team*, let's make a truce and a commitment to work together in unison. To stop all of the inner conflict, and always listen to and support one another as a team, with me as your captain and guide. By consciously working together as a team, we can all have a happier and more productive life to get **All** of what we want: good health, love, fun, success, self expression, and more importantly, internal peace! We need to learn from our friends the geese, who can fly thousands of miles easily by working as a team. By working together they uplift one another, being able to fly 70% more than they could alone; and they are always cheering on the goose ahead of them. And if one falls ill, another team member stays with them and supports them until they are feeling better. This is what we need to do as a team and as a collective system. Each one of us has an important role in the success of this vessel reaching its intended destination; we will never arrive at that destination in conflict or with disrespect for each other. So, do we all agree to put our grievances away; to hear one another, have love and compassion for the other; stop trying to control and manipulate one another or put each other down; and to come together in support and with solutions to each one's challenges, for the overall success of this vessel?"..........

"Yes? Great! Then let's do a proverbial hand shake on this commitment to one another, and let's get started! Each morning, I will close my eyes, put my hands on my heart center and check in with each one of you and see how you are doing and what kind of support you need. I will then express my gratitude and appreciation for you and all that you do, and I will address your needs with the support of our other parts and with our *A Team.* The *A Team* will be able to help us with any of our needs far greater than each one of us could individually! Is that a deal?... Great! And at any point of the day, if any of you are feeling uneasy about anything, just let me know. I will again center myself and check back in with you and the *A Team,* and handle whatever it is! The *A Team* and I are here for you. We will always listen to you and support you. You are no longer alone in this, trying to figure it all out and fight your way through. Your captain is here, and I have brought an army of Divine Beings to back us up! Now it is time for us to finally get into team formation, and soar!"

Take charge of your vessel *Spiritual Self,* and get back on track with your life's mission. You came here for a reason, and all of this programming has gotten you off track, until now. This wonderful journey you are being guided on is beckoning you back. Only our body and mind were created by our parents and society— only our vehicle was programmed with the Human Condition; but not you, the driver. You, *Spiritual Self,* are made from Source and are the driver of this vessel!

Today you liberate yourself from this programming, and you set a line in the sand and say, "From now on we are an integrated system, working as a team to reach this vessel's destination! To run and finish our *marathon*! Daily, we will do our work to liberate ourselves from the labels and programming and get back on track with our mission." There will finally be peace and unison of this Mind, Body & Spirit!

Throughout the history of ancient civilizations, success and triumph has always been symbolized by the coming together of three entities. Win the race by reclaiming your rightful position in your vessel, and by honoring, respecting, integrating and leading all parts of your Being! Only when you take back control of your vessel, and do the work to free yourself from the bugged programming, will you truly have *Free Will*! Till this point, you were under the *will* of your *emotional little kid*, your *intellect* and all of the bugged programming you have picked up! **The Power of Three Will Set You Free!**

The Awakening of Your Spiritual Self

In out of the way places of the heart, where your thoughts never think to wander, this beginning has been quietly forming, waiting until you were ready to emerge.

For a long time it has watched your desire, feeling the emptiness growing inside of you, noticing how you willed yourself on, still unable to leave what you had outgrown.

It watched you play with the seduction of safety and the gray promise that sameness whispered, heard the waves of turmoil rise and relent, wondered would you always live like this.

Then the delight, when your courage kindled and out you stepped onto new ground, your eyes young again with energy and dream, a path of plentitude opening before you.

Though your destination is not yet clear you can trust the promise of this opening; unfurl yourself into the grace of beginning that is at one with your life's desire.

Awaken your Spirit to adventure; hold nothing back; learn to find ease in risk; soon you will be home in a new rhythm, for your Soul senses the world that awaits you.

~ John O'Donohue

Transcend*Transform*Inspire

Inner View

Do you have a different name for your Spiritual Self?

....

What commitments or vow are you, *Spiritual Self*, making to your body, emotional child and intellect? What time each day will you, **Spiritual Self**, check in with everyone?

....

....

....

....

....

....

....

....

....

Do you have a different name for your **A Team,** and who is a part of it? The Divine, Guides, Angels, Deceased Loved Ones? Will you be asking for their help to support what your team needs every day?

....

....

....

....

....

....

....

What commitments did your *intellect* make with your Spiritual Self, emotional child and body?

....

....

....

....

....

....

What commitments did your *emotional child* make with your Spiritual Self, intellect and body?

....

....

....

....

....

....

What commitments did your *body* make with your Spiritual Self, emotional child and intellect?

....

....

....

....

....

....

....

Chapter Eleven

Fifth Step To Freedom
~It's All About Love~

How are you feeling? More peaceful, whole and connected to your *Essence*? Is your mind a little quieter now— not having so much internal conflict? Are your parts working more together as a team? Do they feel more led and supported by you, **Spiritual Self**, and your *A Team*? And how is your relationship with the Divine going now? Are you feeling closer and more connected? Are you developing your relationship with all of your parts, the Divine and your *A Team* every day? Are you practicing **The Formula** and keeping a **Prayer Log**? Are you *seeing* that you are receiving answers to your prayers and requests, and is it strengthening your trust and your relationship with the Divine?

Now that you have connected back to your *Essence*, strengthened your relationship with Source, and have more unity within your Being, we can use the **Growth Formula** to heal the other most important relationship in our life we need to heal, and that is the relationship we have with **ourselves**! Our relationship with ourselves and our relationship with the Divine are the only relationships we have for our entire lives, and for eternity! **Only the love we generate for ourselves, and from the Divine, lasts for eternity.** So, that is **where** we need to focus getting our feelings of love from; *from within*, not from others outside of ourselves. Why? Because the love we get from others outside of ourselves on this earth plane is temporary, even with our family and significant other. Because when they die and cross over, we experience a gaping hole in our love tank and are often brought to our knees. So if we **get our love from within and from Source**, we will never feel unloved or not good enough in some way when someone suddenly is no longer physically present in our lives, or does a hurtful action towards us.

So let me ask you, how do we tend to feel loved now? From people outside of ourselves, right? This is how we have been conditioned to get love from the get go. First, it is with our parents, then our grandparents, then our aunts and uncles, then our siblings and cousins and so on.... When we are first born, for the most part, all we have to do is coo and poo in order to feel connected and loved. Then that quickly changes. Soon we learn that '*these*' behaviors get us love and approval, while '*those*' behaviors cause us to experience rejection, and the loss of love and approval from those same very people! Our parents, caregivers, and the adults in our young lives are like God to us, and their anger, their rejection, the feeling of the loss of their love and approval is so intense for us, that it feels as if it could be the end of us. So our innocent and undeveloped child's mind begins to associate these feelings with potential *death*.

We then grow up and go to school, it all gets worse; now who are we trying to get approval from? Teachers, peers, and coaches. And we start to learn even more things we have *to do* to get their approval and not lose it. And our emotional fear of survival grows and intensifies. We then go to junior high and high school, and it gets even worse, right? Then we really care about **what our peers think,** and who approves of us and who doesn't. Now, their approval could determine the experience of physical abuse or not, outside of what we may already be experiencing inside the home. We start to **work really hard** to get the '*right*' people and the *right peer group* to like us, and we make sure to stay away from the '*wrong*' people and the *wrong groups* that will get us experiencing rejection and perhaps bullying by the said '*in*' crowd. And it's here we begin to learn that one day people love you, and the next day you are their target! This is the time period when our *intellect* is working really hard to develop our **'get love and approval strategies'** and our **'protection strategies'** — strategies to keep from getting further hurt, or risking the loss of love and approval. As we get older and expand all of these approval and protection strategies, they begin to conflict with one another, causing us even more internal struggle and keeping the experience of *real love* away from us all the more.

As we grow up and become adults, it gets even worse. Now we need to get approved by all of society! Now that we are supposed to be an adult and on our own, the fear of survival kicks in all the more. Now we are **really** coming up with ***get love/approval strategies*** for our work, money, success, power, love and life partner. *Strategies* to be connected to the right people *to get all of 'that'*, and ***strategies*** to have all of the right things *to get all 'that'*, etc., etc. And it is **sooooo very exhausting**! Isn't it? All of this work we feel like we have to do, just to feel acknowledged, loved, accepted and even safe. All of this internal struggle we go through, trying to maintain our image and manage all of the various strategies we have for all of the different types of relationships we have in our life. **It is so very tiring!**

Who was taught to just get love from within ourselves or from Source? None of us really, right? Because we were all raised and taught by people who have been conditioned in the exact same way! This exhausting spin in the hamster wheel just gets passed down from generation to generation. Most of us from around the world were taught to get love from our family, and giving us their love usually depended on their approval of us and our behavior. As we grew up, all of a sudden, love, connection and approval had all kinds of rules and requirements. We were taught to be *'good'* boys and girls, which implied we were not that already. We were taught that we were good if we did our chores, got good grades, did as we were told or were the best on the team. Very few of us were taught that we are just essentially good, or given a sense of unconditional approval – a feeling that we're precious because of **who we are**, not because of what *we do* or how we do it. What we were taught instead was *fear*— fear that not measuring up to social standards would cause us disapproval, rejection and great pain in our life.

This depending upon getting love from outside of ourselves is like building a house on sand: one storm of disappointment, and our house, our safe place, totally falls down around us. Unfortunately, this has become a part of the Human Condition. We have all been domesticated into this world like a dog or a cat would be, with punishment and reward. What we call education is really domestication of the human being into the systems of society. We are afraid to be punished and disapproved of, but we are also afraid of not getting the approval and the reward. Before this domestication occurs, we don't care whether we are accepted or not. We just live in the moment; if we are hungry, we let it be known; if something hurts, we let it be known; if something grabs our attention, we become amused with it and laugh and play. If we get hurt or angry, we just express it and then go back to playing with whatever is in our presence at the moment. We are not worried about what others think of our emotions and what the repercussions might be. We are not ashamed of the past or worried about our future; we just experience and express what we are feeling in the moment!

But because of this domestication, we created strategies to feel loved and accepted by our family and society, or at least get some kind of attention. Because, after all, punishment or an intense response can be a real reward for some. For some kids, it was the only way they could get their parents' attention at all; and it felt much better than the far more painful indifference they experienced for years. Whatever the love/approval/acknowledgement strategy is, unfortunately it rarely is a strategy for **how to give love to ourselves or how to feel love from the Divine.** The fear of not measuring up, for someone else's acknowledgement and approval, is what makes us strive to have and be more, all the time; or even to play small. It's what makes us create and defend that image in the top 10% of the iceberg. We are constantly struggling to project that image to the world, according to what society want us to be; pretending to be who we are not, just to feel like we belong and that we are worthy of their time and attention. We don't just create one image, either. We create many different images according to the different groups of people we are associated with, and then we toil to manage them all. Soon we forget who we really are, and we start to live out our images. Unfortunately, we have been so conditioned to claim our identities based on who loves us or who approves of us, that when we don't feel as if we have that love and approval we want from others, we feel real internal suffering. Tell me, how much pain, time and effort do we inflict on ourselves daily, to be accepted by a society that is lost itself? And then we pick up behaviors we learn from that lost society, to either numb our pain or get its love, approval or acknowledgement. How crazy is that, really?

No matter how we slice it, adapting ourselves to fitting in or being a rebel and standing out — all of these behaviors stem from our thoughts of worrying about what other people think. And **living our lives from the perspective of what other people think creates a massive, ongoing pain in our Being.** When we act based on what other people think or what society tells us is right or acceptable, we are acting from a place of a deficit. That is, "I'm not enough as I am, so I am going to change myself to be enough according to your standards, so that I will be accepted and loved by you— and if not, I'm going to do something to at least get some acknowledgement or attention." Always playing a game of *'hide and go seek love and approval.'* For me, it was becoming a *people pleaser* or a *rescuer* and always trying to help others. If I pretended I was strong and had it all together, and was such a thoughtful friend who would always be there for you, then maybe you would appreciate, like me or love me– maybe then I would be *good enough* and have a *purpose* to exist. At the same time I would play small and make sure I didn't shine too brightly, so as to not lose connection, love and approval from peers. These unconscious, yet driving thoughts have caused me **A LOT** of pain and inner turmoil for many years. They have caused me to limit myself, martyr myself, dim my light and not live up to my soul's potential and intention. And I bet this thought, and your constant adapting for others, has caused you a lot of pain and some limiting thoughts and actions throughout the years as well.

We all start out being the smallest, least powerful and the most dependent member of our family. This helplessness at this time is not a theory, it is a fact. To get anything, we needed the help of our caregivers. When we are young, our parents and other adults are the masters of our universe, all-powerful and all-wise. At four, we must follow what they say, please and pacify them to get the things that we need from them because our very life and wellbeing depended on it. To get almost anything that we wanted or needed, we had to win over the love, sympathy and approval of the adults in our life. By virtue of their positions of authority, our parents and other adults were able to dispense principles and rules that we received as unquestionable laws. At that age, what else could we do? This programming has been actively conditioned in us from the time we were very young and is deeply integrated into our subconscious mind. The problem lies in carrying this once true sense of helplessness, and the need to placate others for our very survival and well-being, into our adult lives. What once was a fact has now become a rampant illusion that has cost us dearly. As an adult, everything doesn't depend on pleasing your parents, your family members or others. You don't have to fear your parent's or caregiver's anger or rejection anymore. What others once did for you, you can now do for yourself. **That includes loving yourself, approving of yourself and truly taking care of all parts of yourself!**

Healing our relationships and healing the wounds of our *emotional little kid* will free us of this *Arrested Development*; and allow us to start living life as our adult self, and eventually from our *Essence*. For as long as we unconsciously feel like this small, helpless and dependent child, we will always feel like we are in the presence of all-powerful adults that can control or affect our success and happiness, or our feelings of worthiness and being complete. Unconsciously, our *emotional child* is afraid that, if the parent dis-approves of them, they will go away and leave them all alone. This is the most terrifying thought for a child; it literally could mean life or death, and it completely activates the reptilian part of their brain that is driven by the need for survival. This frightened *emotional child* that didn't get to fully grow up with your physical body, because of its fear, wounding and unawareness of its programming, has been unconsciously driving many of your life responses and decisions.

163

Loving ourselves unconditionally, and feeling the ***unconditional love of the Divine,*** will begin to resolve all of this for us. To heal and transform our relationships with others, we must first utterly and completely **be** ourselves and **love** ourselves. As the Bible and other spiritual teachings tell us, we are to "*love others as we love ourselves.*" That implies we must **totally love ourselves first,** before we are able to truly love others. If we don't have it, we can't give it. If we don't have love within, our love relationships are just horse trading– I will love you, if you will do this for me. Remember, ***our outside world is just a reflection of our inside world***. So where would the mirror get love from, if the very image it is reflecting doesn't have it? Love isn't in the other, love is in oneself. If you have that kind of love for yourself, within yourself, the other person will reflect it back to you. If you don't love yourself, no matter how much love others **try** to give you, it will never feel like enough!

Love brings you face to face with yourself.
It's impossible to love another if you cannot love yourself.
~John Pierrakos

Remember, the Bible says to "**love thy neighbor as thyself**; not '*better than thyself*' or '*instead of thyself*'. Nor does it say to '*love thyself through thy neighbor*'. All of which we more readily, and inherently, do because of our programming. So how do I love myself now? Let me count the ways. Well, I love myself the way I was loved by my parents, by my grandparents, my siblings and my aunts and uncles. I love myself the way friends have loved me, and teachers, coaches and bosses. I love myself the way my parents, TV and movies characters have modeled it for me. I love myself through the perceptions of media and the expectations and conditions of the society around me. I love myself in response to the way significant others have demonstrated their love for me, or by what they have said to me. In short, the education we have received in this area has been distorted and cloudy at best; and for the most part, the examples we have experienced have not been very healthy or uplifting at all. Just like for all of the people we have been learning about love from! It has unfortunately been passed down, all around us, from generation to generation.

So, would you like to be free of this game, and out of this mouse maze trap you probably feel stuck in? Would you like to, instead, **feel so much love from within** that where ever you are, there is love? That you don't require love and approval outside of yourself at all? That you feel this state of love and inner peace all the time, no matter what is going on around you?

Yes? Well, follow me down a different pathway to higher grounds!

The Pathway to Self Love

The first step to self love is *Self Acceptance*. We must first totally **accept all parts** of ourself before we can totally love ourself. All parts — the good, the bad and the ugly! Even all the parts society has labeled as bad, and we have bought into. Being totally honest with yourself on who and where you really are in all areas of life. No longer lying to yourself, buying into your own image — don't pretend to be perfect, have it all together, always being nice and understanding. Don't try to pretend to be above human emotions because you're logical or spiritual, or because you have done a lot of personal development work. Don't try to use a spiritual, intellectual or some other kind of bypass, and be real with yourself. Let your *emotional child* lead the way, and just accept what you see. Be your own best friend and make friends with what you find hiding underneath the waterline. Others will not accept you if you can't accept yourself. And when you are really okay with all parts of yourself, what others think about you won't matter so much to you anymore.

Look under the waterline and face your *Shadow Self*. Acknowledge it and everything that it has been trying to evade and hide. If we fight it, try to avoid it and shove it back under the rug, it just continues to stink up and control our life. Remember, **what you *resist*, persists.** The resisting and pretending that something is not there **is the very thing that keeps it alive and from moving out** of your Being and unconsciously driving your life. If we are truthful about it to ourselves, **if we acknowledge and accept it,** "Yes, that is there. Yes, that happened," **it loses its power over us.** Just like the suffering; when you focus your attention on it and totally face it, the energy just dissipates and moves on out, and you're left with (at your *Essence*) feeling your natural state of peace or bliss.

What should hopefully make all of this easier for you is knowing that you are admitting your limitations to yourself, and to a higher power, and not to another similarly flawed human being. That means it is **safe.** There will be no punishment, judgment, manipulation, blame, rejection, score-keeping, banishment, etc. Just internal awareness and acceptance– and nothing to fear.

Again, it's the **Art of Seeing**– when you shine the light on it, the darkness fades away. Parts of it may still be there, like awareness of what happened and some new wisdom; but the *charge*, the vibration and it being a large *attractor factor* in your life, is gone. You stop silently broadcasting it out. **You stop attracting from it, perceiving the world through it; and more importantly, you stop struggling within to hide it from yourself and from the world!** You begin to feel more internal peace, more self acceptance and eventually *more and more self love*!

To **See** is to *be free*. To truly *see* is liberating for you and for others. When you totally accept yourself, wounds, mistakes, flaws and all, you begin to accept others' flaws as well, and your relationships get more peaceful and flourish. When you stop trying to get from other people what they can't give you, and start giving it to yourself, you begin to just appreciate and enjoy what it is that they *can* offer.

In his book, **Real Love**, Greg Baer talks about how we have learned and use a variety of *'getting love behaviors'* to try and get love, as well as many *'protecting behaviors'* to try and keep ourselves from being hurt or experiencing the loss of love and approval; and that the only thing these **getting and protecting behaviors** get us is **imitation love.**[19] Subconsciously, we know it is just *imitation love*, so we never feel quite loved or fulfilled. (You know, the love and approval we get from others because of the image at the tip of our iceberg?) What we are really looking for and needing is **Real Love**; and that is *unconditional love*. Being loved for *all of who you are*, your good and your not so good. The times we feel **really loved** are when we share with someone something that we are not so proud of (that is under the waterline), and they don't judge us or go away. They love us anyway. That is when we *truly* feel loved and more safe; not when people are giving us love and approval for our image— when we are pretending to be perfect, great and like we have it all together. This is why celebrities can often feel not loved or good enough even though they are getting tons of love and approval from their millions of fans. It is also why all of that attention can actually add to their existing internal pain that they have been spending years of their life trying to hide from!

As a child, when you were clean and obedient, it's likely that the people around you would praise and reward you and, in some way, communicate that they loved and appreciated you. However, when you were dirty, loud, and other-wise inconvenient, undoubtedly you noticed the reactions you received from those same people were quite different. You probably saw frowns, irritation, and anger, and experienced feelings of rejection and withdrawal. And from these reactions, you learned this terrible lesson: When you follow the rules I set, you are *'good'* and I love you; but when you don't, you're *'bad'* and I will retract my love, attention and approval from you. No one *intended* to teach us this lesson, but it was nevertheless taught clearly and powerfully by their actions. We have heard people tell us, with their behavior, that when we made mistakes we were unacceptable; and although that message was incorrect, we still believed it. At our stage of development, we weren't capable of questioning whether these all-powerful adults were right or wrong in what they taught us. When a parent is angry, what four year old is capable of responding, "Now Dad, do you really think this is about me? Isn't it possible that you're just feeling empty and afraid yourself, and that you're taking your anger about it out on me so you can get a brief sensation of power and relief?"

The incorrect and unaware lessons we were taught about our lovability have had far-reaching consequences on our lives. In order to be happy, the one element we all require most is unconditional love — **Real Love**. However, our parents and others clearly communicated that we were worthy of love only when we were *'good'* or if we abided by the set and programmed rules. We were in no position to question that judgment, which meant that only conditional love and approval was available to us. So unfortunately, horse-trading love became our predominant definition and understanding of what love is. Without sufficient **Real Love**, we felt painfully empty and afraid; and most of us have spent our entire lives trying to fill that emptiness with what-ever crutch felt good temporarily: rescuing, people pleasing, praise, power, money, material objects, attention, sex, food, or some kind of substance– and so on. However, these *imitations of love* can never make us feel really loved, happy or fulfilled— a lesson most of us have thoroughly and painfully proven to ourselves on countless occasions. Yet we still keep trying....

This is a universal pain that I have witnessed around the world. Each time I witness it, my heart breaks even more for the Human Condition that is present around the globe. And it makes me even more determined to share this message with the world, so that we can stop this *virus* from continually getting passed down from generation to generation. No matter what personal development event I am at around the world, whenever we are doing an exercise where participants are given unconditional love by some kind of loving touch or powerful and loving words, they break down into a deep soul-level cry! A type of cry that breaks your heart to hear, like when a mother has suddenly lost her child. This gaping hole between the love we desperately crave and the love that we actually feel inside is, unfortunately, ginormous; and oftentimes greater and deeper than the Grand Canyon.

I want you to imagine that you are starving. You haven't been able to eat for a week; you have no money, no one to help you and you have no idea if or how you are going to eat again without doing some kind of dumpster diving. Then a man in a food truck comes up to you and says, "You can have anything you want from my food truck and as much as you want. You just have to do whatever favors I ask of you. Do we have a deal?" You can smell the aromas of food coming out of the truck; you can see some of your favorite foods that you just haven't been able to eat for months; you feel the hunger pains of your stomach; and it begins to rumble, and your mouth begins to salivate, so you swiftly tell the man, "Yes, we have a deal!" You quickly devour up all of your favorite foods, and in that moment you feel very satisfied with your deal. I mean, you were starving and you didn't know when you were going to get another meal, and now you have an abundance of food, whenever you want it; you just have to do what the man asks of you from time to time. But soon you become addicted to this food supply and you can't– you don't want to — live without it. You're afraid you might lose it, so you find yourself doing backbends, sacrificing your time and other things that are important to you, not being yourself, and fighting to keep anyone else from getting too close to your food source, because you're afraid they might take it away from you. You find yourself making decisions and taking actions that are costly and unhealthy for you; perhaps to the point where you become almost unrecognizable to yourself. You don't want to lose this food supply, or feel that gaping hole in your stomach and that desperate starvation you felt once again. You literally become a slave for this food, but you don't know what else to do. You don't know how else to fill this pain and gaping hole in your gut.

This unfortunately is a parable for most of the world. We are love-starved; and we have been conditioned to get love from outside of ourselves, from others who were conditioned the exact same way, who don't have it to give either, and who are also desperately looking for it from you and others as well. Because this Human Condition has been passed down from generation to generation, we are a love-starved world. Begging and horse-trading for love crumbs all the time. Unconsciously communicating **'I'll love you if'** messages like: *If I please you this way, will you then give me love and approval?* Or, *if you do this, I will give you my love and approval, but if you do that, I will take it away.* So we keep pleasing and seeking attention and approval to get the crumbs of **imitation love** that the others are only able to provide. Trying to fill our nearly empty love tank that we just **haven't been taught** how to fill for ourselves. This pain and starvation is so great that it is the source of too many crimes to name, and the mistreatment of others. It is only hurting people who hurt others. And it's only hurting people who take advantage of other hurt people who are not as strong or as hardened as they have become. It's only people who have never felt totally loved; who so desperately want to be loved, but continually get disappointed whenever they try, causing them to incur another wound on their skin to go along with the many others they already have, provoking them to feel even more hopeless and despair. Not knowing what to do to fill the gap and make the pain go away, they feel more anger and rage and just want to relieve themselves of it quickly— like a hot potato– onto somebody else. A person who is hurting another is really desperately crying for help– crying for love. They just want their agony to go away and for someone to at least acknowledge their existence in some way.

Only **Real Love** can fill this painful gap; all of this *imitation love* never will. So that is what we need to give to ourselves— Real Love. **Unconditional love** to **All** parts of us. Flaws, weaknesses, vulnerabilities, shadows, fears and all. Only then will we feel Real Love for our self. When we can stop judging ourselves, then perhaps we can start believing that God doesn't judge us either. Only when we know God doesn't judge us, but loves us, flaws and all, will we feel this unconditional love from the Divine as well. A judgmental God was just a human construct and a tool used to control the masses with fear when the church and government were one. **The Divine is madly in love with you;** you are a part of *It* and a flesh expression of *It*. God is just **waiting for you to see** what *It sees*, and for you to **be in love with yourself as well!** If you create the relationship and allow it, the Divine will be your best friend. And you need to become your own best friend and raving fan as well!

> *Your task is not to seek for Love, but merely to seek and find all the barriers within yourself that you have built against it.*
>
> ~Rumi

I hope you are beginning to see that healing your relationship with yourself is also healing your relationship to the Divine, and vice versa. They are interrelated. Perhaps you are also starting to see, from the fact that all of your feelings about others are *just a reflection of what is inside of you*, that healing your relationship with yourself is also healing your relationship with others. And that loving others is really predicated on *loving ourselves first*. Healing the relationship with our self and giving ourselves the love and approval that we have always longed for from others is **one of the most important things we can do** for our happiness, and to *transform* our life into the one of our heart and soul's dream. When we do, then all other relationships automatically begin to heal, and magic seems to unfold in all areas of our life.

The gift of healing all of this self-denial pain that has been hiding underneath the waterline and controlling our lives, is that we can come back to our true selves. We can stop identifying ourselves based on others´ approval and what they think we should be or do; and instead, finally tune in to our soul's song, and figure out **who** we really are on a heart and soul level. And when we align with our true nature, life comes into balance and our self love and our fullest expression begin to be realized. Now we are trailblazers and trendsetters — we become an example for others and inspire them to uncover their own soul's song, and allow it to be expressed into the world!

The joy of living a *self-approved* life is revealed when we finally allow ourselves to really **Be** ourselves. When we are finally true to ourselves and express our love for who we really are, we put out a different frequency; and as a result, we start attracting and meeting people who are on that same wavelength. We no longer feel the need to chase and people please others. We allow the souls that match our new vibration to now find us, like bees drawn to a flower's nectar.

Imagine yourself now with your own food truck, and a magical genie that keeps it constantly supplied with all of your favorites, all the time. And now, you don't need food from anyone. You have your own constant supply wherever you are, and it's never depleted. And now, you are able to offer food to others, whenever you want, without condition. And now you don't have to do anything to please someone to get a meal. You no longer have to sacrifice yourself or anything to be fed. You are always completely filled up and satisfied and can now just share your abundance, unconditionally, with anyone at anytime. There are no more, *'I'll feed you if'* negotiations. You also don't have to hide and protect your food truck anymore, because you now know your food truck and all of its contents well, and you know that nobody could deplete you of your food no matter what they do. You now know that there is always an infinite and abundant supply from your magical truck, wherever it is, and that you will never feel empty or starved again. And you know you will never need to beg or trade yourself for scraps or breadcrumbs ever again!

> *"Stand out from the crowd, be yourself!"*
> ~Stephen Richards

So let's get into a quiet place alone, and begin having some real *intimacy* with ourselves right now. **Into me I see.** Let's go within and **see** our internal truth, so we can embark on our journey toward *freedom* from this internal struggle and from all of these food brokers. So that we can finally give ourselves some Real Love; return back to our *Essence*; start to receive the endless supply of food from our own magical truck; and finally live our own *self-approved life!* Your task now is to take off the masks imposed on you by society, and just allow yourself to **Be** yourself. When you do, the hidden treasures of your soul will magically unfold!

Inner View

What have you learned about having **Imitation Love** vs. **Real Love** in your life? Do you want to have **Real Love** vs. **Imitation Love** for yourself and in your life?

....

....

....

....

....

....

....

....

....

....

....

....

....

....

....

....

....

....

....

....

....

....

What are some of the wrong beliefs you have had about yourself that have hindered you in your life?

....

....

....

....

....

....

....

....

....

....

....

....

....

....

....

....

....

....

....

....

....

....

....

What have you learned about your own Self Acceptance and Self Love? What is under the waterline that you have been trying to ignore and deny?

....

....

....

....

....

....

....

....

....

....

....

....

....

....

....

....

....

....

....

....

....

....

What have been some of your **get love and approval strategies**?

....
....
....
....
....
....
....
....
....
....

What have been some of your **protection strategies**?

....
....
....
....
....
....
....
....
....
....
....

To See is to be Free. Now that you have opened up, dove under and acknowledged these things, the *charge* around them can begin to dissolve and move out, and the real you, your **authentic self** can begin to emerge. So let's begin the journey of giving ourselves some **Real Love**.

So what do you now accept about yourself that you once denied? What new awareness do you have now?

....

....

....

....

....

....

....

....

....

....

....

....

....

....

....

....

....

....

....

....

....

....

....

....

....

What are some of the things you really appreciate about yourself?

....

....

....

....

....

....

....

....

....

....

....

....

What are some of the things in your life that you are grateful for?

....

....

....

....

....

....

....

....

....

....

....

What is your Reverse Bucket List? Meaning, what are some of the things you have *already done and accomplished* in your life that would be something that someone else might put on their *Success/Bucket List*?

....

....

....

....

....

....

....

....

....

....

....

....

....

....

....

....

Now that we have had some real intimacy with ourselves, we need to move into *accepting* what we found, and apply **The Growth Formula** to move the *cud* out of our subconscious mind. We have the *clear intention* of what we want to heal; we now have to take the *right action* of using the **Healing Process** to allow the *Divine Intervention* to take over and move the *cud* out. So make sure you are in a quiet and private space, grab your MP3 playing device and headset, and go to track #8 or click the link below to download it to continue this Divinely led inner journey. Please do not read forward in this book until you have completed this healing process.

www.HealYourHeartFreeYourMind.com/Self

Now that we are on the pathway to self love through *acknowledging and accepting all* parts of ourselves and honoring all of our attributes, let's really begin to work on our **total self love,** no matter what our past experiences have been. We have to love ourselves so fiercely, as though our very life depends on it— because it does! The experience you have with the *outside world is just a reflection of your inside world*, so your life experience **does depend** on the amount of self love that you have. The relationship you have with yourself, the way you feel about yourself and the way you treat yourself (including the treatment you allow yourself to receive from others), is the most important relationship you will ever have. The rest of your relationships and your experiences of life are just a reflection of that! Just a movie of what you have been silently broadcasting out. So the most important relationship you will ever have (along with the Divine) is desperately craving to be deeply and truly loved by you!

We all carry around with us the cumulative effects of experiencing many wounds, held within our *emotional body* or *child*. Ekhart Tolle, in his book **The Power of Now**, called it the *pain body*. We have experienced uncounted broken promises, unkind words and actions, and many moments when our belief in love and acceptance have been totally and brutally crushed. Through all of this, most of us have picked up an unconscious belief that "*we are not good enough to be loved as we are*." And just as it requires a consistent, focused workout plan to burn off the fat that we have acquired over the years, so does undoing the years of this unconscious programming of not feeling loved and accepted by the standards that have been placed upon us by society. It requires that we make a new vow to ourselves, to do what it takes to uninstall this ancient and outdated *'For Love'* programming, and to upgrade to the supersonic, self-sustaining ***'From Love'*** Operating System!

From this upgraded Operating System we are going to upload, we will no longer buy into the stories of our mind, and we will no longer require the love and approval of anyone outside ourselves. We vow to do the work that it requires to free ourselves from that need, and to **totally accept and love ourselves unconditionally**! To give ourselves ***Real Love***. This has to be greater than a commitment; this has to be a personal oath and a declaration! You must have resolve that **this will be so**! Instead of spending all of your time and energy trying to people please and get love and approval from others, **decide now,** and from now on— **I CHOOSE ME!** I choose my love, my happiness, my peace, my well-being, my goals and intentions, my interests and desires, my heart and my soul. I Choose Me— and **I Approve of Me!** I will no longer be a love beggar, a rescuer or a doormat. I will no longer look for love or approval outside of myself, and instead, **I will look for it within, and I Will Choose Me!**

The *Promise Land* is a fertile land that lies within each human's mind, for it naturally and automatically grows whatever seeds are planted in it. So, the most important conversation you will ever have is the one you have with yourself. We are going to start talking to ourselves **intentionally**, instead of allowing the voice in our head to babble off fear-based nonsense that takes us in directions we don't want to go. Daily, several times a day, you need to declare "*I love me*" to yourself, over and over again! This needs to be your new mantra. As you go to sleep, say this again and again to yourself. When you wake up, **do a half-hour meditation**, saying "*I love me*" to yourself as you breathe in, and letting the *cud* come up, as you breathe out. Continue to say this as you take a shower and get ready for the day, and again in the car on your way to your destination. Say it to yourself as you work out, and again all the way on your drive home. Take any moment you have to yourself to repeat those words, under your breath, over and over again. Say it so many times to yourself throughout the day that this thought becomes the most predominant thought that you have. By doing this, you short-circuit all of the usual negative messages your mind unconsciously replays back to you, day after day. Make sure to say it as you are about to fall asleep, for this is a very powerful reprogramming time of the day. Whatever we focus on in the last 10 minutes before we go to sleep is what our subconscious mind mulls over all night! (Thus, it is also a great time to ask your subconscious mind important questions you are trying to figure out answers to.) Do you remember the tests with the seeds and the rice we showed you in the *Placebo Effect* chapter? Keep picturing those results when you are considering how important this daily exercise really is!

You, yourself, as much as anybody in the entire Universe,
deserve your love and affection!

~Buddha

I want you to say it to yourself, even if you don't totally believe it, because at first your mind will resist. It will try to distract you, allowing the *'I'm not good enough'* **fear virus** to run amuck once again, and take you down some rat hole instead. When you notice the detour, just gently return your focus back onto repeating your mantra, just as you would your breath in your meditation. As you begin to feel more comfortable saying your mantra, take a mirror and look into your own eyes as you say "*I love me*" repeatedly, deeply connecting into your heart and soul!

This needs to be your new daily way of being, so you can switch it up to keep it interesting and inclusive of all parts of yourself. On another day, pull out an old picture of yourself, as a little kid, and tell your little girl or boy how much you love them, how special they are, and that you will always love and be there for them, just as we did for the *Power of Three* integration! You need to give your little inner kid the love they always longed for, that they didn't feel like they quite got during childhood, which stunted their development, so that they can now emotionally grow up with the rest of your body. You're going to love your emotional kid out of its hurt and fear, and into its adulthood!

On a different day, you might decide to say, "*I approve of me*", "*I approve of everything* about me," or, "*I choose me*," over and over again instead. **I choose me** is a great one for us *Rescuer/People Pleaser* types! It was a particularly powerful mantra for me when I had someone in my life whose desires I would consistently put before my own wellbeing — and they gladly took that for granted. On another day, you may add all of the great things that you appreciate about yourself and your life, which you just wrote out in the exercise above; or do the **Body Appreciation Meditation** again. And of course we are loving and taking care of all parts of ourselves as we doing our **Trinity Checks** daily.

Your role is to lay down the new love pathways in your subconscious mind, and make them larger, so that they cover up all of the old "*not good enough to be loved*" seeds and pathways. So that you can free yourself from all of the other *'not'* **viruses** that have been plaguing your psyche. The more you say, "*I love me*" to yourself, the more you will begin to feel it; and the body and mind will begin to respond automatically to these new chemicals that are now flooding the body!

In Native American Folklore, there is a story about a Cherokee elder who told his grandson about the battle that goes on within people. "My son," he said, "The battle is between the two wolves that live inside of us all. One is the **Fear Wolf**, filled with fear, unhappiness, worry, anger, jealousy, sorrow, self-pity, resentment and inferiority. The other one is the **Love Wolf**, filled with love, happiness, joy, hope, serenity, kindness, generosity, truth and compassion." The grandson thought about it for a moment and then asked, "Well, which wolf wins?" The old Cherokee gently replied, "The one you feed the most, of course......" So we need to make sure that **we are constantly feeding the *Love Wolf* with love seeds**, and starving the *fear wolf*, so it can die!

The greatest part of this is that, as you love yourself more and more, life begins to love you back! Your bright light begins to shine and the world starts to reflect that love back to you. Do this consistently for 30 days and you will begin to experience life as magical! With this kind of vibration constantly broadcasting out, the Universe will just begin to respond to your thoughts of interests. Similar to the experience I shared with you about what some of us have when we have a close, loving and trusting relationship with the Divine.

I remember that when this first started happening for me, it freaked me out! I would just think I needed something, and the next thing I knew, somebody would walk up to me and say, "By the way, do you need this?" Or I would go up to buy something from a complete stranger, and they would say, "For some reason, I just want to give this to you gratis." Sometimes, someone would just come up and give me a check to thank me for something I did for them a long time ago! Things I once fretted about would easily work themselves out with very little effort on my part. It was crazy and great all at the same time, and it did seem very *magical*.

And as all of this happens for you, just keep reminding yourself how much you really love yourself. Don't ever stop! So that the old pathways, that have been deeply etched into your subconscious mind over the years, never have an opportunity to take over like unruly weeds again. And **Loving Yourself** now becomes *your natural state of Being*; and you no longer need to look for it outside of yourself. Being totally in love with yourself becomes your new set point, like on a thermostat. We are reprogramming your foundational set point, and the *lens* in which you experience life through!

To increase your thermostat even more, let's pour on some deep gratitude or *great attitude*. Both love and gratitude are two of the highest frequency words and vibrations that there are. So as we begin to experience the world matching our love and blessing us, let's make sure to take notice and express our deep gratitude for each one! Go back and take a look at your lists and start observing all of the blessings you have in your life now, and express gratitude for them. Make the word "*thank you*" a normal part of your everyday vocabulary. Gratefulness means to experience **great fullness**. What we appreciate, *appreciates*! This will magnify the love vibration that you are broadcasting out, and soon the world will be echoing even greater blessings your way! You may be observing how this goes hand-in-hand with our *Prayer Log* and developing our relationship and trust with the Divine.

The quickest way to bring more love, more money or anything else you want in your life, is to raise your vibration and radiate out love, joy and gratitude. Really feel it, and really express it ALL THE TIME! Everything you want is really an inside job; the *outside world is just a mirror of what's within and what you are broadcasting out*. Both the problem and the solution are within! Stop looking for them outside of yourself. **You are the hero you have been waiting for, and the hidden riches are within!**

> *Appreciation is the highest form of prayer,*
> *for it acknowledges the presence of good wherever*
> *you shine the light of your thankful thoughts.*
> ~ Alan Cohen

What is the secret of an alluring person who draws people in? They have thrown the negative thought *virus* out of their Being, replaced it with positive ones, and are living life according to their **own** credo. Their appeal is in the unity of their heart, soul and mind. They are in a state of celebration of life, and love themselves without a hint of egotism. They are not selfish, they are **self-full**. They are constantly filling their cup with self love and gratitude until it overflows. And they can now help and love others from this overflow and not deplete their own cup in the process, as so many of us do. Their *cup runneth over*– and is never empty. They live *'From Love'* and not 'For Love'.

I have a question for you. If you truly loved yourself deeply, would you do things differently? If you really knew your self-worth, would you still limit your life to what you previously thought was possible? Or would you begin to give and believe in yourself more, change your language, and believe that the love within you will attract a better response from the world around you? Would you tolerate less bad behavior towards you from others, ask for what you want and make better decisions? And would you allow yourself to just receive more, without it requiring you to do anything in exchange? As you move into this new state of Being, this is a powerful question to use, to guide your life decisions moving forward: "Does this feed who I want to be— the *love wolf*, or who I used to be the — *fear wolf*? If I truly loved myself, what would I do in this moment?" Then let your love-filled heart guide you and lead the way, not your fearful mind! Everyone has a price, and life respects that price. That price is not measured in dollars or in gold; it is measured in self love. How much you love yourself — that is your price — that is the price life will reflect back to you. When you love yourself, your price is very high, which means your tolerance for self-abuse is very low. If you judge and don't like things about yourself, then your price will be much lower, and the world will respond accordingly.

You are the love that you seek. You are the companionship you desire. You are your own completion, your own wholeness. You are your best friend and your confidant. You are the one that you have been looking for. You are the **only one** who can do what you have been looking for someone else to do for you. Love does not need to come from another. Love is a feeling, it is an emotion, it is a way of Being. That smile, that happiness, that excitement and openness can simply come from loving ourselves! At the soul level— at our *Essence*, we know that **we are love**, and that we do not need others to fill our love tank. Loving ourselves is the most important, loving relationship we will ever have; and the beautiful irony of it all is, the more you love yourself, the more the world will be drawn to showering love upon you! You will begin to see the world through the eyes of love; it will be the *lens* through which you see and experience the world, and everything will have a much brighter and rosier glow about it. No longer will you be viewing the world through those old dark *lenses* of hurt, anger, feeling rejected, loneliness and of not being good enough— no longer through the *lens* of a love-beggar. Now, where ever you are there is love; you see it all around you. When you see a tree– you feel love; when you see the sky or the horizon– you feel love; when you see a bird or a butterfly– you feel love. You see and feel love all around you because it is coming **from within you**, and not from someone or something else outside. No one has any control over you any longer, on what you choose to do and how you choose to live. You will never need to sacrifice or trade yourself off again (prostitute yourself), because now you have your own, never-ending, infinite magical food supply!

> *This above all: to thine own self be true.*
> ~ William Shakespeare

Now go out there and treat yourself as you have always wanted others to treat you!

The **Fifth Step** to Freedom is:

5. Practice **Real Love** with yourself.

- Practice **The Art of Seeing**- be completely honest with yourself, **acknowledging** all parts of yourself and everything you have been trying to hide and deny under the waterline; then **fully accept** them. As you accept them and perhaps give them a silly name, like a playful personality (like *"oh, there goes angry mama again"*), **you will begin to love them**.

- Aggressively feed the *Love Wolf* daily, several times a day and as you are about to fall asleep, showing your gratitude for all that it has brought home to you! Use the *Love Meditation, mantras* and the other tools I gave you daily. Constantly fill up your cup with love and gratitude and love yourself to life! A rich and fulfilled life!

- Create a playlist filled with Self Love songs, listen to them and sing with them daily. A few to start you off with are: Born this Way, Greatest Love of All, Firework, Roar, Hero, You Are So Beautiful, Just the Way You Are, I'm Free, Video, Catch My Breath, Who Says, F*ckin Perfect, Beautiful, Independent Woman, I Believe I Can Fly, It's My Life, I Love Myself Today, Unwritten, Lose Yourself, Girl on Fire, We Weren't Born to Follow, Shine- byAnna Nalick, Anything- by fiZ.

- **Vow** to yourself that you will start doing this NOW and take the **30 Day Self Love and Acceptance Challenge!**

- Jack Canfield, a multiple times New York Times best-selling author of several books, including his famous Chicken Soup for the Soul series, has a company policy to help free his employees from this *virus*. The company charges their employees $2.00 for every negative thought that they have, to give them a physical experience that there is a cost to their negative thinking. They find that the negative thoughts tend to stop after 30 days of this exercise. Go here to learn more about Jack Canfield and all of his powerful teachings and tools: http://jackcanfield.com/about-jack-canfield/

- You will find the **Love Meditation** we referred to, that you can use as your daily meditation, at track #9 or download it here: www.HealYourHeartFreeYourMind.com/Self2

Transcend* Transform* Inspire

30 Day Self Love & Acceptance Challenge Contract

I _____ hereby make a commitment to my Self Love, Self Acceptance and General Wellbeing by accepting this 30 Day Self Love and Acceptance Challenge. Beginning this date _____ at this time _____ and for the next 30 days, I will change how I communicate with myself. I will be honest with myself about things I used to hide or deny. I will acknowledge them, embrace them, accept them and not judge them. Daily, every morning and all day long, I will change my vocabulary, freeing myself from the *virus* and fiercely **feeding** my *Love Wolf* with love, praise and gratitude!

I am doing this and I am making this commitment to myself because I Love Myself, and I want to fully Accept and Love Myself Unconditionally and not *require* any love or approval outside of myself. I know that when I do this, my life and my relationships will be better because they will be reflecting all the Unconditional Self Love and Self Acceptance I have for myself.

I acknowledge that this 30 Day Challenge is designed to create acute Self Love and Acceptance and I agree to grow this Love and Acceptance on a daily basis.

I promise that in the event that I stop giving myself Love or Acceptance and I start using Get Love and Protection behaviors or *virus* words, I will refrain from self judgment and will instead simply observe my thoughts and behaviors. I will then restart my 30 day commitment the following day, until I have completed a full 30 days of completely Loving and Accepting myself.

This agreement is renewable for life.

_____ Signature   _____ Date

_____ Witness   _____ Date

* You will need another rubber band or positive affirmation band for this challenge.

Chapter Twelve

Sixth Step to Freedom
~Forgiveness~

Have you ever been hurt by someone? Are you hurting now?

Have you ever hurt someone else? Have you felt bad about it?

Well don't. I am here to tell you **that it is not your fault**.

It is all of your subconscious programming and conditioning from all of the generational stuff that has been unconsciously passed down to your parents, and then to you. It is your pain and your wounds programmed into your neuro-network that have caused you to create belief systems, usually disempowering belief systems, from an unaware child's mind. And by filtering experiences through this hurt, fear and belief systems, you created wrong perceptions and projections, and thus, automatic chemical reactions in your body take over you. It is not your fault at all. **Thus, you should be forgiven, and you should forgive yourself.**

By the same token— **it is not the fault of others who have hurt you, either.** They too were innocent children who had been unconsciously programmed by their ancestral heritage, conditioned and hurt by unaware adults, who were once programmed and hurt the same way as well. The automatic passing down of the millenniums of human suffering is an unfortunate part of the way a human being is developed. So they should be forgiven too, **and you should forgive them.**

As Jesus said on the cross, "Forgive them, for they know not what they do." How can we carry guilt or blame for a mental disease that is seriously contagious at birth? When you or someone else is physically ill or injured, you don't blame them or yourself for being sick, do you? But the chain of pain can end with you, **if you choose to let go and forgive**! When we realize that our past behaviors were predicated on the automatic programming of the obscure subconscious mind, we can afford ourselves the gift of forgiveness. It's very useful to know that many of our behaviors are programs primarily derived from the beliefs of other people, who in turn were programmed, unbeknownst to them, by others back through time. Neither our parents or grandparents were aware that they were automatically acting out pre-programmed scripts, nor did they know the huge ramifications their actions would have on how we were programmed, and thus, on our life. They too were just innocent children when it happened to them, and this just isn't taught in school! Nor how to heal and transcend it. The truth is that everyone is guilty, but no one is to blame. It is literally a part of the Human Conditioning. And now that *we* have this awareness, **we should forgive them and forgive ourselves,** so that **we can** *transcend* **it and no longer live it or pass it on!**

When we really attempt to walk in the footsteps of others and understand their suffering, like magic, our negative emotions can *transform* into compassion and set the stage for forgiveness to occur. It is when we hold on and refuse to do the work of letting go of the hurt and programming that we stay a slave to it, and pass it on to the next generation— just like what was done to us. Remember, it is only hurting people who hurt others, and we are not here to put on just another band-aid; **we are here to stop the bleeding** for good. Are you going to repeat history, or be the *catalyst for change* in your ancestral heritage?

We forgive for ourself, not for others. Forgiveness is an act of **Self Love**. If you remain a victim, putting out that low vibration, then who is really hurting you? You are! You are continually creating and attracting more of the same from that low victim vibration you hold on to. The past does not equal the future, unless you live there. And if you do, then it does! So if you keep regenerating the same emotions by telling and retelling the story to yourself and to others, then **who** is really hurting you? Sometimes our abusers can be dead and gone for years, but we keep the abuse going on to ourselves for eons. Let go and stop bullying yourself; if you hold resentment towards someone, that hate keeps you emotionally attached to them and keeps them alive in your life!

Holding onto anger is like drinking poison and
expecting the other person to die.
~ Buddha

In Indonesia, the natives have a technique to capture the wild monkeys that raid their stores of food. They take an empty coconut shell and make a small hole in it, just large enough for a monkey's hand. They put some rice into the coconut for bait and tie the coconut up to something permanent. When the thieving monkey smells the food and puts his hand into the coconut to get the rice, he can't get it out, because his clenched up fist is too big to get out of the small hole. To escape, the monkeys must let go of the rice; but because they won't, they don't— and instead become tomorrow's dinner!

Before I became aware of, and really understood, the *Law of Reflection* and all of these teachings, I spent my lifetime being tomorrow's dinner, over and over again. I would spend years pulling away from the world to lick my wounds, tell my mother all about the situation, feel sorry for myself and try to figure it all out. Oftentimes trying to fix the situation, or return it back to my illusion of the way I thought it was or how I wanted it to be. And all that created was my attracting more of the same! Like reliving Groundhog Day over and over again. Yeach!

Forgiveness and letting go is the miracle medicine for the heart, and nothing more than an act of self healing, self empowerment and self love. Letting go of negative emotions you have been holding on to liberates you and stops the poisoning of your mind, your body and your soul, that **you have been doing to yourself for years** by holding on to these grudges, illusions and pain. Remember, **disease** is actually *dis-ease* in the body. Almost all *dis-ease* of the body starts from *dis-ease* of the heart, the mind and the spirit. The medical community is now recognizing the major role that anger and resentment are playing in creating disease and addictions. Dr. Luskin's research at Stanford University suggests that the failure to forgive, holding anger and hatred in one's heart, is one of the risk factors in heart disease. Nearly all cancer patients, besides having a lifetime habit of suppressing and repressing negative emotions, are known to share a marked inability to forgive and let go of their hurt and anger.

Forgiving others then really becomes forgiving yourself for hurting, poisoning and limiting yourself and your life, for so very long! By releasing the past, you unshackle yourself and open the pipeline of love that has been shut off by the hurt, anger, shame and blame. The word forgive means simply to *'give up'* old stories, so you can clean up your energy field and what you are broadcasting out. You *'give up'* all of the hurt, anger and grudges you have felt towards others, and the need to be right. All others! When you forgive yourself, self-acceptance begins and **self love grows**. Which is much better than being Dead Right!

If your compassion does not include yourself, it is incomplete.

~ Buddha

So why is so hard for us to forgive? Why, like the monkey, is it so hard for us to let go?

Well, it's all because of the mind's nature to protect itself. It is very fear oriented and it is always trying to figure out ways to shield itself. In fact, the ego was created by the mind in order to defend the body and itself. The mind does not want you to figure out that you are not your ego/intellect, and the ego/intellect is not you, so it is always operating in defense and survival mode. It fears if you find out that it could be the death of it.

In order to defend and protect itself, the mind is always looking for the problem outside of itself, as well as the solution. And one of the first tools the mind uses is its need to be right! In order to be right, it always feels like it has to make someone else wrong. Not forgiving, and not asking for forgiveness are two great tricks the ego uses to be right and to keep itself in employment and protect itself! A client of mine once blurted out indignantly, "But that would mean I wasted forty years of my life if I so easily forgive them now!"

The ego thinks if we forgive the person, then we are condoning their behavior and we are letting them off the hook. We falsely think if we don't forgive them we are punishing them; that we are hurting them or getting back at them. But instead, we are just punishing ourselves. We get this false sense of power, strength, revenge and an upper hand. We are afraid if we do forgive, it would show a weakness and that we could get hurt again, and we wrongly believe forgiveness means that we are letting the person back into our life. People feel very justified in their anger, and they can give you all the details on how unfairly they were treated. And often times they are right; they did get cheated as children. But what they don't see is that they're now cheating and bullying themselves as adults.

We mistakenly believe that we are imprisoning the ones that hurts us by not forgiving, but really we are imprisoning our self. We are locked in the prison with them, thickening the bars every time we are thinking or talking about it — attracting and projecting from it all the more. We are keeping the pain alive and perpetuating it, continuously hurting and abusing ourselves. Increasing the toxins both in our body and in our Being.

To forgive is to set a prisoner free and discover that...
the prisoner was you."

~ Lewis B. Smedes

So when will you release them? When will you stop abusing yourself and set yourself free?

How about now?

If you are ready now to be free from this self-imposed prison, I will guide you through a short little forgiveness journey.

I want you to imagine that you are walking up to a jail cell filled with all of the people you feel hurt and angry with, who you just haven't been able to forgive, and you are holding the key to the cell. You unlock this old, rusted door, and you walk in. You go up to the first person and you look them in the eyes. See their face now and tell them what you need to say to them, and don't hold back. And when you are done, tell them, "I forgive you and I release you from this prison that I have held you in for so long, and I free myself. I do this because *I love myself and I am done abusing myself, poisoning my heart, my soul and my mind.* Goodbye, I free you forever." Then go to the next person and do the same with them. Release each and every person in that jail cell, until it is only you left in the chamber.

If there is someone in your jail cell that you are really having a difficult time releasing, imagine them as a young innocent child and what their life must have been like: hurt, afraid, confused, perhaps physically or verbally abused, and truly not knowing any better — and realize this is who you're probably really working with, and try again. Remembering that all actions are either love or a desperate cry for help from a once innocent, programmed and mistreated child, and that everyone dreams up their own life from their own programming. The words or actions that hurt you are merely a reaction to their own demons living in their subconscious mind. They are living in their own personal hell, and you are just a secondary character in their dream. Nothing anyone does is really because of us.

Again, suffering is not in the fact, it is the person's perception of the fact. The more we have this awareness with our more logical and matured adult's mind, the less we will take things personally, and the more understanding and compassion we will have. (Which can lead to forgiveness.) If you are dealing with someone who has had an addiction, know that you are working against the *disease of shame and denial,* and that shame and denial most likely

191

started from something that was done to them as that once innocent child — and just passed down. Knowing that it is the job of the mind and ego to be right and protect itself, it would be unpragmatic to expect full admission and sincere regret from someone who has lived such a plight.

Once you have forgiven everyone and are alone, find the mirror in the corner of the cell and look into the eyes of your jailer and say, "I forgive you and I free you, and I will never return here again. **I do this because I totally love myself,** and I realize I can't move forward in my life with my mental gears stuck in reverse. I am done looking in the rearview mirror, because that is not the direction I want to head in. It is all forward moving from here on out, free from this prison I have sentenced myself to, never to return back again!" Then walk out of the cell, close the door, lock it, and throw the key inside, where you can never open it up again!

Tools of Forgiveness

So how do you feel? A little lighter, a little freer — not carrying so much trash? Across all spiritual teachings from all ancient civilizations, forgiveness of self and others is the critical element to healing, to health, to love, and to higher consciousness. **It is the pathway out of victim consciousness, healing the heart and liberation of the *Spiritual Self.*** Here I will share with you a few powerful tools to use to forgive from the *bird's eye view* and from your higher consciousness. As I impart this information, see if you notice any similarities to the teachings I have been sharing with you in this book.

Radical Forgiveness

Radical Forgiveness is a powerful tool that was developed by author Colin Tipping.[20] Its intent is to magnetize us away from the victim archetype and the world of illusions that our mind spins for us. To do so, we need something that will take us beyond the drama of our lives, so we can see the *bigger* picture and the truth that lies hidden from us. When we awaken to that truth, we will be able to *transcend* the victim consciousness. Victim consciousness is defined as the conviction that someone else has done something bad to you, and as a direct result, they are responsible for the lack of happiness and peace in your life.

For traditional forgiveness, we take the evidence from our five senses and use our *intellect* to come up with the conclusion that we have been wronged. We then have to go through a process to try and let go, the best that we can, and 'let bygones be bygones'. But with this type of forgiveness, there is still a residual need to condemn the other person and to be right.

Traditional forgiveness is based on the premise that something wrong happened. *Radical Forgiveness* takes the position that nothing wrong really happened; thus there is nothing to forgive, and in fact you should be grateful to the person instead. That is why it is radical!

Radical Forgiveness looks at the situation from a very spiritual perspective, from the *bird's eye view*. It says that we made agreements with others, at a soul level, to heal something in our energetic Being — be it a wound, a disempowering belief or a karmic issue— and that we should be grateful that this other soul was willing to play the bad guy to help us heal our old wounds and limiting belief systems, for our soul's growth and evolvement.

It further goes on to say, that this person is just mirroring back to you an old hurt or belief that needs to be acknowledged and healed— an old *charge* that needs to *be allowed* to be expressed in order to move out. That in fact, this person is acting as your **Healing Angel** to help you *transcend* this pattern or vibration, so that **you can evolve and expand**. Thus, this is why you should be **grateful** to them for being willing to play that role for you— because who really wants to play the villain?

The Universe is designed to expand. It is only the fear of our mind that prevents us from doing so. So whenever a situation happens, or whenever we look at an event of the past, we have two choices. We can make the choice that most people take— to be the victim and make the other person wrong, which in turn allows you and the mind to be right. Or, we could choose instead to recognize that beneath what *seems* to be happening on the surface (the worm's eye view), something else more meaningful, and perhaps supportive for you, is what's really going on at the spiritual level (from the bird's eye view). That instead, this could be an **opportunity** to heal and grow, and is actually a real *gift* for you.

To take this second option means you have to recognize that your beliefs or perspective have no real basis to them. That it is simply a story your mind has made up, based on a few facts and a whole lot of interpretation. We do this all of the time. We experience an event, make interpretations about it, then put the various pieces together to create a largely false story about what happened, and react as if it is so. (Remember my story about the man in the audience with his arms folded?)

Let's take another example from my life. When I was young, my dad did drink, he would accuse me of things I didn't do, he would hit me when I argued with him, my mother didn't stop him and told me, "You know better than to argue with a drunk"; those are a few of the facts. But none of that meant what my childhood interpretation became, that "*my parents did not love me,*" or that, "*something was wrong with me and I wasn't good enough to be liked or loved.*" That was a made-up story, from a preprogrammed naive child's mind, from which I formed a belief that unconsciously drove my life.

We all have a voice within us that is either pathetic or prophetic, and it is our choice, at any given time, to decide which voice we want to live our life by. It is normal for a child to come up with those kinds of wrong belief systems because of the way a child thinks at that age, and because of the development of the brain. In fact, every one of us has these kinds of wrong beliefs driving our lives – until some life event happens that causes us to go underneath the waterline and **SEE** what kinds of beliefs are really hiding there. Young children are very egocentric and wrongly believe that the world revolves around them. So anytime anything goes wrong, they believe that it's their fault – that whatever happened is because of them (i.e. my dad must be hitting me because there is something wrong with me). A lot of what we attract in our life, how we perceive the world and how we react and make our decisions is determined by wrong interpretations made long ago by a 3-year-old!

As you are making your decision on which path to take, it is very important to remember that if we choose to be right instead of grow, our soul will just attract someone else to mirror this *charge*; and you will just have to **re-live** it again with a different name, a different face and at a different time. So when now is a good time to *transcend this pattern*, let go of the pain and be free of all of what has been trapping you?

> *An ordinary man behaves like a dog which upon entering*
> *a hall of mirrors barks at all the other dogs.*
> *The Sage entering the hall of mirrors sees only himself.*
> ~Gurunathan

Pratikraman

Pratikraman is a Jain spiritual belief and practice to clear out negative karma in order to reach what they call *moksha* (being free from the death to rebirth cycle). They believe that anything that is happening in their life is just the Law of Attraction (they call it Scientific Circumstantial Evidence) automatically playing out to burn away negative karma. They do not get involved in the blame game story that their mind tries to tell them; instead, they are very excited about the opportunity to burn away their negative karma, so that they can go to their next level of consciousness, and don't have to come back to Earth to relive it again. They are very careful to **not** react to things that happen, in order to **not create** any new negative karma. *This belief system keeps them out of victim consciousness*, and very honest and careful of not hurting others. It would be a better world if more of the population took up this belief and practiced it. It can be compared to one of Jesus's teaching, *"If someone slaps you on one cheek, turn to them the other also."* Again, they are looking at the world from a *bird's eye view*, and are not caught up in the worm's view.

> *An eye for an eye only ends up making the whole world blind.*
> ~Mahatma Gandhi

Ho'oponopono

Ho'oponopono is an ancient Hawaiian indigenous practice and belief system that was shared with the mass public by author **Joe Vitale** in an article he wrote back in 2006, *"The World's Most Unusual Therapist,"* and in his following book, **Zero Limits**, published in 2007. The article was about a therapist in Hawaii who healed an entire mental hospital full of some of the roughest, criminally insane patients. It was impressive enough that **Dr. Hew Len** was able achieve this feat being that before he was hired, the hospital could not even keep enough staff to run it— they had become so frightened of the patients that they would just quit or call in sick all the time. But what really made this article go viral was *how* he was able to accomplish this huge triumph.[21]

You see, **Dr. Hew Len** never met with one patient to accomplish this seemed miracle. He would merely read the patients' files and then use tools to heal whatever he read in their file, within himself. He also taught the staff how to do the same. Whatever they saw in the patients, or however they judged them, he taught them how to heal that in themselves.

Before he arrived, these patients were so violent and criminally insane that they were drugged and hand-cuffed to their beds. They weren't allowed to have visitors or outside privileges, and the hospital wasn't able to keep enough staff to take care of all of the patients. They were in a constant state of having to hire and train new people, who would never last very long.

As Dr. Hew Len continued the Ho'oponopono practice and persisted to teach the employees how to do the same, slowly but surely things began to change. First the patients were able to be un-handcuffed from the beds, and then they were taken off the sedatives. Soon they were able to start having visitors; and shortly after, they were able to go outside and enjoy the sunshine. Then, it got even better. They started to be released!

One by one, as their mental wellbeing improved, they were released. Soon there were too many staff members for the number of patients that they had, so they had to start letting employees go. Even those patients who had no prior chance of ever being released, were being freed. And that kept going until only two patients remained, and they closed down the entire ward! This all happened within four years.

Amazing, huh? So what were the tools he used to heal what he saw in their files, in himself? What did he teach the staff to do whenever they had a negative thought or view of one of the patients? He just taught them to say four little phrases over and over again, whenever a negative thought or charge came up, until the feeling dissipated. Those four phrases are: "Thank you", "I'm sorry", "Please forgive me", and, "I love you".

And this is why you say those four phrases. *Thank you*– for showing me something that I have inside of me that still needs to be seen and healed. *I'm sorry*– for seeing you as bad and wrong. *Please forgive me*– for seeing you as bad and wrong; and *I love you*.

Does all of this sound familiar? Doesn't it sound a whole lot like the *Law of Reflection* and the **Healing Process** (*The Art of Moving Blocked Energy*)? That whatever negative thought and feeling you have about someone else is just a reflection of what is inside of you, and when you heal it, it **magically transforms**. Dr. Hew Len explains, "Simply put, Ho'oponopono means to make right or to rectify an error. According to the ancient Hawaiians, error arises from thoughts that are tainted by painful memories from the past, and Ho'oponopono releases the energy of those painful thoughts, or errors, which cause imbalance and disease."

Joe Vitale shared this immediate experience he had the first time he tried it. "One day, someone sent me an email that upset me. In the past, I would have handled it by working on my emotional hot buttons or by trying to reason with the person who sent the nasty message. This time, I decided to try Dr. Len's method. I kept silently saying, *'I'm sorry'* and *'I love you'*. I didn't say it to anyone in particular. I was simply evoking the spirit of love to heal within me what was creating the outer circumstance. Within an hour I got an e-mail from the same person. He apologized for his previous message. Keep in mind that I didn't take any outward action to get that apology. I didn't even write him back. Yet, by saying *'I love you'*, I somehow healed within me what was creating him."

I, Brandy, have shared this healing process with hundreds and hundreds of students, and the **magical** healing stories that come back from these students who practice this are both heart-warming and unbelievable. One student was scheduled for his third bypass surgery and had totally given up on life. He was getting his affairs in order and was totally inconsolable. His wife was inconsolable as well, because nothing she would say or do would cause him to have any hope. He had totally given up. But he found his way to my class and started incorporating what he was learning immediately.

His father was also on his deathbed in the hospital and not expected to make a recovery. He had been estranged from his father for years and both of their impending deaths motivated my student to try this Ho'oponopono tool to heal his relationship with his father, before one of them met their demise. He just started practicing saying, "***Thank you, I'm sorry, Please forgive me, and I love you,***" over and over again, as he thought about all of the hurt and angry feelings he once had about his dad. And a ***miracle*** happened; his father got better and was released from the hospital! They talked on the phone and everything seemed to be **magically** better between them. The energy was different, and they didn't have to talk anything out. They just shared what they physically had been going through, comfortably, and their closeness and bond began to grow. My student ***miraculously*** healed as well, and never had to have that third bypass surgery! (Talk about the power of healing the heart!) His father lived for another two years, and they were able to build a deep and loving bond during those years. That was seven years ago from the time of this writing, and he and his wife are doing great, and are happily enjoying life together.

Another student had been estranged from her sister for years. They had lost their mother years before, and they each had a separate relationship with their father. My student started to practice these tools with both her sister and her mother, and **magically**, one day her sister called. The energy was different for the first time in years. It was lighter, it was calm, and it was comfortable. They just started sharing stories about their father and their lives with their husbands, but nothing about their past was discussed. There no longer felt like there was a need on either side. The more they talked, the closer they became. It was like a **magical** upward cycle. Quite the opposite of the downward cycle conversations they used to have in the past. My student was loving having her sister back in her life, someone who really knew what her family and childhood was like.

This healing was in Divine timing. Shortly after they drew close, their father fell ill and died soon after. Luckily, they now had each other to go through it together, healing as a whole family in their father's last days, and growing even closer. Which was another Divine timing, because soon after, her sister's husband fell ill and died as well. Her sister was devastated, and my student was able to be there for her sister through that very rough time. For the first time in years, my student's sister came out to stay with her for a while, and they were gifted with the time and the proximity to grow an even closer and deeper relationship.

Time and time again, I see powerful examples like this, where families that were once estranged **magically** heal and come back together after these tools are used. Nothing ever needs to be talked about; thus the old stories aren't kept alive nor the old flames kept burning. Just simply by not getting caught up in the story, and instead saying these four little phrases, "***Thank you, I'm sorry, Please forgive me and I love you***," love is restored. You can buy Joe's song as he is singing the above at:

www.cdbaby.com/cd/joemrfirevitale/GotaProblemtheHooponoponoSong#.Uo_Vfn8 RobU.email

You will find several examples of how this tool has helped many others in Joe's book, *Zero Limits*. For more information go to: http://zerolimits.info/

> *"The weak can never forgive.*
> *Forgiveness is the attribute of the strong."*
> ~Mahatma Gandhi

Summing It All Up

So with all of these ancient forgiveness tools, you should notice one common theme. The practitioners **do not get involved in victim consciousness** or the blame game. They all take full responsibility for whatever is going on within themselves, and between them and the other person, and they apply the ***Law of Reflection***. They know the problem is not *'out there'*, and that both the predicament and the solution lie within.

They all operate from the **bird's eye view**, a spiritual perspective, and not from the deeply-rooted physical realm and the everyday human illusion of reality. This is **how** they *transcend* their present day physical reality, and no longer re-live it over and over again. And this is how what seems like miracles and magic unfolds in their lives.

When we have recently experienced great hurt or harm from the action of another, such as a tragic death or if we've just been physically assaulted, we can't be expected to accept, in that moment, that the experience was something for our greater good and for our soul's growth and evolvement. The five senses will automatically react to the situation, and we will not have that kind of receptivity. But in time, as the trauma and physical senses calm down, the sixth sense can take lead, and true healing and evolvement can unfold and take place.

I shared with you that when my mother died, I was very angry at God and at the people I blamed for her death. I was reactive, I retaliated, and I could not believe in a God who would take my mother away from me at such a young age. But by applying these forgiving and healing processes, I began to see the gift in my mom's early passing. I was able to see that through our soul agreement, my mother chose to leave early for my soul's growth and evolvement. It required my mother's death to get me to where I am today. You see, I thought I had it all figured out before she died, and nothing else would have gotten me here so swiftly. Nothing else would have forced me to really heal my victim consciousness, and heal my relationship and grow closer with my father. Nothing else would have forced him to heal and grow along with me. And nothing else would have forced other loved ones in our family to grow as well. In hindsight, I was able to see that there was a Divine order to all of this, and although I greatly miss my mother, I am profoundly grateful to her for being willing to shorten her time in this world, for all of our souls´ growth and evolvement. Life is much better when seen from the ***bird's eye view***, out of victim consciousness and from a greater state of gratitude.

In fact, what if we took on the perspective that everything that has happened in our life was a ***gift*** of our soul's choosing, for our soul's growth and evolvement? That actually, everything has been just preparing you for your *Spiritual Self's* vision and mission. That life has not been beating you up, but preparing you for your soul's next step and for the great contribution you are to share with the world. How about if the things of life weren't happening TO you— but instead, were happening **FOR** you? That the Universe is working on your behalf to give you opportunities to *transcend* your once upon limitations and to **up-level** your life and soul's evolution. An opportunity to reorganize your thoughts and beliefs and restore your life back to your soul's original intention. How about if this is all a set up for a **step up**, instead of a set back? Would that be a more powerful and beneficial belief to have?

This is the belief held by two very influential men of our day, Nelson Mandela and Tony Robbins. When Tony was interviewing Nelson Mandela, he mistakenly asked Nelson, "How did you survive through all those years of suffering in prison?" And Nelson Mandela abruptly answered, "I didn't survive. I prepared." How would things change in your life if you altered your perspective from *surviving* something **to *learning and growing*** from it, and **seeing** how you can ***utilize it*** to make the world a better place to live in? Tony knows that it was his own childhood trauma that has driven him to understand human suffering, how to break free of it, and to then share that awareness with others. He knows all of his childhood suffering has prepared him to be the powerful and passionate teacher that he is today! Oprah says the same about her own life experience as well. They were being prepared to be able to sing their soul's song.

The truth is that almost every great teacher we have ever had was birthed out of the pain and struggle that they went through, and the solutions they discovered to *transform* their suffering. They found a way through it and out of it, and discovered a greater meaning for the experience rather than the typical victim's story. They discovered that, like the metamorphous of a caterpillar into a butterfly, gifts often come through the appearance of a problem and the struggle out of it. For instance, the thought process could be– because I had that experience, I now have this greater awareness, this compassion, this knowledge, this learning, this strength, this drive, or this commitment to help liberate others from that same experience or pain. They realized that within every adversity lies the **seed** to greater possibilities.

These teachers have created new and more powerful meanings for their apparent toil— meanings that *transformed* their life experience, and in turn, ended up improving many lives around the world!

Forgiveness, and looking at things from the **bird's eye view**, from your **Spiritual Self's** perspective, instead of from the worm's eye view, is the pathway out of the victim consciousness and into your greatness, towards your soul's intention. Wayne Dyer, at the age of 34, drove to Biloxi, Mississippi to visit the grave of his father, an alcoholic and abusive man who had abandoned him, his mother and his two brothers the day he was born. Although his father had died 10 years earlier, Wayne had only just learned about his death. With a level of anger so great and deep from years of built-up pain, he drove to his father's grave with two tasks in mind: to find out if it was even acknowledged on his death certificate that Wayne was his son, and to literally piss on the grave of the father that he held such anger, hatred and resentment towards for the past 34 years.

But instead, Wayne was taken through a powerful forgiveness process that changed his life forever. Most people today know Wayne Dyer for all of his bestselling books (having sold hundreds of millions of copies), his PBS television specials, and his heart-warming, thought-provoking talks..... But most don't know that, up to that point in his life when he visited his father's grave, he was overweight, drinking heavily, and describes himself as "basically on an involuntary suicide mission." Through the power of forgiveness and healing his heart, he was able to radically transform his entire life to one of abundance that inspires millions of people around the world!

What if everything that has happened to you is actually a set up for a **step up to something greater,** instead of a set back? And all that is required is making a different *choice* to take a different road to a higher ridge, with a greater perspective? To make the *choice* to move from the wound, ***to the gift.***

> *"Forgiveness is the fragrance that the violet sheds*
> *on the heel that has crushed it."*
> ~ Mark Twain

In his seminars, Tony Robbins often shares a story of two brothers, very close in age, raised in the same family with the same experiences, who grew up to live very different lives. Their father was a drug addicted, alcoholic philanderer who would often be in jail for theft. One brother pretty much followed in his father's footsteps as an alcoholic philanderer who was in jail for robbery; while the other brother was a loyal husband, father and upstanding citizen of his school board and community. When Tony asked each brother separately why they think their life turned out the way that it did, each one gave him the same answer, "Well, with a father like that, how else could my life have turned out?" So it is not the events that determine our life, but the story and the meaning we give them. You have a *choice point* to make. You can choose to continue down the victim's path and keep yourself stuck on that same road, or you can instead choose to use it as a **stepping stone** to a greater life purpose. As **preparation** for the *gift* that your soul has to share with the world. An opportunity to break the chain of pain that has been passed down within your genealogy. And instead of feeling like a victim, you can ask the Universe, "What is the gift in this that I have not been seeing? What gift does this have to offer me right now?" You can also **choose** to *transcend* this victim and limiting pattern by being **grateful** to the person for being willing to play the role that they did, for your soul's growth and evolvement.

Thomas Edison, America's famous inventor, sold candy and snacks on the train as a young boy. One day, a man lifted up Thomas and his load of snacks onto the train by his ears — and that was the beginning of the end of his hearing. Thomas Edison could have easily dwelt all of his life on this cruel and damaging experience, like most would, but instead he saw it as a blessing. He would tell people, "Deafness has been a great help to me. It has saved me from having to listen to a lot of worthless chatter, and it has taught me to hear from within. To hear the voice of the Infinite Intelligence and receive guidance on my creations." Every adversity has the seed within it to greatness. You have an important *choice point* to make. Are you going to be a mere survivor of your circumstance or a **catalyst** for change? For inspiration, passionately sing along to this song:

www.HealYourHeartFreeYourMind.com/Stronger

The key to *transforming* our life *is transcending* the **victim consciousness** that is a part of the Human Conditioning that was just passed down to us. Refusing to forgive and let go is a trick the mind/ego uses to keep us in this victim consciousness. The mind/ego does this because it is fearful of its own death and it is always in a state of protection and defense. Victim consciousness comes from this fear. Fear is just another one of those *virus* words that we need to alter, so that it no longer has the physical effect on our body that it does right now. To the extent that the *virus* continues undetected and untreated, our survival symptoms multiply, the vibration and the energy around it multiplies, and fear then becomes like a negative prayer that we are broadcasting out, and drawing the like into our life. Just like if someone desperately fears dogs and sees one, the dog will sense that fear and immediately attack— but that same dog would respond differently to a person who loves dogs and has no fear associated with them. Anything you fear is much more likely to find you and do harm than it would if you never had that fear. When you fear failure or rejection, you will attract or create it; and when you focus on success and having raving fans, you will attract more of that instead.

So tell me, what is the actual biological purpose of *fear*? To protect us from physical danger, correct? Just like that of an animal that is suddenly presented with a predator, the sympathetic nervous system automatically activates the adrenal glands to mobilize us in either fight or flight. However, because our subconscious mind (our ego and our identity) has become a part of our physical body, we can turn on the same fight or flight response at the flick of a negative thought, whether we see a lion or we're afraid we are going to lose something we deem important. Fear has unfortunately become the mind-made devil. At the moment the ego hears the mere mention of something that threatens its survival within society's rules of acceptance and approval, fear surges through our body in order to protect itself. The body *Turbos* up. The purpose of this surge of energy is to increase our physical power, so that we can excel in our performance for our very survival or the protection of something we love. Like that which allows a mother the strength and power to lift a car off her child. This energy boost just gets misplaced and misunderstood due to all of our subconscious programming.

For us to feel fulfilled, we must grow and make progress. And for us to grow and make progress, we must take steps into uncertainty and out into the unknown — out of our comfort zone. When we do that, guess what happens? That's right — *fear* arises. I am not talking about, "OMG, there is a mountain lion" kind of fear, although it may produce the same type of bodily reactions; I am talking about the more subtle feelings of fear, like *"I'm not safe,"* that have become pervasive in our psyche like worry, insecurity and anxiety.

Fear is not a bad thing in and of itself; fear is a precursor to growth and expansion. Right before any major awesome thing came about in my life, I was first anxious and would feel that surge of energy. But when fear psychologically controls us, limits us and sends us down a negative spiral, we have stepped away from and lost its true gift and purpose. It now becomes more like cancer — in its attempt to save itself, it ends up destroying itself.

Now let's look at this word **Turbo** we referred to above. What is its purpose? To provide more power to quickly improve the performance of some kind of vehicle, correct? Perhaps, to get out of a tight spot quickly. Very similar to the purpose of fear or our auto-adrenal system for our vehicle (our body). So, what if we started associating the word *fear* **to** the word ***Turbo***? What if you changed the phrase, "I am fearful" to, "***I am Turbo***." Would that create a different feeling within your body and mind? If you started to feel those old fearful feelings and you changed your vocabulary from, "I am feeling fearful, or I am feeling anxiety" to, "***I am feeling Turbo charged***," does that create a whole different response in your body and Being? Do you feel a little more excited and powerful? Do you feel as if you have a little more oomph to achieve what needs to get done? See *fear* as **FUEL** — the jet fuel required to take you where you need to go – and be grateful for it being there! Fear is just excitement, with more power and a faster energy to support the transform-ation that has the opportunity to happen at that moment. The master will use *fear* as **fuel**, unless they are in mortal danger; then they use it to get the heck out of Dodge!

The difference between some of our greatest athletes and performers is how they define the energy that surges in their body, and how they let that energy affect their actions. The great achievers like Tiger Woods, Michael Jordon and Lance Armstrong utilize this energy pumping in their veins to drive and catapult them to their next evolution. While the person stuck in victim/safety based thinking labels that energy as fear and anxiety, and hides and pulls back instead.

Now if you found poison somewhere in your home that was threatening your wellbeing, you would take immediate action to remove this poison from your dwelling, correct? So let it be the same for freeing yourself of this poisonous thought affecting your body and life. Watch this transformative Ted Talk given by Kelly McGonigal, a Ph.D. psychologist from Stanford, on stress and the power of belief to give you a new awareness and perspective on *fear*:

www.HealYourHeartFreeYourMind.com/Stress

When you have this greater awareness of what this feeling **really is** and **give it a more positive supportive meaning,** you can now *transform* that feeling, that once debilitated you and kept you from your dreams, **to *strengthening and empowering you*** towards them instead! So exchange the word and the feeling of fear **to *Turbo***, and **supercharge your life** to your next evolution! This is another powerful tool to get out of the Matrix, the *safety zone* and this victim programming!

Just as we said in chapter six, the first step to *transcend* the obstacles and live more of a joy-filled, magical life is to completely uninstall and free yourself from the victim consciousness. It is not an easy task because of our generations upon generations of programming and our societal conditioning integrated into our physical bodies. It requires new awareness, new languaging and new behaviors. It also requires **taking responsibility for everything**, getting out of the Blame Game, forgiveness, and actually applying the *Law of Reflection* into your life. It calls for no longer participating in the tricks of the mind like the Drama Triangle or making someone wrong in order to feel right. It entails **letting go** of old stories and letting yourself and others out of your self-imposed prison. And beyond forgiving, it requires getting out of your myopic view and taking a ride to a higher and grander perspective. To a view from the heavens where you can transmute your anger into **gratitude**!

The Sixth Step to Freedom is:

6. Step up to the *bird's eye view* and use one of these **Forgiveness Tools** to **heal your heart** and any animosity you feel with any one that has ever been in your life, currently alive or not. Since our life started from our parents, begin your forgiveness journey with them and move forward in your life from that point on. Don't forget to include forgiving yourself!

   - Continue the liberation from *victim consciousness* by **forgiving** everyone you once held captive. Always remembering the *Law of Reflection* and seeing them as your *Healing Angels.*

   - Create new meanings for your adversities. Ask the Universe, "What is great about this that I have not been seeing? What is the *gift* and how has this served me? How can I learn and grow from this? What great work have you been preparing me for?"

   - Change your vocabulary and *transform* your relationship to *fear* and **Turbo Charge** your life experience.

   - Now that you have greater perspective, re-read chapter six on **Self-Empowerment** to liberate yourself from *victim consciousness.*

*Transcend*Transform*Inspire*

Inner View

What have you learned both about Forgiveness and Gratitude?

....

....

....

....

....

....

....

....

....

....

....

....

....

....

....

....

....

....

....

....

....

....

....

List all the people alive or not that you still need to forgive or need forgiveness from:

....

....

....

....

....

....

....

....

....

....

....

....

....

....

....

....

....

....

....

....

....

....

Now begin to **See** the *Gifts* they have given you as your *Healing Angels* and use one of the tools you just learned to forgive them and to forgive yourself.

....

....

....

....

....

....

....

....

....

....

....

....

....

....

....

....

....

....

....

....

....

....

....

....

Chapter Thirteen

Seventh Step To Freedom
~The Conception of It All~

So how are you feeling after that forgiveness process? A little lighter? A little freer? More liberated and empowered? Through it, we have laid down a strong foundation for what's next.

It is very important to heal our relationship with our parents, whether they are alive or not, whether you are close to them or you keep a distance, because our relationship with our parents determines our relationship with everybody else thereafter. All challenges in our life and in our relationships with others is a reflection of the challenge and *charges* we have or have had with our parents, and other primary care givers we had growing up in our young years. The key to *healing our relationship with others and to transforming our life* is to heal our relationship with our parents, our primary care givers, and any other significant family relationships we had from our childhood.

It doesn't matter if you grew up with your biological parents or not, they still are primary contributors to your development as a human being. Their lineage is a principal factor of your subconscious programming and what is unconsciously driving your life; remember that 50 percent of our personality is already created by the time we are born. Remember my eye-opening example I shared with you about my friend who never knew anything about her birth mother until she was 27, and the uncanny duplication of mannerisms between them? Because of how a baby is imprinted and psychologically developed through their subconscious mind from the point of conception, and because of how things get passed down through the generations, healing our relationships with our parents is crucial to healing our subconscious programming and what we are broadcasting out into the world!

Any feelings, *charges* and belief systems you have about either one of your parents, and why they weren't directly involved in your life in any way, will have a heavy influence on your life and your relationship with others. It is the root cause of the patterns that continually show up in your life. Whatever the reasons are, it is bound to be very emotional and perhaps even traumatic. Because of the egocentric nature of a small child, there are likely several stories you have in your mind, that don't behoove you, of why they weren't there. These types of situations can often bring up feelings of abandonment, not being good enough, or not wanted or loved. None of which we want to be unconsciously broadcasting out and having the world mirror back to us.

Remember, after birth, we are still primarily in a hypnagogic trance state until after the age of six; so our subconscious mind is still just recording and storing for later playback whatever it hears and experiences, without the analytical capability to discern between right and wrong or put things in a right context. The most influential perceptual programming of the subconscious mind occurs from conception through the age of six. These are called the **Imprinting Years**— perceptions acquired during this time period become the fundamental subconscious programs that really shape the character of an individual's life. So, whatever happens with your parents, primary caregivers and other family members during this time period, and whatever beliefs you create from this egocentric, naive, undeveloped child's mind, will have a life driving influence on how you perceive and experience life and others.

It is not until somewhere between the age of 6 and 7 that the Alpha waves become more dominant, and the analytical mind begins to develop and draw conclusions about its experiences with the outside world. Between the ages of eight and twelve, the Beta waves become more and more active, and this is when the real conscious and analytical thinking begins. This is when a child's conscious mind filters all of its experiences through its database of all of the subconscious programming it received since conception (*the cud*), and comes up with decisions and belief systems that then get stored in the subconscious mind for later playback. By the time children reach adolescence, their subconscious minds are filled up with data that ranges **from** *how to walk and talk* **to being told**, "*They can't,*" and, "*They will never be good enough,*" **or** "*They can do anything they set their minds to,*" in which to process their life experiences through and come up with these driving belief systems.

Usually, we do not go back and re-examine these naive beliefs systems or decisions with a more aware consciousness until we hit some kind of dark night of the soul event, and are prompted to through some kind of healing or personal development process (like this). So all of these wrong childhood belief systems of *'no, can't do, can't have, rejection, not being good enough or not as good as another, not wanted, not important, not liked or loved,* etc.', are unconsciously running our lives, determining what we draw into our life, blocking us from reaching some of our major life goals, and actually causing us to reach this dark night of the soul.

Because so much of our subconscious programming happens through our parents and primary caregivers as we are growing up, these are the primary relationships we have to heal to transform our life experience. These relationships are the source of most of our core *charges* that we are attracting from and filtering life through. These *charges* will continue to be reflected back to us by the Universe until we acknowledge them and allow them to be processed, so that they can move on out.

Our relationships in life replicate our relationship with our parents.

It's like you are in a business meeting and all of a sudden you are feeling uncomfortable and not very confident; you just want to either keep quiet or slip out of the meeting, and you're not sure why you are feeling this way. All of these old stories are running around in your head, and it's like your little girl or boy is tugging on your sleeve, saying, "That man reminds me of dad. Dad use to say I can't do anything right and that I will never amount to anything or succeed. He would tell me that I was dumb and that my ideas were stupid. I don't feel so good right now; I'm not feeling too confident; I don't want to be here; I don't want to talk; they will just shoot down my ideas." You start to experience the old feelings you used to feel in your body, when your father would say those unkind words to you, as if it was happening all over again. That experience, those thoughts and feelings being felt in your body, is called ***transference***, which is a very common occurrence in the human psyche. It is when a stored *charge* gets triggered by something in the external environment that is picked up through the five senses, and comes back up, like *cud*, for processing.

Transference— *the process by which somebody unconsciously redirects or transfers feelings about something onto another object.*

When we are matching each other's *charges,* this ***transference*** can become mutual. I remember I had a boss who took a liking to me right away during our interview because, he said, I reminded him of his daughter. He developed a strong instinct to protect me instantly when, within two weeks of hiring me, an alcoholic employee in my office starting hitting on his female colleagues. I was one of them, and another lady in our office reported him and included my name as one of his targets. From that moment on there was a strange relationship between my boss and me that became more like a father and his teenage daughter, than a boss with his employee. He was suddenly managing my life, without telling me, in order to guide me and protect me. I would experience strange disciplines and him talking down and correcting me as if I was his daughter. I soon began to feel as if he was trying to control me like my father would. I could tell that he cared about me as a person, but I could never get his approval— I was never quite good enough in his eyes, and thus I would rebel. This working relationship was so odd that I called HR to step in and get involved, and they were able to clearly see all of the **transference** that was going on between us.

Since we are not taught about this tendency for **transference** of our wounding onto others, we tend to justify these experiences, shove them back down and try to forget them— which they temporarily do, until the feelings and story (*pattern*) shows up again at a different time, with a different face. Oftentimes it is really difficult to admit and face the fact that we have hurt or anger towards one of our parents. We may clearly and admittedly have anger towards one, but the other one that we felt the most loved and connected to, we have a hard time admitting that we have any anger towards them as well. Yet it is important that we look at these charges too. Just because we don't acknowledge it, doesn't mean that hurt or anger vibration is not broadcasting out to the world like a radio station, and affecting our life experience.

I shared with you that, although I felt as if my mother were my soul mate and I loved her more than life, I still felt very hurt and not totally safe or protected by her when she didn't protect me from my father when he was drinking. Because of my deep love for her, I did not want to admit that I had this *charge* with her, so I only focused on healing my *charges* with my father; yet that charge with my mother kept affecting my life no matter how much work I did on my charge with my dad. That *charge* kept getting mirrored back to me by the world, and I would continually attract experiences that would validate my feelings of not having a safe place, and that I had to guard and protect myself.

This fear to acknowledge a *charge* with a parent became the main obstacle with a boyfriend of mine as well. We were both very aware of his hurt and pain with his father, and we kept doing a lot of work on trying to heal those *charges*. But what we discovered, and what he refused to look at for a long time, is that he had a lot of hurt and anger with his mother too. That he actually blamed his mother overly doting over him as the cause of his father being jealous of him, and so vehemently rejecting him. He was angry that she leaned on him and did not stand up to his father and leave sooner, so he wouldn't have had to live with his father's jealous rage his entire childhood. It is so difficult to admit that you are angry at the only parent that you felt totally loved by. But it was this anger he had with his mother, and her not standing up for herself against his dad, that he kept playing out with the women in his life and with me; unconsciously he wanted her (through us) to finally stand up to his father (him). That *charge* kept showing itself to him, wanting to be healed, and wanting to be processed so it could move on out— but because of his fear of losing the love and approval from the one parent he felt he had it from, he could not bring himself to take a look at it.

This is an example of another emotional abuse that is rampant in our society, that does not get as much attention amongst all of the physical abuse, but is definitely just as debilitating to a child's future as a thriving adult, and that is **Emotional Incest**. Emotional Incest is when a parent leans on their child as an emotional crutch, in order to feel loved and better about themselves and their life, or for some physical help. It often happens when there are problems and relationship dysfunction between the parents of the child, be it: control and abuse, addictions, bad communication, mental or physical illness, an emotional or physical absentee parent, relationship issues that cause anger and hurt, divorce, being and staying single, the death of the partner or an immediate family member. Because all of these things are fairly common incidents in families, and much of the world is love-starved from the love they feel they didn't receive as a child, Emotional Incest is unfortunately quite prevalent. This is where we get *'Mama's Boy'* and *'Daddy's little Princess'*.

Consider a scenario where the mother and father are fighting, and the father leaves in a storm and the mom is crying in her bedroom. Her four-year-old toddles into the room, confused and terrified about what is going on with mommy, and says, "Mommy, don't cry! I'm sorry, I love you mommy!" Mom looks up at her child, her tears dry up and her eyes fill up with love, and her face breaks into an instant smile and she says, "Oh honey, I love you so much. You are my little angel. Come here and give mommy a big hug. You make mommy feel so much better. I don't know what I would do without you; promise me you will never leave me!"

A touching scene?

No! It's the beginning of Emotional Incest! The child has just received the message that he or she has the power to save mommy and make her smile when she is hurt and sad, and thus, is responsible for her happiness. The child, who is already egocentric and thinks everything is because of them, will readily take up this responsibility and become the *'big man'* or *'big girl of the house'*. Parents leaning on their children for their emotional needs creates an enmeshment that fosters unhealthy co-dependency between them, and it is also carried into the child's other relationships in their adult years. Often-times with individuals of the same sex as the parent that was leaning on them.

Making a child the stand-in surrogate for the spouse that *'left'*, and leaning or *'dumping'* on them about it, be it from divorce, break up, emotional distance or death, is unfortunately quite common. Those who are using their children to get their emotional needs met probably believe that the new arrangement is beneficial and win/win. They think they are present for the child, the child gets to feel useful and loved, and they are getting their own needs met, all at the same time. Unfortunately, the ramifications of the parent's neediness on the child's life are far greater than any benefits that the child feeling important and needed *might* have. Not only is an unhealthy co-dependency pattern created that follows the child through life, but they also lose their childhood and become adults way too early— which tends to cause them to lose their sense of play and the ability to explore their own self-expression. They tend to identify who they are through others and become quite the people pleaser. When a client's parents divorced, he suddenly became the only child left at home of his five older siblings. His mother, who was already distraught about having an almost empty nest, leaned heavily on him as the surrogate husband and made him the "man of the house." Before seeking help, he spent three decades of his life anticipating and meeting his mother's every need. He even went so far as to live right next door to her, with his wife and daughter, so that he would be close enough to come running whenever she called. That was until his wife had enough, took their daughter and left, and was threatening divorce!

As another example, look at the account of a concerned grandmother who came looking for help. She said, "My son married a young widow with two boys. Throughout the marriage, my daughter-in-law would never allow my son to have any kind of fatherly relationship with her eldest son, although he was the sole father of her younger child. The oldest boy is now twenty years old and won't leave his mother's side. He has to sleep in the bedroom next to hers, he paces the floor until she gets home from work and then follows her around the house. He sits outside the bathroom door while she bathes. He calls and texts with her constantly when they are away from each other. And when he graduated from high school, he attended a local community college because he didn't want to leave her. But it became too long of a drive, back and forth between school and the house for him, so he quit and got a close by minimum wage job instead. She takes him everywhere she goes and he refuses to have a relationship with his younger brother or my son. It's as though he resents their presence in the home and wants his mother all to himself. He has had only one girlfriend in his life, and she was the daughter of a close friend of his Mom's that she spent a lot of time with. Please help!"

Unfortunately the mother created a deep co-dependency with her oldest son when she treated him as a 'surrogate husband' after she was suddenly widowed and in despair. In his own grief and fear and with her encouragement, he has clung for dear life to that job role, ever since. This decidedly unhealthy relationship will greatly hinder his life if they don't both actively heal the great entanglement she created; but his great love and co-dependency with her, and the great fear of the loss of that love and approval, makes it very difficult for him **to admit and see the pain and limitations it has caused him in his life.**

So, is there a parent or a primary caregiver that you still need to heal with, that you haven't wanted to admit or take a look at? Have you experienced some Emotional Incest that has been difficult to define as a type of abuse? Through it, have you developed a co-dependency that has been difficult to see or admit? Now is the time for us to **choose the stepping stone** towards a different path in our life, to a higher road. Just because you refuse to acknowledge something doesn't keep it from causing havoc in your life. Now is the time to transcend the *patterns* and renovate your life experience. We have begun this journey, as we started using some of the forgiveness tools. Do you now see you need to add one of your parents or caregivers to that list you wrote up in the last chapter?

Have you done the research and looked at your parents' childhoods and upbringing that we asked you do in Chapter 3? Did you find out more about what their lives were like at the point of your conception, during your mother's pregnancy, and about your delivery and reception into the world? Were you able to find out what some of their belief systems were from their upbringing? And, did you find out more about your grandparents' childhood and belief systems that they passed on to your parents?

Since almost fifty percent of our personality is already created by the time we are received into the world, and so much of it is ancestral and societal stuff being unconsciously passed down to us (the mental disease), this is essential to understanding what we are unconsciously broadcasting out into the world. We truly don't have any references and awareness of a large percentage of what is driving our life! For example — I have always attracted people with mother issues, and I always tend to bring those *charges* up for them. This did not make sense to me at first, since I had a great relationship with my mother and my grandmother (her mother), and most of my charges were with my father. It wasn't until many years later that I realized that, although I did not have any major issues with my mother, my mom did with hers! In fact her charges were far greater with her mother (my grandmother) than with her father, and that just got downloaded into my neuro-network while I was in utero — and it was unconsciously driving my life experience. In fact, my mother did experience Emotional Incest from my grandmother when there were marital issues between her mother and father and when he left the family to marry another woman he had worked with. My grandmother *dumped* her anger and rage on my mom, became depressed, and my mother had to become 'the big girl' and 'the man of the house' to take care of my grandma and her little sister. When my mother was going to marry my father, and while I was in the womb, my grandmother became fearful that she would lose control of her *crutch*. Thus, she would constantly try to sabotage my parents' relationship and poison my mother's mind, by saying that my father was going to resent having to marry her because of her pregnancy, and would leave and abandon her just like my grandpa did to her. Phew! No wonder I had all of that 'burden' programming!

This information about our parents' and grandparents' upbringing is vital to our healing and to our forgiveness of our parents' mistakes. Everything is inter-connected, and it all greatly contributes to our development, from the point of conception and into our growing-up years. It is a critical element for us to discontinue broadcasting the victim consciousness out into the world, so we can stop attracting more of it. This awareness will launch the liberation from your *patterns* and *obstacles* that have hindered you from being able to live the life of your heart and soul's intention. This knowledge was so critical to my healing of all the victim programming that I had been unconsciously broadcasting out for so many years. When I took a look at all of my grand-parents' struggles, from one of them being one of thirteen kids growing up on a cotton plantation deep in the south and a manic depressive, to others being alcoholics, to some of them being married and divorced several times, to another disowning their family and calling themselves the black sheep of the family, to another one having their father commit suicide while they and the rest of the family were downstairs in the living room— I knew there had to be a lot of pain and victim consciousness running deep in my bloodline that I needed to heal, because my family before me never had. If you were adopted, it would be very beneficial for you to learn more about who your birth parents were and what was going on in their upbringing and in their life at the time of your conception. If you can ask the parents that raised you more about what they know about your adoption, that would be of great help. Otherwise, just capture everything about their childhood (and their parents' childhood), and how life was for them as couple when you came into their life.

So if you haven't gone out and captured that information yet, do so now before continuing on this healing process. This information is that vital. Go back now and re-read Chapter 3 and Chapter 4, *How Is Our Life Created Anyway* and *Why Our Life Has Been Unfolding At It Has*. In those chapters, I have given you a lot of examples of how this subconscious programming, since conception, replicates and shows itself in our daily lives. You will have a greater understanding of all of this when you re-read those chapters now, in this context. And this new understanding is going to shine light into all the areas of your life that were once confusing to you and hiding in darkness.

I shared with you how deeply driven my mother was by the programming of not wanting to be a burden, based on the parameters of her conception; that she would first choose to be a single mother, in a time period when women weren't even allowed to have a credit card on their own, let alone own a house, and would choose to die before ever feeling like a burden to anyone. I also shared with you how deeply that belief system got passed down and unconsciously programmed into me, and drove so many years of my life, until I became aware of it. These little mischievous varmints are rampant in all of us, and are the most difficult to uncover and evict. They are buried so deep and have been building up, veiling themselves from generation to generation for eons; so much so, that it requires a new *awareness*, more information and a whole lot of Grace to draw them out from their fortress. This is why we have been strengthening your relationship with the Divine and doing all of this pre-work, preparing you for this moment of true liberation.

You're about to do some real intense emotional work. **To begin this deep internal journey we are about to go on, you need to dedicate a couple of days to it — like a weekend.** If you haven't done your research on your parents and family yet, go do that now, answering the questions in the **Inner View** in Chapter 3, starting on page 43. Please **do not go any further in this process until you do so**. This is very important! And when you're ready to start this intense two day process, make sure you go to the bathroom, grab some water, create a comfortable space for yourself with lots of pillows and perhaps a Wiffle bat (totally optional) and get into a quiet and private place where you can feel free to express your emotions.

When you are ready to begin this sacred journey, first get out your favorite picture of yourself as a little kid that you really connect with, taken somewhere around the age of 7 or 8. Then invoke your Divine, asking them for guidance, support and the awareness to **SEE** whatever you need to. If you feel up for it, it would be divine to sing the moola mantra three times to summon the Grace, so the **Healing Process** can begin to flow. If you would like to hear it sung instead, you can find it under track #6 or download it here.

www.HealYourHeartFreeYourMind.com/Mantra

OM
SAT CHIT ANANDA PARABRAHMA
PURUSHOTTAMA PARAMATMA
SRI BHAGAVATI SAMETA
SRI BHAGAVATE NAMAHA
Three times

The adoption of our parents' patterns begins in the mother's womb and accelerates after birth. From the point of conception until around seven, we are like human sponges just absorbing everything around us. As we become toddlers, we tune into the emotional vibe of our family and home, and our emotional body absorbs up their frequency. This programming continues until after puberty, by which time we have either adopted our parents' and primary care giver's patterns or rebelled against them, which we then carry out into the world in our adult lives.

We are either *adopting* our parents' patterns to get their love and approval, or we *rebel against* them, to either get their attention and some kind of connection from them, or to protect ourselves from being further hurt. Longing for our parents' love and approval is at the basis of all human pain. Even Michelangelo felt the need to please his father. He once wrote to him, "I am the most famous artist in the world... I have worked night and day and undergone hardships of every description...... but I still do not know what you want of me." This sense of almost desperate willingness to please, to get the love and approval we always sought from our parents, stays with us as we grow older, because its pain is still locked inside of us, still un-fully expressed, as our hurt *emotional child.*

Because of our egocentric nature as a small child, we always think things are our fault; we are always unconsciously trying to take care of and save our parents and heal our relationship with them, so that they will see us, love us, approve of us and not leave. This *charge* is always living within us, unconsciously trying to get healed and unawarely driving our life. A powerful example of this was demonstrated in the Walt Disney movie, ***Saving Mr. Banks*** — the true story of how the Mary Poppins movie was finally made between Mrs. Travers, the story's owner, and Mr. Disney, and why there was so much resistance from Mrs. Travers until....... Until they finally found the right story ending that her *emotional child* was always trying to recreate — *the saving of her beloved father, Mr. Banks,* who died of alcoholism and caused her entire family to fall apart. Mr. Disney shared with Mrs. Travers that he was always trying to improve the story ending with his father through all of his stories as well.

We unconsciously broadcast out these *charges* and attract similar situations to ourselves in the attempt to heal them. People who had an abusive parent will often find themselves in a similar situation with a significant other. It has the draw of the familiar, and how they were conditioned by what a person who says they "love you" does; and now they also have the unconscious hope that, "this time it will be different and I will finally get the love I always craved for from my mom or dad." Of course that doesn't happen, and the *charge* just gets larger, and they attract from it all the more, creating a vicious cycle of the same *pattern* in their life, time and time again.

We tend to project, or *transfer*, our childhood wounding onto all of our various relationships in our adult life. Onto our lovers, life partners, our friends, our associates, our colleagues, our boss or any other authority figure in our life. This is why **your suffering is not in the fact, it is in your perception of the fact.** This is why *the outside world is just a reflection of your inside world.* And this is why your life is the way that you perceive it to be now!

To free ourselves from this programming and pain, we have to face our truth and be totally honest with ourselves. No longer living on the river of denial as our family most likely did! We must dare to face the emotional pain of our childhood because that is where the roots to all of our life challenges reside. Welcoming all painful remembrances of it. It is better to face this sting head to head, once and for all, than to carry the burden of this pain into the rest of our life, to be mirrored back to us. The emotion at the time will be intense but short-lived, and the end result will be inner peace and freedom!

Freedom from the internal war we have been secretly fighting. Like in a war where soldiers are forced to deny their emotions in order to survive, this emotional denial works to help the soldier survive the war, but later can have devastating delayed consequences. The medical profession has recognized the damage that this emotional denial causes, and have coined a term to describe it— ***Delayed Stress Syndrome***. Soldiers have to deny what it feels like to see their friends killed and maimed, what it feels like to kill another human being, and the fear of having them attempt to kill you. The stress caused by this intense trauma, and the effect of denying it to yourself and others, eventually surfaces in ways which produce a new kind of trauma, such as: anxiety, addictions, fear, anger, uncontrollable rage, depression, inability to maintain relationships or hold jobs, suicide, etc. And instead of blood and death, what may have happened to us as children was more like a spiritual death, an emotional maiming, a mental torture or some kind of physical violation. Whatever the form was, we were forced to grow up denying the reality of what was really happening in our homes.

We were forced to deny our feelings about what we were experiencing, seeing and sensing. We may have grown up in a home having to deny the emotional reality of our parents' addictions, mental illness, anger, rage, depression, abuse, abandonment, betrayal, deprivation, neglect, emotional incest, etc. Or, perhaps it was dad ignoring us because of his workaholism, or our mom smothering us because she had no other identity than being a mother or another safe emotional outlet. Perhaps it was abuse of one parent on the other, and/or on us or one of our siblings, while the other parent didn't protect us. Whatever the pain or shame may have been, we were born into the middle of a war where our sense of self was battered and fractured, and we felt like we had to hide and deny it all to ourselves and to the world. We grew up in the middle of battlefields where our being was discounted, our perceptions invalidated, and our feelings ignored and nullified. And the battlefield each of us grew up in was not in some foreign country against some identified "enemy" — it was in our *'homes'*, which were supposed to be our safe haven, with our parents and caregivers whom we loved and depended on.

The trauma of feeling like we're not safe in our own homes makes it very difficult to feel like we're safe anywhere. And feeling as if we're not lovable to one of our own parents can make it challenging for us to believe that we can be lovable for others. This internal war we went through probably didn't last just for a year or two — most likely, it lasted about seventeen or eighteen years or so. And it probably wasn't a battlefield because our parents were bad— it was a battle because they were at war with themselves. Because they too were born into the middle of a war they did not create, nor did they choose. By doing our healing, we are breaking the cycle and becoming the emotionally honest role models that our parents never had the chance to be. We are doing our part to break the cycle of The Human Condition– the mental virus, and the self-destructive behaviors that have dictated human existence for thousands of years.

So now I invite you to look honestly at the reality of your childhood experiences, and give yourself permission to re-experience the past and any of its unhappiness and pain. These patterns were just recorded and learned, and like Nelson Mandela said during his freedom speech— "No one is born hating another person because of the color of his skin, or his background, or his religion. People must learn to hate." So look at your picture or visualize yourself as young as you can, and re-experience what it was like to be *you* at that age. What kind of things were you being taught by your parents and family that you just picked up by what you observed and experienced? Invite your *emotional child* to no longer hide, and take lead in this process. You made all of these life-defining decisions at emotional highs and lows through an unaware, undeveloped child's mind, at a time when your parents were God to you, and you innocently trusted and depended on them fully. So we need to look at our childhood experiences and our relationship with our parents from this innocent child's view, and not as a logical, understanding adult. It's now time for your emotional child to express itself freely in a safe environment, completely supported by the Divine and your *A Team*.

So, *emotional child*, look at the picture and into your own eyes, and remember. What do you see? Did you feel like you were wanted and taken care of by both of your parents? Did you feel loved, accepted and important to them both? Did you feel loved unconditionally *or* were you always trying to get their love, attention and approval to no avail? Did you feel uplifted *or* always put down? Did you feel safe and protected, *or* did you feel abandoned and unsafe by either one of them? Did you feel rejected or ridiculed? Were they both present for you, *or* aloof? Were you allowed to express yourself and did you feel seen and heard? Allow the memories just to flow up, and express whatever emotions that want to come out as they do. Remember, the only way out of suffering, is through. Let the charges express themselves now.

What would happen when you asked your mother or father for their attention or for something you wanted? Would they give it to you, or was it always a sharp "no!"? What were your parents' attitudes and emotions like? Did they always seem happy and positive *or* angry and depressed? How were you disciplined? Were you afraid of either of them? What did you learn to do to try and escape punishment? What was life like when you came home from school? How was your parents' relationship together– were they loving and affectionate *or* fighting and distant? How was life like with your siblings for you, and with your parents? How about with your grandparents? Your aunts, uncles and cousins? What was life like growing up in your family– fun and joyful *or* fearful, depressing and lonely? What kind of attitudes and beliefs did your parents have about others, and the world, that affected you?

Allow all of these memories and emotions come up freely. Remember all the details— see them, hear them and feel them completely. Don't hold anything back. Let all of the hurt, confusion, memories and anger to rise up, and the tears to unceremoniously fall. **Get your journal out now and start writing out some of the answers to these questions, and the awareness that comes up around them**. Just allow whatever memories that want to come up, to come up. Keep writing until you feel complete. And when you are done, take a bathroom and water break before you move on to the next session of this process.

Inner View

So now is the time to let all of this clutter that has been limiting you and weighing you down rise up from underneath the waterline, so that it can move out and float away. In this next session we are going to set **you**, *inner emotional child*, free to totally express yourself! Bar none!! It's time for you to express all of your anger, hurt, pain and rage! **Get your journal out** again, listen to track #10 on the audio program, and for the next **45 minutes,** you are just going to vent and rail on all of the hurt, anger and pain you have towards **your mother!** Forget all of the great things about your mother right now; all you're going to focus on is all of your *Mama Trauma*. All of her shadows that got passed down to you, and how they screwed up your life! In this part of the process, you are going to blame her for the problems that you have in your life. Write her from your hurt, angry and scared emotional teenager, letting it all out, full of expletives and all! Start off with something like, "It fucking hurt me when you did '*this*', and now my life is like '*this*' because of it! Fuck you, mother!" And just keep writing quickly, whatever wants to come out, not thinking or filtering anything; just express whatever bubbles up, for at least 45 minutes, until you feel you have exhausted all that you needed to say. Don't worry about her ever seeing it, we will burn it after. But for now, just let all of the hurt, anger, confusion and rage come out in a stream of flow. Start writing now, and don't go forward in this process until you complete this.

You will find track #10 here, if you don't have it downloaded already:

www.HealYourHeartFreeYourMind.com/WriteOut

We may not be able to solve everything we face, but
*we can't solve **Anything**, unless we Face It!*
~David Corbin

Inner View

Now we are going to do the same with our father. Listen to track #10 again and **continue writing in your journal, to your father**, about all of your *Papa Trauma*. About all of your hurt, anger, rage and blame, starting off with something like, "You fucking hurt me when you would do '*this*', and now my life is like '*this*' because of it! Fuck you, dad!" And just let whatever needs to come out, out. Don't hold anything back. Keep writing intensely, in a stream of thought, for at least **45 minutes** or until you have exhausted all that you want or need to say!! *Emotional kid*, this is your time to express yourself fully and get everything off your chest and out! Again, don't think about any of your father's good attributes right now, just focus on all of his shadows and all of your hurt and pain because of them, and rant and rave! Don't worry about him ever seeing this, we will burn them all after we are done. Don't move forward until you have finished this very important, very powerful process. And after you finish this, you may want to take a little time to your-self before you go on to the next part of this process. Go to the bathroom, get a glass of water, and notice the relief you are already beginning to feel from this release.

This tool we just used, ***The Write it Out of Your System***, is a powerful tool **Napoleon Hill** (author of *Think and Grow Rich*) would use to clean out the basement of his subconscious mind, to get out any anger and resentment that he was carrying. So instead of just pretending it is not there and shoving it back down like the ego/intellect likes to do and have it still affect your life, or taking it out on someone else or numbing yourself from it, it is a very useful tool to move the garbage out of your body without hurting anyone in the process. I invite you to use it anytime you feel any hurt, anger or resentment towards someone before you take any other actions you may feel like doing!

So now that we got all of that hurt and anger out and expressed, and we are more in touch with all the different emotions we experienced with our family as a small child, let's take a closer inner view, so we can heal all of these *charges*. Put on your headphones and listen to track #11 on the audio program as you are going through this exercise.

www.HealYourHeartFreeYourMind.com/InnerView

Inner View

What are some of the patterns you have in your life?

....

....

....

....

....

....

....

....

....

....

....

....

....

....

....

....

....

....

....

....

....

....

....

....

....

....

What are some of the major *charges* you found hiding under the waterline and which ones are associated with these patterns?

....

....

....

....

....

....

....

What did you learn about your grandparents' upbringing and some of their core beliefs?

....

....

....

....

....

....

....

....

....

....

....

....

....

....

What did you learn about your parents' upbringing and their core beliefs?

....

....

....

....

....

....

....

....

....

....

....

....

....

....

....

....

....

....

What did you learn about your parent's love affair and journey together?

....

....

....

....

....

....

....

....

....

....

....

....

....

....

....

....

....

....

....

....

....

....

....

What did you learn about your delivery, time in the womb, and your reception into the world? Watch an example of how critical our reception into this world is on our Being. www.HealYourHeartFreeYourMind.com/womb

....

....

....

....

....

....

....

....

....

What did you learn about what was going on within your family your first 5-6 years of life?

....
....
....
....
....
....
....
....
....
....
....
....
....
....
....
....
....
....
....
....
....
....
....

Now looking at all of your family history, when did you get some of those *charges you listed*? Is it generational or from the birthing process? Is it post birth from 0-7, or from 8 and older? You may not logically know the answer, but just write down whatever comes up when you ask the question. Your subconscious mind and your *A Team* know the answer.

....

....

....

....

....

....

....

....

....

....

....

....

....

....

....

....

....

....

....

....

What charges from your childhood do you now see/feel you projected onto the Divine?

....

....

....

....

....

....

....

....

....

....

So now that we have done all this deep and generational inner mining, let's really begin this metamorphosis back to our *Essence*. Again, pull out your favorite picture of you as a small child so that you can really reconnect with yourself as this little girl or boy, and all that you experienced. Remember how you were feeling at that time and what life seemed like in that moment. And as we go through this process, just allow whatever memories and feelings that come up, to come up. It is time that we allow our child within to be heard by our parents and receive a little bit of what we have always longed for. Before we get started, go to the bathroom, make sure you're in a quiet and private place where you can fully express yourself, grab some water and pillows you can beat if you need to, and plug in your smart phone/mp3 player to some speakers so you can be wire-free. Go to track #12 or download it at the link below to be guided through this powerful inner journey. Do not read further until you have been guided through and fully engaged in this life changing journey!

www.HealYourHeartFreeYourMind.com/Parents

Inner View

So how are you feeling now? A little lighter, a little freer? Are you feeling a little more connected to your parents now? Do you feel a little more compassion, understanding and forgiveness for them? Are you feeling more love? Do you have more awareness of where some of your *charges* and *patterns* come from? Great! Because now we want to build off of that, so that everything can transform in your life to the way you want it to be! Remembering that almost everything that has been showing up in your life, and all of the challenges you've been facing with some of your other relationships, have just been a mirror to the *charges* you have had with your parents. And as we heal those *charges*, your life will reflect something anew. It will begin to mirror back a lot more love, joy and peace.

So for this next part, **get out your journal again,** and I want you to write two more letters; one to your mother and one to your dad. But this time, **your Spiritual Self** is going to connect with **their** Spiritual Self, and they are going to tell you the story of their childhood, with their parents and caregivers, and why their lives have unfolded the way that they have, and why they have done some of the things that they did as your parent. And as you write, just let whatever comes up, come out, even if you're not sure if it is true. Your **Spiritual Self** has a connection and an intuition that your *intellect* does not have. So just allow your parents' Spiritual Self tell you more about their childhood experience and all of their fears and pain of making mistakes with you as their child. Let them express their fear, their shame for their mistakes, their guilt for not knowing better, and their apology. Keep writing for at least 30-45 minutes for each parent until all that they need to say and apologize for is complete, and you feel more compassion and internal peace. When you complete a parent's letter to you, grab your pillow and re-hear those words of love and apology from them to you right away, and imagine that they are holding you as a child, saying those words to you as they tear up and hold you tightly to their chest. When you feel complete with that, move on to the next parent's letter.

This was such a powerful exercise for me! When I took a look at my parents' childhood, I became grateful and in awe of what a wonderful job they did in comparison and in spite of the childhood experience they went through! I became in awe of how well they didn't transfer all of their wounding onto me. Because I know how negatively my childhood pain has impacted me, and mine was a mere fraction of what each one of them went through; yet they never really shared that anguish with me. For the most part, they sheltered me from much of their sorrow. Please do not read forward until you have completed this process for both parents. Please grab your headphones and listen to track #13 while doing the next couple of exercises to help you connect from your *Spiritual Essence* and get some Divine support.

www.HealYourHeartFreeYourMind.com/Letters

Inner View

So now that you have completed all of this beautiful work with your parents, and you are feeling so much more healed and connected to them, you get an alarming call. It is from one of your family members, and they tell you that there has been an accident and you need to come down to the hospital right away. They tell you that your parents were driving together and they got in a terrible accident, the doctors say that their condition is grim and you need to get their affairs in order because they don't have long to live!! You rush to the hospital, and when you arrive, the doctors tell you that you'd better get in the room quickly to say your last goodbyes, because they don't have much time.

They are in separate rooms, so you go in and see your father first. He is happy to see you, and as you begin to talk, he says, "My child, please let me speak first. I have something important I need to say to you before I go. I love you. I always have. I am sorry I wasn't always the best dad or husband, and I made many mistakes. I am sorry that I didn't heal all of my childhood wounding before becoming your parent. I am very sorry for all of the mistakes I have made with you and your mother and our family. I hope you can forgive me and won't hold a grudge. I hope that you free yourself of my mistakes and don't follow in my footsteps; and instead, only take the good that I gave you. How is your mother doing, is she going to make it? Tell her I have always loved her, and I am sorry for the mistakes I made with her too. I will always love you, my little one."

You don't have long, so *tell your father now everything you need to say to him.* Tell him if you feel love for him; tell him if you have compassion for him; tell him if you forgive him and tell him what you are grateful for. Tell him about all the things you appreciate about him, and if there is something you are sorry for, tell him now, before you no longer can:

....

....

....

....

....

....

....

You then run over to your mother's room and you begin to tell her what your dad asked you to share with her. She smiles a weak smile in gratitude and says, "My dear, I have always loved you too. I know that I haven't always been the best mother to you. I know I have made many mistakes, just as my parents did with me. I am sorry I didn't do better, that I didn't heal my child-hood wounding before having the privilege of being your mom. I, too, have made many mistakes with your father and our family, and I just hope you can forgive me. I hope you will let go of any pain we may have caused you and not carry it into your life as I did. I love you deeply my beautiful child, and I always have. I am sorry I allowed my fear and pain to get in the way of always showing that to you. I am sorry my time with you is over, and I can't make it up to you, but I will love you for eternity and will be cheering you on from the other side. I don't know what it's like over there, but if I can, I will always be there to help you whenever I'm able."

So what are the things you need to say to your mom before she goes? Do you have messages of love, compassion and forgiveness for her too? Do you have messages of understanding, gratitude and appreciation? Are there any regrets you have with her? If so, tell her now. This could be your very last chance.

....

....

....

....

....

....

....

....

....

....

....

....

....

....

Inner View

So, what are the great attributes about you parents? In what ways were they great people? Were they a great parent? What great things did you learn from each of them? What *gifts* did they give you? What great legacy are they leaving you? In what ways did they *transcend* some of their upbringing and not pass it on to you? What are you grateful to them for? What great thing has your relationship with your parents prepared you for?

Write them down for each parent below; and when you feel ready, write it in a letter and send it to them. You may see their heart melt and your relationship with them begin to flourish. They, too, have only wanted to feel loved and appreciated by their parents first, and then secondly, by you. And you have the gift of knowing that what is appreciated, *Appreciates*! As we just experienced, we never know when we will lose the opportunity to tell someone our truth, and what we love and appreciate about them. I have seen one too many people's greatest regret being not telling their parents their truth and how much they really loved and appreciated them, before their parent passed. That lost opportunity haunted them and caused them a lot of pain for many years. If you have a parent still living don't miss this opportunity; if they have already crossed over, know that they can still hear you. We may not be able to hear them because of the limitations of our five senses, but they no longer have those limitations.

What I appreciate about my mom is:

....
....
....
....
....
....
....
....
....
....
....
....
....
....
....
....
....
....
....
....
....
....
....
....

What I appreciate about my dad is:

....

....

....

....

....

....

....

....

....

....

....

....

....

....

....

....

....

....

....

....

....

....

....

....

....

If you had other primary caregivers or stepparents who were really influential in your growing up years, then do this entire process over with each one of them.

Before we end, let's take those angry letters we wrote to our parents and burn them. The purpose of a prescribed fire is to burn away the dead and old, and regenerate new growth; so that is what we are going to do in this fire ceremony. We are going to release and burn away all of those stories, all of those passed-down patterns, all of the *charges* and pain, and watch them burn away. And as we do, we are going to claim back our pure *Essence* and our **new truth,** and watch that regenerate growth and new life for us instead! **So burn those angry letters now, any way that works best for you, and....**

What new Truth are you now claiming for yourself?

....

....

....

....

....

....

....

....

....

....

....

....

....

....

....

The Seventh Step to Freedom is:

7. Heal your relationships with your parents and your primary caregivers.

- Look for patterns in your life to indicate *charges* that need to be healed.

- Invoke the Divine and use **The Growth Formula, The Healing Process** and the other tools we just gave you to do the healing.

- If there are other people you have a lot of hurt and anger with, that you still need to heal with and forgive, you can use **The Write It Out System** with them too, before you try to forgive them from the *bird's eye view*.

Transcend*Transform*Inspire

Chapter Fourteen

The Eighth Step To Freedom
~Your Angel of Transformation~

Who is this Angel of Transformation, you ask? Well, it is your significant other. The relationship with your life partner can be the most important relationship for your growth, healing and expansion into truly living your soul's life mission and intention. Most people go into relationships from a place of lack. Looking for what they feel they need, and hoping to find it in the other person, only to discover that it's not there. In romantic relationships, un-confronted, unaccepted aspects of yourself come to the forefront more easily and much more frequently than in any other relationship. Emotions that you otherwise can choose to ignore, feelings that you could otherwise suppress or emotions that you have not recognized, but are definitely dominant within you, tend to come to the surface in this relationship more often than in any other. This relationship mirrors the love and approval we have been trying to get our entire life from our parents or primary caregivers, more than any other relationship we have. Thus, this relationship is going to bring up our childhood wounds and programming, both the ones that we are aware of and the ones that we aren't, more than any other. That is why this relationship, consciously managed, could prove to be the most effective tool in knowing yourself, healing yourself and restructuring your life to the one of your heart and soul's intention.

Remember my cute story about Todd and his wife and how, over time, the whole neighborhood was listening to them *'talk'*? And we asked, "Why is this a story that most of the world can totally relate to?" We asked, "Why is it that all of our relationships that first seem to be great and wonderful and are our dream come true, slowly begin to diminish and demise? Why do we always say, "We feel the most hurt by the ones we are the closest too," or "We tend to hurt the ones we feel the closest to"? Well, this is why. Our partners are our biggest mirrors to our childhood wounds and programming. They will push our buttons, our *charges*, more than any other person. Not only because we spend the most time with them, but because we tend to attract the person who is the perfect mirror to our *charges*. Like vibration attracts like vibration. For example, a *Victim* will tend to attract a *Persecutor* or a *Rescuer*. At first, it may be hard to **see** what you are mirroring in each other, but if you dig deeply and are honest with yourself, you will find it.

For instance, when I was at my lowest, I attracted a controlling, abusive boyfriend. At first, before I had a greater understanding of the **Law of Reflection**, I could not see how we were mirroring each other because I didn't have an abusive, dominating personality. I was more of the Pollyanna people pleaser. However, after deeper digging, I realized that he was mirroring back the *charge* I had with my father that I had not totally healed— because I tried to heal it with my logical adult mind. He was mirroring back my victim consciousness that I hadn't completely resolved. I was a people pleaser because I was still in victim consciousness, and what more perfect mirror is there for someone who wants to dominate and control someone, than a victim people pleaser? I also became aware of how he was mirroring back my own controlling issues. Although being a *Rescuer* has a prettier bow than a *Persecutor*, it is still another form of control. As a *Rescuer*, I am trying to get you to live as I think you should, and I am wanting you to be grateful, dependent and indebted to me.

When I got really honest with myself and really looked within at what he was reflecting back at me, I was able to ask for the Divine Intervention to heal it, so I didn't have to experience that being mirrored back to me anymore. He became one of my biggest **Healing Angels** in helping me heal my childhood stories — my childhood wounds and wrong beliefs. At that **choice point**, if I chose to follow the old path of feeling like a victim and participating in the blame game, then I would have just kept attracting more of the same in my life, instead of *transcending* it as I did.

> *Life is a mirror and will reflect back to the thinker*
> *what he thinks into it.*
> **~Ernest Holmes**

So, are you moody? You don't want to answer that, do you?

Well, have you experienced *'someone else'* as being moody? Have you ever, at one time in your life, completely *'lost it'* — said and did crazy things and later said to yourself, "Who was that person? I don't even recognize that person. That wasn't me, I don't act that way!" Have you ever done that?

Yeah, I have!

We think we are one person with a bunch of moods, but actually we have a bunch of personalities within one body. We may have the little kid, the adventurer, the business woman, the scared little girl, the courageous woman, the selfish woman, the compassionate woman, the tomboy, the lady (ok, these just happen to be my old ones) — each one tied to a different neuro-network in our subconscious mind and body. When a charge connected to the neuro-network is triggered (when your button is pushed), the associated personality gets activated, and parts of the person's body, perceptions and attitude can completely change. Just like a person with *Multiple Personality Disorder,* everything within us can change when that personality becomes engaged. We see everything differently, we process information differently, we make decisions differently, and our beliefs and even our values may become very dissimilar in that moment. We literally become a different person.

A person with *Multiple Personality Disorder* can have different identities with a different age, sex, and demeanor— including their own postures, gestures, voice tones and distinct ways of talking. Several personalities, sharing one body, may have different heart rates, blood pressures, body temperatures, eyesight and even eye color. Whenever a new personality takes over, the otherwise healthy host can suddenly have allergies, asthma or other signs of disease, like diabetes. The wonderful gift from studying MPDs is having a better understanding of how powerful our mind and beliefs are, and how they can completely change our physical bodies and experience. (Similar to what we observed with *placebos.*)

The only difference between us and a person with *Multiple Personality Disorder* is that we are aware of the other personalities, meaning we don't completely lose awareness of the actions of a personality. We just tend to think they are moods, or that we were triggered. We may be shocked and confused by our behavior and where it came from, but we don't lose complete awareness of it. We also don't disconnect with our core identity and take on a completely new one when a new personality is engaged. A person with MPD often is not aware of the other personalities or their actions. They usually disassociate completely from the other personalities.

These different personalities all come from the same source, through great pain, fear and trauma. Our trauma just tends to be less severe than that of a person who developed MPD in order to protect themselves. Or at least our biology was able to handle the trauma better. It is a defense mechanism that the mind uses to protect the child from feeling overwhelmingly intense emotions. Similar to the reasons why our ego/ intellect/controller was created. Each cluster of *charges* tends to have a common emotional theme such as anger, sadness, or fear. Eventually, these clusters develop into full-blown personalities, each with its own connected memories and characteristics. In both cases, the personality tends to be triggered when a *charge* (a button) gets pushed from the host's surrounding environment.

Our personalities are formed through our relationships throughout the years. It starts from conception with our parents, then continues with our primary caregivers, then other family members, and continues with others we have had emotional interactions with during our childhood and teenage years. And from that baseline, these unattended personalities just begin to grow and get stronger and affect our other relationships all the more. I am going to share with you a little story about a couple, and the dynamics of it may sound pretty familiar to you:

A husband and wife were going on a picnic at their favorite park, on a warm, summer Sunday, to celebrate their anniversary. They were both excited to have this time to be together and just relax, because their schedules had been so busy for the last 4 months that they barely had any time to really connect. The wife packed up all of her husband's favorites, and she was excited to surprise him with a few.

As they sipped on wine and nibbled on cheese and crackers, they took a trip down memory lane, remembering how much they loved to go on picnics in nature during their courtship. They remembered how much love they would feel when they would get out in nature together. As they sipped their wine, all of the beautiful memories came back about their courtship and how they fell in love. They joyfully relived the engagement, the announcement, the wedding, and oh, the wonderful honeymoon. They relived the moment when their first child was born and how they fell even more madly in love with each other. And as they stared into each other's eyes holding each other's hand, it felt like they were falling in love all over again!

Suddenly, the husband received a phone call that interrupted their special moment. "Oh honey, do you mind if I take this? This is about the big deal I have been working on for the last three months that we are having our final meeting about tomorrow. I wouldn't take it if it weren't so very important," he said. "Sure, honey, no problem — I will just get our surprise dessert ready for us," she responded.

He goes off and takes his call privately and she proceeds to prepare his surprise. She is feeling so much gratitude for this wonderful day and this special moment to be able to really connect with one another. She is just reveling in the deep love that they just shared and is excited to surprise her husband with the dessert they had on their very first date.

As he approached her, she jumped up holding the dessert saying, "Look what I brought for us. Does it look familiar to you?" He quickly slaps it out of her hand and says, "I don't care what it is— we are out of here now!" She just stood there dumbfounded, thinking, "What the hell just happened, who is this man? This isn't my husband!" Little did she know that the kind, loving husband that left to take the phone call was no longer around; the call went really badly, and he found out the deal he had been working so hard for was going south, and so the Ruthless CEO (*personality #89*) came back to their party.

Well, that brought up her scared little girl personality #54, and she reacted to him with that. Which brought up his personality #27, and he reacted back to her with that personality. She yelled back at him, "Who are you? You're crazy— I don't even know who you are," from personality #88. Well, that really infuriated him and brought up personality #77, and he launched back at her from that personality. This shocked her even more, and she unleashed personality #55! And so on, and so on it went....

Does any of that sound remotely familiar? Have you ever experienced something like that with someone who was close to you? Did it seem shocking and like the unfolding of a very bad dream? We always think we are having a relationship with just one man or one woman, but really we aren't; we are having a relationship with an entire crowd! A crowd of personalities.

These types of interactions happen because our *inside world* is just interacting, and reacting, to another's *inside world*. Because **our** '*button*' is just reacting to **another's** '*button*'. **Our** *charges,* with their associated beliefs, are just reacting to the **other's** *charges* and associated belief system. Our minds are just **filtering** everything through our *charges,* and we are experiencing each other through our *cud*. This is the dance of our wounded *emotional kids*. This is why the people we are the closest to and spend the most time with, are going to be our biggest mirror to our *charges*, and they can bring up our *charges* **more than anyone else can.**

So, it doesn't matter if you change partners; you are still going to be mirroring each other's *cud* and filtering life through it if you haven't yet healed it. You will just have the same feelings and experiences with just a different face and a different name, at a different time. This is why a relationship that first seems like our dream come true, can seem to slowly diminish and demise. Because we don't have this awareness and we get caught up in the victim consciousness and the blame game.

The *ego/intellect* always wants to blame the other, and wants to lead you to believe that it will all be better if you just traded them in for someone else. And when you do, at first you think, "Wow, see, I was right! This new person really gets me and everything is great now." But soon enough, we are seeing the whole cycle replay itself again, and again, and we say *what*? Exactly! *"Why does this always happen to me?"*

It's like we are running around out there in the world with our wounds on our skin, and we are trying to keep others from hitting them, so that they won't cause us a sharp pain. But then they get close to us and accidentally (or sometimes not accidentally, if one of their own wounds was hit) knock one of our wounds; and we get upset with them and blame them for the pain that we are feeling, instead of taking the procedures we need to heal the wound. Instead of being grateful to them for letting us know that we still have an open sore that needs our attention.

> *When I heal my wounds, it heals my father's,*
> *and it heals the wounds of future generations to come.*
> *The cycle stops.*
> ~Thich Nhat Hahn

Because of the programming that is living in our subconscious mind and dominating our being, **transference** is happening between people, all the time. However, it is particularly prevalent in our romantic relationships. **Transference** is when we see another as being like our parent, primary caregiver, or like another family member we have a heavy *charge* with, and we automatically react to them as if they were actually that person we had the experience with. This is mostly happening at the unconscious level, so oftentimes we won't realize we are doing it until we take a deeper look at it later. Mostly it is our *emotional kid* that is doing all of the automatic reacting. What triggers *transference* could be a similar look, a tone of voice, a mannerism; or they may do or say something that reminds us of something a parent or family member would say. When we are in *transference*, we tend to blame the other person for the way we are feeling, and we are *certain* we know what they are really up to! (Remember, just like I was certain that the man in the audience was bored and hated my talk?) The initial trigger sets our pattern, our *personality* in motion, and it just starts taking over our body and mind. The chemicals are released in the body, and we are positive we know all about what they are thinking and feeling and what their agenda really is; and we react automatically as if it were so, without talking to the person at all about the situation!

There is also something called *positive transference*, which is something we tend to do when we are first falling in love, in like, or deep admiration. We tend to *project* our dreams and our ideals on the person. At first, the individual seems to be our dream come true and have everything we have always wanted and needed (from our parents). When we are in this state, we are certain we know who they really are, what they are all about, how they are feeling, what they are thinking (like: they're thinking and feeling the same way as you are), and that we are seeing all of the real person. We are so positive we know who this person really is, that we cannot listen to anyone say anything that contradicts our perception of them; we may even distance ourselves from anyone who says a disparaging word about them. That is until our illusional bubble bursts and again we say— *what*? You got it, "*Why does this always happen to me?*" Does any of that sound familiar to you?

The key to having a great relationship with your partner is to **know** that **they are your greatest mirror, your greatest teacher and your Healing Angel!** To not get involved in your mind's illusion, the story, the blame game, trying to change them or have the need for them to agree with you and to be right. To instead, always **practice** the *Law of Reflection* with them and utilize the *Healing Process* for every *charge* that they are mirroring back for you. Also, to put into practice the **Art of Listening**– that is the art of listening to oneself.

When you are interacting with your partner or others, listen to your mind, your body and your heart. Listen to how you are feeling, and what *charges* they are bringing up for you— what fears, what beliefs, what memories, and how you are reacting. What *charge* from your parents, from your family, from your life experience are they reflecting in you that still needs to be **seen and expressed** — what is still needing to be healed?

When someone is yelling at us or hurting us in some way, we should not listen to what they are saying. Instead, we should listen to what **we are saying inside**. *Transcendence* of our past and our patterns is listening to oneself. Whenever we are disturbed by something, there is a story, a *charge* and perhaps even a personality behind it that is trying to come out and be healed. Remember: if the reaction is hysterical, it is definitely historical!

So, let's practice **The Art of Listening** so we can have a greater awareness of it when we try to use this with our partner or someone else in our life. Call up a friend or family member and have them tell you an emotional story about their life that has really affected them. As you are listening to their story, you're not going respond, try to reassure them, or give them any advice. You are just to be present with them and **listen to the feelings and stories you are**

telling yourself as you're hearing their words. After they're done, just note down **everything you noticed about your experience within**. You will begin to learn a lot about yourself in this encounter. You can ask them what their experience was when you didn't talk back to them. What you will probably hear from them, especially if this was in person, is that it felt great and that they finally felt heard. You could then share with them what you are doing and ask if they will practice it with you, so you can have that experience on the other side of the equation as well.

What did you experience when you practiced the *Art of Listening*?

....

....

....

....

....

....

....

....

....

....

....

....

....

....

....

....

....

....

....

We need to remember that we cannot change anyone; we can only experience them as they are, listening to ourselves as we do. Always reminding ourselves that trying to change someone is futile and damaging to the relationship, and only keeps us stuck in our *patterns*. We need to relate to our significant other and other family members as we would with our cat. Now, a cat is a cat— it's not a dog. And no matter how much you try to make it like a dog, it will never be one. Trying to make your cat act like a dog would be very frustrating to both you and the cat. The cat might get so annoyed that it begins to avoid you. It certainly wouldn't feel loved by you. I mean, how could you feel loved by someone who wants you to be like a dog, when you're a cat? If you, as an owner, want the traits of a dog— well, then you should just get a dog; and not try to turn your pretty little cat into one!

So why is it that you love your pet, like a cat or dog, so much? You love it because it loves you unconditionally, exactly the way you are! It doesn't try to change you, and you don't have to adapt yourself at all to get its love and attention. Now, why does your dog or cat love you so much as well? Because, for the most part, you accept them exactly the way they are as well! You aren't trying to make your dog act more like a cat. You aren't projecting all of your programming onto it, like telling it, "Oh, you should be taller; you should be skinnier; you need to be cuter; you should have less hair; you're stupid; you need to clean yourself this way; you need to eat this way; etc." And they're not doing that to us either— they're not trying to change us at all! They are just experiencing us, sharing themselves with us and adjusting their actions to our mood. They aren't telling us that our mood is bad and that we should change it; they are just letting us be in it and adjusting their interactions with us in accordance. All of this unconditional love is why our relationship with our pets is so great, and why some people love their pets the most!

How other's love us, does not define us; It merely defines them.
It's how we love, in which we are defined!
~Brandy Faith Weld

So here is a powerful exercise for you and your partner to do together whenever you are experiencing any conflict. In this **Transference Exercise**, each one of you needs to write down what behavior your partner has that really bothers you and *charges* you up, and see how it feels akin to the experiences you had as a child with your parents, caregivers or perhaps other family members. As you do this, identify the person their behavior reminds you of — like mom, dad, step-dad, grandma, older brother, etc., and why. What's the *charge* or belief you had around that family member? Also, take a look at your standard reaction to the behavior. Where did you learn that reaction? Did that come from a parent or caregiver too? Is that a patterned reaction you have to an old wound and story that has played in your head for years, and that you have played out with others? What patterns and wounds from your childhood are you guys mirroring to each other?

For example, on my side, my ex-boyfriend mimicked the dominating, intimidating and controlling behavior of my father, and I copied the behavior of my mom— trying to take the high road, managing it myself internally and hiding it from everyone else; pretending everything was ok. On my boyfriend's side, he was copying the behavior of his controlling, angry and insecure father, and I was replicating the behavior of his mother, a people pleasing doormat that his father would just walk over and take for granted — which would just make him angrier (and rage more, like his father). Because what his little boy **really** wanted was his mother to finally stand up for herself against his father (him). When I would hit a breaking point and take a stand, the tables would turn instantly, and he would become the peacemaker/people pleaser and would get the biggest smile on his face! He would instantly become happy, because at an unconscious level his little boy finally had his wish come true — his mother was finally standing up for herself!

Now the key in this exercise, and when you are sharing, is that you are taking full responsibility for your perception of the situation and your reaction to it, knowing that your *suffering is not in the fact — it is in your perception of the facts*. That the feelings and situation are just a mirror to your *charges* and programming, and a helpful indicator of a healing that still needs to transpire. You may *see* you have had a pattern of feeling a similar way with others and that you have had a habitual reaction as well, which you may have learned from another family member or in reaction to that family member's behavior. When you share with your partner, you are using *'I'* statements and not *'you'*. The intention is to clear the air, heal with each other, and begin to heal the *charge* that is being mirrored, not dump on one another. You're being authentic and open, and as you lower the waterline and begin to share your old wounds with one another, you provide each other the opportunity to experience **Real Love**. If the other person provides a safe space for you, doesn't judge and doesn't use the information to attack or leave in some way, and instead they hold space for your healing and growth, then that is unconditional love— **Real Love**. The type of love we feel with our pets, and the type of love we can experience with the Divine. By sharing this way, we are demonstrating that we are more interested in love, peace, and each other's growth than we are in power and being right!

Inner View

So how does your partner mimic or remind you of a wound or old story that you have with your parents, caregivers or other family members? Which one? Which family member are you modeling in your reaction to them?

....

....

....

....

....

....

....

....

....

....

....

....

....

....

....

....

....

....

....

....

....

....

....

....

....

....

....

....

....

....

....

....

....

....

....

....

....

....

....

....

....

....

....

....

....

It's important to know that you don't have to share with the other to use this **Transference Exercise**. We are always unconsciously using *transference* in many of our relationships. So we can use this same tool to help us get out of our stories about some of our other relationships as well. This can be a helpful tool to **see** *what we need to heal* and what our *intention* should be for the **Growth Formula** and the **Healing Process**.

The 7 Step Communication Process for Life Partners

If you and your partner are both aware of these teachings and are consciously supporting each other's growth and evolvement as partners, then you could practice this **Seven Step Communication Process**:

1. Enter into the discussion as your *Spiritual Selves*, realizing that you and the other intrinsically have the same wants and needs, to love and be loved, and are **Healing Angels** for each other's growth and evolvement.

2. Invoke the Divine and take the intent to connect to the other, heart to heart, soul to soul, for each other's greatest good. Keep looking at the other person's face, preferably eye to eye, and don't turn away. (Turning away can cause them to feel rejected and not heard.) You will have a far deeper sense of compassion seeing the real being, their *Essence*, through their eyes.

3. Remember the teaching "**The outside world is just a reflection of your inside world,**" and vice versa with your partner. Become aware of what is happening within you and **listen to yourself**. What feelings and charges are coming up for you? This is how you are going to be able to **respond** and **communicate from your higher consciousness** and not *react* from your lower consciousness.

4. Also remember the teaching, "**Your suffering is not in the fact, it is in your perception of the fact.**" It is how your mind is interpreting the information, as it filters it through your *charges*. So, the first thing you need to do is calmly and lovingly tell them what your *perception* was from a place of **total responsibility**. For instance, I have a negative reaction when you do **x**. I experience you as **y** (your perceptions and judgments) like my **z** (family member). The patterns I went into were **y** (your reactions) which I learned from **z** (your family member) or in reaction to **z** (your family member). I still have this *charge* from my childhood and could use your understanding and support in healing it.

   For example: I had a negative reaction when you **wouldn't listen to my beliefs and needs**. I experienced you as **rigid in your rules and not open to hearing my beliefs, understanding me at all, or being willing to adapt to my needs** like my **father** would. The patterns I went into were, "**Fine, I will do it my way anyway, and you're not a safe place to share my needs and who I am with. You're not really interested in knowing who I am and won't listen or try to understand me, so I just won't share with you anymore,**" which I both learned from my **mother** and in reaction to my **father**. I still have this charge from childhood and could use your understanding and support in healing it.

5. Now allow them to give you clarifying information on your *perception*. We will normally find that it was a total misunderstanding, a story of our mind from our *charges*; and through this clarifying information you can get to the beautiful

truth, and **respond** from that place instead, creating a positive win-win plan for moving forward. A great start-off response to give the person clarifying information is, "Oh, I can see by your history how you could have perceived my actions that way. What my actual thoughts and intention was *x*."

6. From this state of awareness, respond with a desire to help one another. "So we can see we are both just bringing up each other's *charges* from the past, but we don't mean to hurt one another, correct? What we both want is to feel love and happiness and for the other to feel the same, right?" "Now that I can see that I still have this *charge* affecting me and my *perceptions*, I will go do my work to heal it. **Thank you for being my wonderful mirror**! Let me know if there is any way I can support you in healing your *charges* as well."

7. Now share what you appreciate about the other with each other.

Now knowing what your partner is going through, you can give your partner the space to deal with it, and not take anything personally. This will help your relationship a lot. The truth is, nothing our partners are doing is personal. They are just dealing with their own garbage they picked up and perhaps are crying for help. You are only responsible for your dream, and you give your partner the space to deal with their own. By utilizing this **Communication Process**, you are now applying everything you have learned and are catapulting each other in your growth and evolvement. You are letting go of the stories and staying out of the victim consciousness, the blame game, and the mind's need to be right. Instead of keeping the *charge* and *pattern* stuck, you are becoming aware of them and can now consciously handle them using the *Healing Process,* so that you can *transcend* them and no longer experience life through them. You are taking responsibility for everything, and no longer further damaging your relationships by reacting or by trying to change or fix the other. Our individual healing is relational healing. You are just supporting each other doing your own work with the Divine, so that you can now experience life through your pure *Essence,* **at cause**, and will no longer be stuck living life *in the effect*!

So let's begin healing these patterns and *charges* we have around our significant other, so we can *transcend* them and begin to have a different experience of **Love** with a life partner! Let's start off by going within and having a little Inner View.

Inner View

What patterns do you have in your relationships with a significant other, past or present? Do you have the pattern of blame, victimhood, needing to be right, wanting it your way, always seeing the other person wrong, always trying to fix others, strong attachments, jealousy, co-dependency, fear of abandonment?

....

....

....

....

....

....

....

....

....

....

....

....

....

....

....

....

....

....

....

....

....

Is there a story you always tell yourself about your relationships with a significant other? A common feeling you have had? What do you think is the source *charge* for that story and feeling?

....

....

....

....

....

....

....

....

....

....

....

....

....

....

....

....

....

....

....

....

....

....

....

So we're about to take you through a healing process with your significant others, past and present. Before we do so, please watch this video and allow whatever *charges* that come up around it be a mirror into what's within that still needs to be seen.

www.HealYourHeartFreeYourMind.com/Woman

Now make sure your sitting comfortable in a quiet and private place, grab some water and pillows, plug your headphones into your smart phone or MP3 player and go to track #14 or download at the link below, to be guided through this journey towards greater love. When you are done going through this process, answer the following questions below.

www.HealYourHeartFreeYourMind.com/Partner

What old *charges* do you now see that you still need to heal?

....

....

....

....

....

....

....

....

....

....

....

....

....

....

....

....

....

....

....

....

....

List out the names of the partners you have had these patterns and stories with in the past and now practice *Ho'oponopono* with each one them, asking them for forgiveness for blaming them. Begin to feel **gratitude** for their willingness to play the role of your *Healing Angels*. Practice until you feel a shift in your energy with them and send them love from your heart to theirs, feeling the virtual healing.

....

....

....

....

....

....

....

....

....

....

....

By seeing and utilizing your life partner(s) as your *Healing Angel* for your soul's growth and evolvement, and for *transcending* all of your childhood subconscious programming, you can re-install **Love** — that which you really are, onto your hard drive, as your new Operating System. Once you do, your partner, and the world, can begin to mirror that back to you instead. Here is a playful metaphor I received in an email about installing **Love** on our hard drive:

Tech Support: Yes, how can I help you?

Customer: Well, after much consideration, I've decided to install **Love**. Can you guide me through the process?

Tech Support: Yes. I can help you. Are you ready to proceed?

Customer: I think I'm ready. What do I do first?
Tech Support: The first step is to open your Heart. Have you located your Heart?

Customer: Yes, but there are several other programs running now. Is it okay to install **Love** while they are running?

Tech Support: What programs are running?

Customer: Let's see, I have Past Hurt, Low Self-Esteem, Grudge and Resentment running right now.

Tech Support: No problem, **Love** will gradually erase Past Hurt from your current operating system. It may remain in your permanent memory, but it will no longer disrupt other programs. **Love** will eventually override Low Self-Esteem with a module of its own called High Self-Esteem. However, you have to completely erase Grudge and Resentment. Those programs prevent **Love** from being properly installed. Can you erase those programs?

Customer: I don't know how to. Can you tell me how?

Tech Support: With pleasure. Go to your start menu and invoke *Forgiveness*. Do this as many times as necessary until Grudge and Resentment have been completely erased.

Customer: Okay, done! **Love** has started installing itself. Is that normal?

Tech Support: Yes, but remember that you have only the base program. You need to connect to the **Higher Consciousness** server in order to continually get the upgrades.

Customer: Oops! I have an error message already. It says, "Error - Program not running on external components." What should I do?

Tech Support: Don't worry. It means that the **Love** program is set up to run on all Internal Hearts, but has not yet been run on your Heart. In non-technical terms, it simply means you have to **Love yourself** before you can **Love others**.

Customer: So, what should I do?

Tech Support: Pull down **Self-Acceptance**; then click on the following files: **Forgive-Self; Realize Your Worth**, and the virus protection software **You Are Protected and Safe.**

Customer: Okay, done.

Tech Support: Now, copy them to the "My Heart" directory. The system will over-write any conflicting files and begin patching faulty programming. Also, you need to delete Verbose Self-Criticism from all directories and empty your Recycle Bin to make sure it is completely gone and never comes back.

Customer: Got it. Hey! My heart is filling up with new files. Smile is playing on my monitor and Peace and Contentment are copying themselves all over My Heart. Is this normal?

Tech Support: Sometimes. For others it takes awhile, but eventually everyone gets it in their proper time. So **Love** is installed and running. One more thing before we hang up. **Love** is Freeware. *Be sure to give it and its various modules to everyone you meet. They will in turn share it with others and return some cool modules back to you.*

So that basically describes in an amusing way what we have been doing. Healing your relationship with your significant other and utilizing them as your biggest **Healing Angel** for your soul's growth and evolvement. Seeing others and utilizing them as your **Healing Angels** as well will get you the rest of the way, changing the electromagnetic signature that your heart is sending out to one of love, instead of hurt, fear and anger. And as we change our vibration to love, we can now interact with our partner and others *from love* **versus** *for love.*

When we get to this place of operating in our relationships from self love and a full truck, we can now further improve our relationship with our partner by expressing our love for them in their **Love Language**, not ours. We tend to give people what *'we want'*, so however they are expressing love to you is a great indicator of what their *Love Language* is. But it is best to have the discussion with one another about what actions make the other feel loved and cherished directly, and break the habit of habitually expressing our love in our language. Life partners rarely have the same *Love Language*, and speaking two different languages is often a big part of the relationship problem. Things get lost in translation. It's kind of like two people being married to one another, yet one speaks French and the other speaks Russian, and neither one speaks or understands the other's language. There is a great book that describes the various *Love Languages* that you and your partner can read together, called ***The 5 Love Languages*** by Gary D. Champman.[22]

The Eighth Step to Freedom is:

8. Practice seeing your partner as your biggest mirror and your primary **Healing Angel**, and apply the teachings to your relationship.

- Apply the *Law of Reflection.*

- Remember, **suffering is not in the fact but in your perception of the fact**, for both you and for the other.

- Practice the *Art of Listening.*

- When a conflict comes up, practice the *Transference Exercise.*

- Apply *Ho'oponopono* or the **Healing Process** to the *charges* that are being reflected back to you.

- Always remember that you cannot change someone, you can only experience them, and trying to do so is damaging to the relationship.

- If your partner or other people who are close to you are aware of the teachings and willing to practice them, use the **Seven Step Communication Process.**

Transcend*Transform*Inspire

Chapter Fifteen

Ninth Step To Freedom
~From Transcendence to Transformation~

Now that we have done all of this healing and *transcending* of your subconscious programming and what you have been broadcasting out, we can begin to create your dream life from your **Higher Consciousness**— the **Pure Love**, **Pure Spirit** that you **truly BE**. From your *Essence*, instead of your mind's programming. This is when we really begin to **stop** living life *at the effect* and **start** living life *from cause*. Moving from living in the Matrix (the land of programs and at *the effect*) to living in Zion (from Higher Consciousness and *at cause*). Moving from a world based on the lower consciousness of fear and limitations, to a world based on love, faith and infinite possibilities.

Before we were able to help you *transform* your life into the one of your heart and soul's intention, we had to get you back to zero. **Zero limits,** that is. Clear out the *cud* and return you back to being the clean slate that you were before the programming began in the womb. Return you back to the pure, unsoiled *Spirit* that you truly are! When Michelangelo was asked how he created a sculpture, he answered that, "*the statue already existed within the marble. God Himself had created David; my job was simply to get rid of the excess marble that surrounded God's creation.*" The same goes for you. Your true **Essence**, your *Spiritual Self,* isn't something you need to construct. Your job is to simply **allow the Divine to remove the debris**, the fearful programming of your subconscious mind that has been weighing down your perfect Being, just like the excess marble that surrounded Michelangelo's perfect statue. As you are freed from this debris that got passed down to you and that you have been carrying, your true *Essence* of **Pure Love** can shine through and light the way for your new life's unfolding.

> *What lies behind you and what lies in front of you,*
> *pales in comparison to what lies inside of you.*
> ~Ralph Waldo Emerson

The fact that this joyous, peaceful, love-filled state is, in reality, one's own inner *Essence*, has been the basic tenet of every great spiritual teaching. For example: "*The kingdom of God is within you*," and, "*You are gods; you are the children of the Most High*," and, "*God created man in His image and likeness to think like Him.... and man became a living soul.*" People have experienced moments of this blissful state of being one with Source through a myriad of ways — it could have been through a spiritual experience, with nature, through a sexual experience, or with some kind of substance assistance— and they long to get back to that feeling, so they keep searching for things outside of themselves to regain that feeling of bliss. This high state that people are seeking is in fact their true *Essence*. If their intellect is in control, and they haven't really become experientially aware of their *Spiritual Self*, they will believe the feeling was created by something outside of themselves that they need to get back. But all that happened is that, through some special circumstances, they have experienced their own **true self**— their **Higher Consciousness**. Perhaps you've experienced some of that through a few of our meditations. Unfortunately, most people in the world have been so divorced from their *Spiritual Essence* that they don't recognize *it* when it peeks its head, because they have spent most of their lives buried under, and identified with, their lower conscious programming. So instead, a false negative self-image has blotted out the joyous brilliance of their true nature.

Sir David Hawkins M.D., Ph.D., a renowned researcher on Human Consciousness, gives us a vivid model to refer to for the different levels of consciousness in his book **Power vs. Force**. Both Power and Force are elements of energy. In fact, if you lookup synonyms for energy, both of these words will come up. One is just a lower representation of energy and is more visible than the other is. **Force** is an influence that produces a change in an object's motion or state of rest — a push or pull upon an object resulting from the object's interaction with another object. Force has a lower frequency and requires endless effort and renewal. The more you use it, the less energy you have, and it always requires more and more of it to get the same result done. It is demanding, laboring and not empowering at all. **Power,** on the other hand, has a high frequency and is a source or a means of *supplying energy*. With *Power*, the more of it you use, the more of it is generated— it is infinite, endless, and it just naturally flows. You can pull from it effortlessly whenever you need it, and it influences conditions without any force. In physics, it is the rate at which energy is transferred, used or transformed; and in social studies, it is the ability to influence people's behavior.

In his **Map of Consciousness**, David Hawkins shows that the greater amount of pain and wounding (debris) we have, the less amount of our *Essence*, our **Life Force** or energy, can come through our physical body, and the lower our vibration is. From my near death experiences, I would say that this is true. When I crossed over to the other side, I experienced a love that is indescribable in human terms, a love that is all-encompassing, a joy and a bliss that engulfs you. The ineffable sensations I was experiencing were limitless and infinite. For me, there was nothing but this feeling of love, bliss, knowingness and peace. Pain, fear, limitations and all of those lower emotions did not exist. It was like this infinite energy I was feeling was the real me, and the **state of my body** was only a *barometer* for how much of this **Life Force** I was able to express through my physical vehicle. When I returned to the body, it felt as if my body would implode — that it couldn't contain that much love or energy. And for the first time in my life, I felt absolute love and bliss for no reason at all — just for being. Wherever I was, there was love, and it didn't require me **to do anything** or require anyone outside of myself. The love-filled energy I was experiencing was too overwhelming for my body for a couple of months, then I think it got squeezed out by the limitations of the present consciousness of my body at the time.

	Level	Scale (Log of)	Emotion	Process	Life-View
	Enlightenment	700-1,000	Ineffable	Pure Consciousness	Is
	Peace	600	Bliss	Illumination	Perfect
P O W E R	Joy	540	Serenity	Transfiguration	Complete
	Love	500	Reverence	Revelation	Benign
	Reason	400	Understanding	Abstraction	Meaningful
	Acceptance	350	Forgiveness	Transcendence	Harmonious
	Willingness	310	Optimism	Intention	Hopeful
	Neutrality	250	Trust	Release	Satisfactory
	Courage	200	Affirmation	Empowerment	Feasible
	Pride	175	Dignity (Scorn)	Inflation	Demanding
F O R C E	Anger	150	Hate	Aggression	Antagonistic
	Desire	125	Craving	Enslavement	Disappointing
	Fear	100	Anxiety	Withdrawal	Frightening
	Grief	75	Regret	Despondency	Tragic
	Apathy	50	Despire	Abdication	Hopeless
	Guilt	30	Blame	Destruction	Condemnation (Evil)
	Shame	20	Humilation	Elimination	Miserable

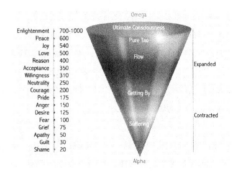

Sir David Hawkins' Map of Consciousness

This would also make sense for my other near death experience, my first one, when I was in my twenties and I thought I had a terminal disease. It was a time when I was stuck in fear and victim consciousness, and a fearful event took place that threw me down even lower on Sir Hawkins' scale into lower consciousness — squeezing out even more of my *Life Force*, like a kink in the hose. The more I went to doctors, the more fearful and confused I would become, and the more dis-ease I would feel in my Being and in my body. The more dis-ease I felt in my body, the less *energy* I would have to bring it back to homeostasis. It wasn't until I started to alleviate some of the fear and give my body some more healing *Life Force* — by finding God, limiting the toxic food, working out and oxygenating my body, becoming a vegetarian and eating high vibrational food and drinking alkalized water— that this dis-ease went away, and more and more of my **Life Force** came through.

My many experiences going to an ashram in India would also show me that this is true. When I first went to India, after my mother died, and I was in deep grief, blame, existential suffering and at my lowest vibration, my body could not take all of the enlightened, peace, bliss, love energy that was contained at that ashram, so it would just shut down and go to sleep. I slept in my room for a couple of days, thinking I was rested, and within 20 minutes of being in front of the awakened monks, I would fall asleep again right in front of them!! I literally could not hold my head up. But as time went by, and I began to heal all of my wounding, removing all the debris I had accumulated throughout the years, I would feel less and less sleepy when I returned to the ashram— until there was a day when the vibration of the ashram and all of its enlightened inhabitants no longer made me sleepy. Instead, their high vibration would only escalate my own, increasing my state of internal peace, bliss and awareness!

For people living from the fearful mind (and *Force*), a high feeling is any state of consciousness that is above where they have customarily spent a lot of their time on the **Map of Consciousness**. So to a person who lives in fear, moving up to courage will give them a high feeling. To a person who lives in hopeless apathy, anger is a high state. (For example, rioters and looting in a ghetto.) At least fear feels better for someone in despair, and pride feels way better than fear!

So that is what we have been doing: clearing out your debris so more of your **Life Force** can come through, and you can start experiencing more of life from this *Power* versus all of the *Force* you have been using from the fear-based, survival-focused, reptilian mind. We have been cleaning up all of the lower conscious programming and making room for more of your *Essence* to take lead over your vessel! So that you can start feeling and experiencing all of what its natural state is — love, peace, joy, openness, limitless and togeth-erness. And you can start creating and experiencing life from this state of Being and vibration, this *Power*; instead of the states you have been operating from, by *Force* – the fearful *intellect* and your *emotional little kid*.

You are, *your Essence is*, this **Pure Love** and **Peace** at the top of the scale. When this truth is clouded, what we see as a world of chaos is simply the *Field* mirroring back our subconscious mind's internal turmoil and its belief that *peace* is missing. Thus, our fear-based plea of, "Let there be peace," echoes back to us as chaos. This understanding of how the mirror works can encourage and teach us not only to heal our fears and our subconscious programming, but also to change our languaging we have with the Universe. *Transforming* our life is based on the understanding that the energy under- lying all of creation is a malleable, invisible form that accurately reflects what we transmit out vibrationally, consciously or unconsciously. Our life stands the way that it does today because of what we have been programmed with, and because of what we have been unconsciously broadcasting out. For many centuries, indigenous shamans have tried to teach us this, and have taught that we need to **pray the results we want** to the Divine or Universe, and not the problem. They urged people to focus on the outcome **as if it were already a reality**– to pray *gratitude for total health* instead of praying for healing; to pray *gratitude for all of the water and rain* instead of praying for rain.

> *Therefore I tell you, whatever you ask for in prayer,*
> *believe that you have received it, and it will be yours.*
>
> ~ Jesus

Praying **for** something reinforces our *perceived lack of it*. Feeling love and gratitude for the desired outcome **being so** visualizes it from our **Power**, from our *Higher Consciousness*, as if it is already there. Our infinite and abundant Universe always contains sufficient amounts of love, peace, health and happiness in some form. Effective prayer hones in on these positive possibilities, viewing the world with appreciation and gratitude, as if the perfect outcome already exists. By doing so, we increase our vibration, open the door, and call in these greater possibilities we are gratefully holding in our mind. So from a continuum perspective, we are not praying for something in the future to happen for us, not even a minute into the future. **We are praying from the past**, as if it has already happened and we are just flashing back on the memory of it, and expressing our gratitude for it **now**.

| Past | Now | Near | Distant |

When millions of people prayed their gratitude for the world's peace, for instance, their collective focus on this present peace had a profound effect. In 1972, twenty-four cities in the United States with populations over 10,000 experienced meaningful drops in crime rates when as few as 1% (100 people) in each city participated in a peaceful prayer. During the Israeli-Lebanese war of the early 1980s, researchers with the International Peace Project in the Middle East trained a group of people to *feel* peace in their bodies rather than to simply pray for peace. At specific times and days, participants throughout the war-torn areas of the Middle East focused on **feeling peace** in the midst of conflict. During each such time period, terrorist activities stopped, crime declined, emergency room visits dropped off, and traffic accidents decreased. When participants stopped their experiment, the statistics reversed.

From the findings of these studies, researchers extrapolated how many people are needed to *share the experience of peace* before peace is mirrored in their world. What they found is that it only required the square root of 1% of the population. In a city of one million people, this is about 100 people. In a world of 6 billion people, it requires only about 8,000 around the world! Collective prayer, or meditation, can be a powerful force to change the *Field* to that which is collectively held in mind. This square root of 1% is considered the **Tipping Point** of consciousness. **The more people that focus collectively on a desired outcome, the faster such an effect will be created**. In Senegal West Africa, the prison system required 11,000 of their inmates, in thirty-one prisons, to meditate every day– and after a year, they had to close down three of the prisons! They then had eight others operating at only 30% of capacity, which they then had to figure out how to consolidate.

Through David Hawkins' research, he found that about 85% of the world's population calibrates **below the critical** *Courage* level of 200 on the scale in the above chart; yet the overall average of the global consciousness is at approximately 204. The discrepancy between these two statistics is due to the great vibrational **Power** of the relatively few people living at the top of the scale (from 350 up), which counterbalance the lower vibration of the masses. The influence of a few individuals at *Higher Consciousness* **counterbalances** the whole. Conversely, the extreme negativity of a few individuals can sway entire cultures and produce an overall drag on the global consciousness, as history has illustrated for us several times. (And as you may have experienced personally, within your own families and communities.)

That is why, as each one of us heals our own hurt, fear and subconscious programming, *we are doing our part* to heal the global consciousness that runs through us all– and thus, we are *transforming* the world. As the square root of 1% of the population changes what they are predominantly transmit-ting out (fear, anger, hatred and hurt) to the Universe, it will change *what* the world mirrors back. The Earth desperately needs healing, and each one of us is assigned a corner of the world *that is ours to transform* – that is, our life, our relationships, our *charges*, our fears and our belief systems. Whatever energy system we find ourselves a part of, it's our job to heal it – to raise up the thought forms of the global consciousness, by purifying and lifting up our own. By healing our lower conscious thought forms and **Being** the change we want to see in the world!

The practice of *forgiving* ourselves and others is the first step of our most important contribution to the healing of our lives and the world. Hurt and angry people cannot create a peaceful planet; they just pass on the bleeding. As each one of us has the resolve that "*the buck stops here; I will no longer pass on this spirit of hurt, anger and fear,*" and as we each do our own work, we become **The Incredibles**– the world's super heroes that we all have been waiting for. Just as each cell is designed for the greater good of the body, and as each cell restores itself from malignancy to perfect health, it strengthens the body's ability to **restore its self to total well-being**.

> *You must be the change you wish to see in the world.*
> ~Mahatma Gandhi

Lower Consciousness Versus Higher Consciousness

Let's describe in greater detail the difference between merely existing in life from the bottom part of the scale of the **Map of Consciousness**, from *Force* and the lower consciousness— **versus** creating and experiencing life from the top of the scale, from *Power* and the **Higher Consciousness**. Living life from the lower consciousness is operating from our fear-based mind (the *intellect*) and our subconscious programming. It is wrongly believing that you **are** your mind, instead of knowing that the mind is just an organ that has been programmed, and is an instrument to run the body. It is thinking that the thoughts that you have all the time **are you**. This is just a sign that the instrument has fully integrated into your body and has taken over as the master, and now you have become its slave. The truth is, the mind or *intellect* is just filtering what it picks up with its five senses, through the *charges*, beliefs and knowledge the subconscious has recorded, coming up with a story and sending out chemicals into the body as if the story were true, and the body reacts. Most of your thoughts come from your *charges* and your associated belief systems that were triggered by something picked up through one of your five senses.

The lower consciousness totally identifies with the body and the identity that you, your family and society have created for you, starting with the name they gave you at birth. It is your ego, the top 10 percent of the iceberg. It buys into the illusions and stories of the mind **as reality**. It thinks **it** is the *Doer* (or *Force*) and believes in the illusion of control. It's always trying to protect itself and believes it needs to control things and others in order to do so. It does not accept the '*what is*' and greatly struggles to try and make things the way it thinks it '*should be*', based on its programming from society. Always feeling internal struggle while doing so, thus always causing external struggle as well.

The lower consciousness is very fear-based, reactive and always in protection mode. A lot of this fear is driven by the **reptilian brain**, the most ancient and primitive part of our brain. The reptilian brain is instinctual and in charge of survival and reproduction. It has the same standards and behaviors as reptiles do, and operates from a binary *'fight or flight'* response. It is driven to define and defend territory. **When it is activated, it takes priority over *all* other systems of the brain**, like the limbic, neo-cortex and the cerebellum. Unfortunately, our reptilian brain is overactive nowadays because it has been conditioned to fear by our government and society. This conditioning has caused our reptilian brain to now react as if social psychological pressures **are** actually physical threats — automatically activating our fight or flight response system at the drop of a negative or worrisome thought.

The lower consciousness operates from victim consciousness, always blaming others and situations for its problems. Always looking for what's wrong, and is constantly trying to figure out how to fix it and protect itself from the always looming danger. Thus, it is always in the state of survival and competition, continuously looking for both the problem and the solution outside of itself. It believes, "*I have to be in control, and I have to be better than you. So I need to be right; and to be right, I have to make you wrong.*" The lower consciousness is very repetitive, compulsive, and circling in loops. It feels all of the emotions we find below the ***Courage line*** on the **Map of Consciousness**— scarcity, worry, hurt, fear, frustration, anger, shame, guilt, depression, confusion, anxiety, uncertainty, self-pity and despair.

The lower consciousness is run by the *ego/intellect*. The ego is built on fear and wounding and was created in order to protect the *body* and the *emotional child* from being further hurt. It has a pseudo-life of its own, and like all life forms, fights very hard for its survival. Thus, in order to protect itself it has become the controller, the master trickster and illusionist — always trying to get you to think that *it is **you***, and ***you* are it**. It is a silver-tongued devil and has a slew of tricks up its sleeve to try and convince you, starting with saying things like, "Hi, I'm your adult, mature, rational self. I'll help you look out for number one," as it pulls out all the stops **to sabotage you from figuring out who you really are**, and continuously projecting thoughts on where you '*should be*'. Giving itself a perpetual lifetime of employment of — "When I get that, *then* I will finally be happy."

This *identity* that was created from the time you were named, that the ego is protecting, is like a wall that feels and appears to be real, but isn't. The term *wall* is just another concept created by the mind. What appears to be a *wall* is really a bunch of wood beams, insulation, drywall, nails, perhaps bricks, cement, siding and paint, connected to one another and given a name — *wall*. Our identity is the same; it is a bunch of various experiences and information recorded in our subconscious mind, that was named when our body was born. Your ego is afraid if you find out that you aren't this *'wall'* and that you are really this **Pure Love** and **Pure Spirit** instead, that it will mean the death of it — so it hasn't wanted you to know. That is why it has worked so very hard for so long, to distract your *Spiritual Self* from clearing away the picked-up debris and emerging to take back its rightful place as **the captain of your vessel!**

Brandy Faith Weld

"Read and discover that what you thought you knew, was merely an illusion."

Fairy tales like Snow White and Sleeping Beauty are metaphors for the relationship between lower consciousness and Higher Consciousness. The wicked stepmother, which is the ego, can put the Sleeping Beauty or our *Spiritual Self* within us to sleep, but she can never destroy it. You can turn the faucet off, but the water is still there, ready to flow *powerfully* whenever it gets turned back on. She can cast a spell on us, distract us, trick us and manipulate us, but the *Pure Love* inside of us will never die. It just goes to sleep for a long while, until the right Prince Charming (or Princess) arrives and awakens us! His or her kiss reminds us of who **we really are and why we are here** — that the *Love* that we are is the energy of creation, the same energy that creates babies and life. Our Prince or Princess comes in various disguises (like this program), and the right one, in the right form, at the right time, will eventually awaken us with their unique kiss for us, reminding us of this truth.

Once we realize that we never were all of those old stories we got programmed with, the **Higher Consciousness**, our *Spiritual Self,* can take lead in our life. The Higher Consciousness is declutched from the mind and **knows** that it is not the mind. It knows that the mind is a **superb instrument** and a tremendous asset when rightly managed. It just uses the mind as the powerful tool it was designed to be, and it doesn't get caught up in the mind's stories. It knows that it is not its thoughts, and that they automatically run from the programming of the subconscious mind. It knows that it's not the body, and that the body is just a vehicle to have a physical experience in this earthly realm. It also knows that it is not its *charges*, or the pain the body or the mind feels. It detaches from the *concept* of self that has been created by family and society, and doesn't get caught up in the ego's created identity.

The *Spiritual Self* knows that it is really the *ghost in the machine*. That in truth, **it is Pure Love**, no matter how it feels or appears at the moment. It knows that in true reality, outside of the Matrix, it is an **Infinite Being** with *infinite possibilities*. That it isn't limited by the finite and just by what the *intellect* knows or what appears to be real at the moment. It knows that it is **one with Source** and connected to the *Universal Intelligence*. It knows, just like the wave, that although it isn't the entire ocean, it is a part of and made up of all of the same elements as the sea. It knows that it is connected to and is a part of the **All**. It is 'we-oriented', focused on the good for all and win/win. It knows that together we can get through anything, and in separation and competition, we will destroy ourselves. When you operate from your Higher Consciousness, you will experience all the emotions above the *Courage line* — unity, internal love, joy and peace, a calm comfortable confidence, awareness, acceptance, forgiveness, a knowing and trust.

People operating from their Higher Consciousness **know** that the Universe will provide infinitely if they **ask, believe and are totally open to receive.** They do not live from a linear construct and because they believe and are open to the infinite possibilities, **they live life in the question** and not in the preconceived answer. Doing so bypasses the limited answers that the mind can only provide.

When you ask a question, you are inviting the *Field* to give you an answer from its ***bird's eye view.*** You trust in its greater intelligence to guide you and deliver the best answer, because from your Higher Consciousness you can see the array of mechanisms that the Divine runs with a brilliance of design and ease. Our hearts beat, our lungs breathe, our ears hear, our hair grows, and we don't have to do anything to make them work — they just do. Planets revolve around the sun, seeds become flowers, embryos become babies, and acorns become oaks with absolutely no help from us whatsoever. This is true ***Power.*** Their natural evolvement is built into an intricate system that **we are integral parts of.** We can let our lives be directed by this same intelligent power that makes the flowers grow if we choose; or we can continue to try and do it using our *Force* and by the limitations of our mind. **It's our choice.**

> *I know this world is ruled by infinite intelligence.*
> *Everything that surrounds us- everything that exists -*
> *proves that there are infinite laws behind it.*
> *There can be no denying this fact.*
> *It is mathematical in its precision.*
> ~Thomas A. Edison

What if we could see, in our daily lives, the working of that ***Power***? What if we believed that it loved and protected us so much that we could totally trust and relax in it? If we fully believed that the Universe is on our side and that it always has our best interest in mind, with a greater *awareness*— and that our attempts to direct this ***Power*** only interferes with the greater perspective that **It** has to answer our requests? Your *intellect* is the problem that we want to circumvent; it can only deliver answers based on what it has previously recorded. It's finite, so its answers are finite. It is not infinite and unlimited like the Divine and the Universe. When you live in the answer, or from your mind, whatever it knows is the sum total of what can show up for you; instead of the ***infinite possibilities*** that actually exist in the Quantum Field. The more that we can trust in what appears to be invisible, the more these possibilities can be revealed to us in physical form. And in truth, what appears to be visible is really made up of a slowed down version of the invisible.

You don't ask the Universe for help from your lower consciousness and the linear worldly constructs you have been taught, thinking your answer can only come through the means in which you know. It's not, "I need more money, and I either need to get it from my job or by borrowing it from 'x'. Instead, it's, "*OK Universe, what is it going to take for $50,000 to show up in my life by the end of this month? I am excited to see how you are going to bring it to me! I am grateful for it and ready to receive. I will pay attention and respond however you guide and direct me. Thank you. I feel so much love and gratitude for all of the abundance you provide for me all the time!*" Then just let the Universe respond, guide you and bring things your way. Don't try to anticipate and figure it all out. You will just limit what can unfold. We are just constantly trusting and turning things over to the ***Divine Intervention*** that can make things bigger and better than we can begin to imagine! It is **The Success Formula** in action!

It's about staying within your Higher Consciousness no matter what is going on, seemingly good or bad, and asking, "*How does it get even better than this?*" Not dropping back down into the fear of the lower consciousness and what appears to be real; knowing that by asking this question, whatever appears to be '*bad*' will just turn ***better*** and whatever seems '*good*' will quickly turn to ***great***! The pilot doesn't fear that there isn't a horizon to land on, just because he can't see the horizon past all of the clouds in front of him. Whenever something shows up that feels negative, instead of reacting to the stories your mind feeds you, you ask, "*What is great about this that I am not quite getting or understanding? What is this trying to show me or help me with, and how does it get even better than this?*" Then listen to the answers and guidance you get to this question.

To live from your ***Essence***, you utilize your *intellect* to get clear and specific about your intentions, to take some right actions in alignment towards them, and in asking the Divine the right questions on how to best receive your intention. But after that, everything is turned over to the guidance and ***intervention*** of the Divine, the Field, the Universe, God, or whatever name you want to give this **Source** that you are a part of. Let go of the *doership* and be excited about the ***Powerful*** adventure the Divine is going to take you on, based on your intention, your **trust and reliance**, and your open question of '*how?*'! And of course, whatever shows up, just say, "*Wow! Thank you- and how does it get even better than this?*" And just wait for the answer and follow it, thanking the Universe and asking the question again! **Endlessly.**

People living from their lower consciousness don't have a money issue, a love issue or a success issue; what they have is a *reliance and receiving issue*. Like most of us, they bought into the wrong beliefs passed down to them about who they are and what their worthiness is to receive. In fact, studies have shown that even when people who previously struggled with money win the lottery, they find themselves in the exact same financial position they were in before they won, within one to two years after winning. The money did not change their wounding, fear and subconscious programming that is unconsciously driving their life. Poverty or scarcity consciousness is not about the amount of money you have; it's about the way you see yourself, how you treat yourself, how fearful and guarded you are, and what you think your deservedness is to receive.

People with scarcity issues haven't realized **who they really are**, how powerful they are, and that they are more than worthy to receive all of the bounty of the Universe! Their conscious mind may have been told it from time to time, but their subconscious programming always overwrites it before they begin to believe. Your unconscious belief about worthiness and receiving is the problem for the lack of abundance in your life. Unfortunately, so many people have retained the old-world view that poverty and self-sacrifice are pleasing to God. They also seemed to pick up the wrong concept that after the six days of creation, God finished His work and could not create any more —that the majority of men had to stay poor because there wasn't enough to go around. They hold so much of this erroneous thought that they feel fear and shame to ask for wealth and abundance.

The truth is that God is infinite and abundant, and always creating and expanding; it is the nature of the Universe and of life.[23] In fact, It is expressing itself **through you** and It wants to **give you anything you ask for**, because that is *how* It creates— **through us**. That is also how It *experiences* Its creation as well— **through us**! God wants you to make the most of yourself, for yourself and for others, because *making the most of yourself is how you can do the most for others* — **other expressions of Its self**! Got it? If not, read that again! I know it can be a little confusing. All things are possible when you free yourself from this old and erroneous programming, know who you really are, and **are totally open to receive** the abundance that is available to you! Once you really get this, it will be a paradigm shift in both your thinking and your life!

Love is what we were conceived as. Fear is what we have been programmed with since we've been living within a body. The *'original sin'* (missed the mark) was when we were disconnected from our *Spirit Self* and *Source* and were taken over by our fear-based programmed mind. When we operate from fear, we shut everything out; we shut down our receiving. The hero's journey is an internal one from the head to the heart; it is the relinquishment of the fearful programming and the return back to the **Pure Love** that we really are, that resides in our heart space. The return to our **Essence** is the great cosmic drama, the personal journey from illusion to Truth, and from internal pain to inner peace. Love is the ultimate reality and to experience Love in ourselves and **as our self,** and in others, is the grandest achievement at a soul level!

Love isn't material; it's energy. *Love* isn't seen with the physical eyes or heard with physical ears, but people can usually tell you when they feel it and when they don't. It is perceived through another kind of vision, and it requires a different kind of *'seeing'* than we're used to. It requires a knowing from the heart's brain — the intuition of our heart. The knowing from a vague memory of an enchanted realm that we all secretly long to return to — a knowing from our **Essence,** that lives in the chamber of our heart.

The truth doesn't stop being the truth just because we can't see it. We can't see radio or television waves, but we know that they exist. *Love* is within us, it is what we really are; that is our true wave. It cannot be destroyed; it is only hidden by the clouds of our hurt and fear. Fear is to *Love* as darkness is to light. The only thing that has kept us from our *Love* and our *Light* is all of the fear and darkness we got programmed with. As we have removed the fear and darkness, more and more of our *Love* and *Light* has been able to break through and shine.

In truth, there is no such thing as a gray sky— the sky is always blue. There can be gray clouds that cover up the beautiful blue sky, which makes us wrongly perceive the sky as gray — which wrongly made us believe that we were our mind and our thoughts. **Love** is an infinite continuum of energy; the *Love* that is in one of us is the *Love* that is in all of us. There is no place where the Divine stops and you start. You do not end at the edge of your skin. Just like a wave can't separate from the sea, at our **Essence** we can't separate from the whole. We are all part of a vast ocean of *Love*; we are all made of the same subatomic particles. We may have different pollutants we picked up in our section of the sea, but our quintessence is all the same. I know it is so difficult to **know** this when we are in these earth suits; but when you cross over, as I did, there is no question to this truth.

Like a fingerprint, and because of your soul's experiences, you are a unique expression of God with unique qualities to share with the world— to share with the whole. When you begin to **receive** the **vastness of who you truly** *are*, everything in your life starts to change, and the world and the Universe begin to shower you with love and abundance. Reflecting back, that which you are vibrating out — *Love and Limitlessness*. When you finally accept your own greatness and allow the world to see it, the world will gift your greatness back to you. You just **ask, trust** and **allow** the Universe to bring it to you in a way that you never imagined with your limited *intellect*.

You have to **know** who you really are and be **committed** to *Being it*. Committed to allowing your bright light to shine for the world to see! No more playing small in fear of losing the safety of the comfort zone or approval from others. There is nothing unique at all about a human being feeling afraid and playing small. It's like Marianne Williamson's famous quote from **A Return to Love**:

"Our deepest fear is not that we are inadequate. Our deepest fear is that we are powerful beyond measure. It is our light, not our darkness that most frightens us. We ask ourselves, Who am I to be brilliant, gorgeous, talented, fabulous? Actually, who are you **not** *to be? You are a child of God. Your playing small does not serve the world. There is nothing enlightened about shrinking so that other people won't feel insecure around you. We are all meant to shine, as children do. We were born to make manifest the glory of God that is within us. It's not just in some of us; it's in everyone. And as we let our own light shine, we unconsciously give other people permission to do the same. As we are liberated from our own fear, our presence automatically liberates others."*

Life truly begins right outside of your comfort zone. So if you are feeling uncomfortable, you should get excited; it is the beginning to greater things! The anxiety you feel is just the *Turbo Charge* you need to support you in your expansion. You have to step up and step out of the green zone and decide to be more — no matter what others think or say. No matter what their fearful and limiting thoughts and beliefs may be. You can live in fear or you can live in faith— **it's your choice**— and the Universe will just reflect that decision back to you.

To live a grander life, you have to get clear about **WHO you really are** — *a Spiritual and Infinite Being that is Love and one with Source, that has an entire Spirit Team assisting you upon your request*— and make the **choice** to be your glorious self, larger then you have ever been willing to be in the past! You have to be willing to rock the status quo in your life and in others around you. You have to stop limiting yourself by defining yourself based on who you *'used to be'* and by the labels that others have given you. You have to **let go** of the old *'concept'* of you (the wall). The past does not exist now, unless you choose to **re-**create it and **re-**live it. You have to **be willing** to be bold, fabulous, outrageous; to *think differently* and be more of *YOU*, **according to you!** Stir the pot and stop refusing to be **All** that you truly are! You playing small does not help the world at all; you playing your greatness does! So make the jump from the safety zone and the people pleasing to the bigger waters that await you!

When you **decide and commit** to *Being* **All** that you are and letting your bright light shine, the Universe will respond accordingly. Just be **open and ready to receive**, and the ways to do so will begin to show up in your life and guide you. Across spiritual teachings, the universal description of God is **I Am That I Am.** I AM are the two most powerful words there are. The Divine or the Quantum Field merely responds to, and reflects back, whatever *Stand* you are taking. A **Stand** is when your heart, mind and Spirit are all in agreement. So whatever words you put at the end of that I AM from this alignment, the Universe just responds, **"*OK, I AM THAT!*"** Which means, you give birth to and shape your reality by whatever *Stand* you take, by whatever words and emotions you attach to the back end of that almighty **I AM.**

"And what-ever you shall ask in my name, that will I do."

Mahatma Ghandi took a *strong stand* for the rights of the Indian people and for peace, no matter what the circumstances looked like. He believed in a future that he could not yet see with his senses, but was so alive in his desire and vision. No matter what was done to him in response, he stood strong and in alignment with his *stand*. His *stand* from his Higher Consciousness— from the high vibration of Love and Peace. Mahatma Ghandi was a peaceful soldier who used his heart and Spirit instead of his fists, and persuaded hundreds of thousands to do the same. From this consistent higher vibration, no matter what low vibration the British threw at him, eventually the Universe mirrored back this *stand*, with the British military peacefully withdrawing from India and returning the country back to its original people after 200 years of ongoing turmoil.

You see, **mahatma** means *great soul,* and it's inside of each one of us, awaiting to be **seen and unfold**. It is a *Creative Life Force* that is constantly and forever flowing through you, picking up the vibrations of your consciousness – your **stand**, and expressing that frequency in a visible and physical form. *"As within, so without."* This energy is impartial, it just reflects back. It does not care about your mistakes of the past, it only knows how to create in accordance with your consistent **present consciousness**. So when it is flowing through the **Pure Love** and **Light** you are, instead of all of the fear and childhood programming, it has no choice but to manifest this love, peace and the intentions of your heart and soul. *"As a man thinketh in his heart, so is he."*

You now know that you are more than a physical body; **you are consciousness** living in a body. Like clay, the energy of *infinite possibilities* is shaped by this consciousness, which was powerfully proven by the **Double Slit Experiment** we shared in Chapter Nine. All of us broadcast a distinct energy pattern or *soul signature*. Your fluctuating states of consciousness change that signature. **I AM THAT** which I *feel*, heart, mind and soul that I AM. You are **declaring** yourself **to Be** the second part of that **I AM** statement. I AM **love, peaceful, joyful and abundant!** Change the conception of yourself at the subconscious level, because we know that it is over a million times more powerful than our conscious mind or intellect, and you will automatically *transform* your life experience! You will alter what the Universe delivers to you and what the world reflects back to you. Love, value and adore yourself, and the world will confirm that vibration back to you! (So keep up with your Self Love Mantra!)

You need to keep doing the work to heal your relationships and your *charges* so that both your heart and subconscious mind are liberated from the negative thought patterns, and your *awareness* of **Being *Pure Love*** and **one with Source** dominates your thought sphere and becomes your master blueprint from which you build. We need to be really careful about what words we are attaching to the back end of our **I AM** statements. Be very careful not to repeat old programs you might've once said, such as, *I am so stupid, accident prone, hurt, sick, afraid, worried, clumsy, poor, ADD,* etc.. We need to take out the old film reels from the projector and replace them with new and improved film reels that have nothing to do with past stories or what *appears* to be our reality today. This means we need to take the mantra meditation we introduced to you in the *Self Love* chapter to the next level. You now need to flood your mind and awareness with these types of mantras: "**I AM Love**", "**I AM Pure Love**", "**I AM Pure Spirit**", "**I AM one with Source**", "**I AM an Infinite Being with Infinite Possibilities**", "**I AM happy, magical and blissful**", "**I AM peaceful**", "**I AM radiant and strong**", or whatever you want *your reality to be now!* **I AM** is the language of **Power** from our *Spiritual Self*, and I WILL is the language of *Force* from our *intellect*.

What mantras are you now going to use to create your new reality?

....

....

....

....

....

....

Throughout this book you have been taken through processes to be liberated from your *charges* and many of these destructive thought patterns, and you have been given the tools to free yourself from the ones that still remain. With this freedom from the debris we once carried, we can now look at our life again in all the different areas we looked at in Chapter 6 – *Self Empowerment*– and now consciously create anew. This time we will create **at cause**, from our Higher Consciousness. "*As within, so without.*" The Universe is already responding to us, we just need to give it better direction. So now that we have a greater awareness of **who we really are** and how we have been creating our life thus far, and now that we are lighter, carrying less debris and vibrating higher up the **Map of Consciousness** and choosing to create our life through our *Power* and no longer through *Force*— how do you want your life to be? What *stand* are you **now going to take for yourself** in each one of these areas of your life, from a place of abundant receiving?

    a.   Health and Fitness?

....

....

....

....

....

b. Career?

....

....

....

....

....

c. Finances?

....

....

....

....

....

d. Material Items and Life Style?

....

....

....

....

....

e. Relationship with Significant Other?

....

....

....

....

f. Relationship with Family?

....

....

....

....

....

g. Relationships with Friends and Community?

....

....

....

....

h. Relationship with Source?

....

....

....

....

....

Creating Our Life as An Infinite Being

We are now going to create this new life you want to live from your Higher Consciousness, and birth your **Life Vision** from your *Spiritual Self* as an **Infinite Being**! To do so, we need to **apply** what the ancients have been teaching us about how to effectively pray **to our life,** through the unity or the *coherence* of our mind, heart and Spirit. We need to *stop* focusing on how our life is at this moment and praying for it to be something different. And **START seeing it how we want it to be** and *FEEL such gratitude for it* **Being So, Now!**

The word **feeling** is the key ingredient, and **feeling it now** is the secret sauce of the recipe! Because that is the only language the subconscious mind understands. The subconscious mind is literal and sensory-based, and can only know things through the five senses of seeing, hearing, feeling, tasting and smelling. Effective communication with the subconscious mind is achieved by using one or more of these senses in alignment with the intended communication. For example, the conscious mind may have a goal to be happy; however, without further clarification of exactly what happiness means, the subconscious mind is at a loss to assist in accomplishing that goal. It's like planning a fun vacation with your best friend but not defining what each one of you considers *fun*. Their idea of fun might be lying on a warm beach with a pitcher of margaritas, and yours is climbing up Mt. Kilimanjaro! (This sounds like me and my best friend!) So the word fun, like happy, is too abstract; what one considers fun, the other considers their worst nightmare! The notion of happiness or fun has little meaning to the subconscious mind until the idea is translated into sensory-based language. For instance, if you were to feel happy, what kind of things would you be **seeing** with your eyes? Perhaps you **see** yourself playing volleyball with your friends on the beach, joking around and laughing. What kind of smells might you be smelling? Imagine yourself **smelling** them as we did with the lemon. What kind of things would you be **saying** to each other? **Hear** those words, now. What kinds of **emotions** would you be feeling as you are playing and joking with each other? **Feel** those feelings in your body, now. Close your eyes and remember a specific time where you **felt** this kind of happiness. You want to feel and experience it all over again, relive the **emotions and feelings** you felt in your body at that moment. This is the *language* in which you need to communicate to your subconscious mind for change to happen, just like the athletes do to increase their performance!

So as you are creating this new Life Vision, **feel** all the feelings you would feel if that ideal life **was so, right now**; and express your excitement and gratitude for it! Be in love with your Life Vision— **feel** your love, your passion, your excitement and your gratitude for **how fabulous your life really is now**. See yourself living this Life Vision without fear or limitations, and celebrate it! Let the waves of enthusiasm roll through you, over and over, throughout your body. Don't ask and pray for it to happen at some later date; **it's all here now and you are just remembering it and celebrating**. The Divine, the Quantum Field works in the **NOW** but as if it already happened in the **PAST**; and you're just fondly remembering, expressing your gratitude for it now. If you ask for something to come in the future, it will forever be a day away. **The Power is in the Now as Already So!**

Again, **we have to marry thought with emotion**. At the heart, thought and emotion merge as a *feeling*, and a vibration is broadcasted out to the Universe by the heart, the largest magnetic field of our body. The *feeling vibration* is the language the Universe recognizes, and it's the way to communicate with the *Field* to have our prayers answered, **and not the words** (a lot of the western world has wrongly believed the power of their prayer came from the words that they spoke). (Hmmm, the subconscious mind and the Field has the same language, imagine that!) The communication through the heart is a real-time application — *'as if'* it is already done. The heart is just expressing all of its excitement that **this possibility**, out of the millions of possibilities available in the Quantum Field, **is happening now.** The heart center is our Spiritual Self's home, and the language of the heart has a powerful and immediate effect on our world and our life experience! It is the wind in the sail of our Life Vision and soul's mission. At my live events you will get a very powerful experience of this. www.HealYourHeartFreeYourMind.com/programs

To *transform* our life to the one of our heart and soul's intention, we are going to leverage this power and **Visulate**™ (visualize and meditate) on this new exciting life we are going to create from our Higher Consciousness, **every day**. Preferably every morning, just as we are waking up and still in Theta or a low Alpha state. First, we will invoke the Divine and connect to Source from our ***Spiritual Self*** by getting our *Life Force* moving throughout our Energy Centers, until we quiet our mind and bring all of our awareness to our crown (the top of our head). And as we do, we will begin to feel our Higher Consciousness become **unified with Source**. And from this place of *Love*, we are going to feel the excitement and gratitude for our life being the way we have envisioned it **now,** throughout our body and *Beingness*. Seeing and **feeling** the deep love, passion and exhilaration of it all, and then reverberate that feeling out in stereo into the Universe! Being as **thankful** for it in our body, mind and spirit as we expect to feel when it has taken form. The grateful mind continually expects good things, and the nature of expectations breeds **faith**. And the Universe responds very well to this high vibration of expectation, this *stand*. Like a positive, self-fulfilling prophecy!

Your **body and your subconscious mind** need to **feel** and be convinced that your visualized experience is happening to you **now**. Just like the athletes do, and just as we did when we were visualizing pointing at the wall and turning further. You have to use all of your senses to recondition your subconscious mind to this new state of *Being*. You have to **see** what you would see, if it were happening in this moment; you have say the words you would say and **hear** the words or noises you would hear, if it were all happening now. **Feel** the texture, **taste** the tastes, and **smell** the aromas— **fully experience it all** in your mind's eye **now**. When you hold clear, focused thoughts about your intentions, accompanied by the passionate emotions in your heart and body, you broadcast a stronger *electromagnetic signal* that pulls you toward a potential reality that matches your vision, influencing the subatomic particles all around you!

When we tap into this Universal Intelligence through our Higher Consciousness, we make direct contact with the *Field of Infinite Possibilities*, and we are giving it a clear signal of the life we **expect** to experience, no longer filtered through all of our fears and charges. To **expect that it is done is key**! It is your *stand*, and what the Quantum Field of Infinite Possibilities most responds to. Your subconscious thoughts are electromagnetic, and your heart is 5000 times more powerful electromagnetically than your brain. So your heartfelt, **grateful expectation, as if what you desire is so,** from your cleared up Higher Conscious Heart *aligned* with your subconscious mind, is one of the most powerful electromagnetic pulls there are! The energy making up all of matter, including us, is electromagnetic, so every material thing acts as a magnet and attracts like vibrations.

By **Visulating**™ every day from this clear and cleaner slate, you are now living life *at cause*. You're drastically changing something inside of you to **cause** *an effect* in the world outside of you. You're intentionally and radically changing your vibration and the message you are delivering out to the Universe and to the Divine. Because everything is made out of subatomic particles, matter or energy has a plastic quality, and so what you **impress it with**, it becomes! So, you are going to live in your new house mentally every day, until it takes form around you physically! And now that your heart and mind are in coherence and you have taken a *stand*, and are **taking right actions** in alignment with this *declaration*, you have **changed your electromagnetic signature** and what you are broadcasting out to Universe; so now the Quantum Field will draw you and this matching potential out of the infinite possibilities that exist, together. I compare it to being like a satellite dish, remote control, and television. There are many channels of consciousness available to us through the satellite dish; we just need to push the right buttons on our remote control to experience the new programming we want to come through our monitor!

Everything is energy and that's all there is to it. Match the frequency of the reality you want and you cannot help but get that reality. It can be no other way. This is not philosophy. This is physics.

~Albert Einstein

I know from personal experience how frustrating it can be when life seems to bring you an endless succession of the same type of unwanted outcomes. But as long as you stay the same and broadcast out the same *electromagnetic signature*, your patterns will remain plaguing your life. This is not praying for what you want for a moment and then going about your day as it was. To unfold this new Life Vision, you have to get up from your visulation different than you were yesterday, **every day**. You have to get up *as the person* you just visualized. This is a continuous and interactive **living prayer**. You have to see the world from *that version of your self's perception*. You have to make decisions and take actions from their mind set. Just like an MPD (a person with Multiple Personality Disorder), you see and respond to the world, physically and emotionally, differently. You respond and take actions **as** this new identity you just created; you think, speak and plan in terms of actually having everything you visualized now! You not only create a *'to do list'* from this place, but you also create a *'to Be list'*. **You are creating a new imprint on your *Being*—** overwriting the old imprint you picked up from your childhood. You act the part and make decisions from this new confident and powerful state daily— excited and grateful that your life is going just the way you have always dreamed that it would. That all of your life goals are coming into fruition and you are finally living your idealized life!

"To dream by night is to escape your life. To dream by day is to make it happen."
~ Stephen Richards

A new state of *Being* **will** create a new reality! Just like the professional athletes that have achieved new records because they performed their new time, or skill level, over and over in their mind beforehand. Fully feeling all they would feel in their body, as if it were really happening, then getting up and doing exactly what they have envisioned. But we are going to apply this practice to our entire life experience! We are going to live out this new life and this new way of *Being* in our subconscious mind every day until it becomes automatic and effortless, just like walking and driving have become for us. This is how we, the ***Spiritual Self***, will biologically change our mind, heart and body to no longer live in the past and at *the effect*, but to rather chart out our future from the place of **Power** (from the place of **I AM***)* and **at cause,** in coherence with the Quantum Field.

As we do this, we have to remember that we are only taking care of the vision or the ***'order'***; the Divine will handle the *'how'* and *'when'* it is delivered. Do not try to direct the way your vision should unfold or be attached to how it should look. Just like in a restaurant, you make your order and wait, knowing that the waiter will bring your order to you when it is perfectly ready. You don't go back in the kitchen and try to direct the Chef on how to make it! We are following **The Success Formula** and just taking some *Right Action* towards our vision (our *Clear Intention*), and following the guidance of the *Divine Intervention* and fully *expecting to* **Receive.** Be open and receptive to the voice within, speaking to you through your intuition. If you feel an urge to call someone or write them an e-mail, do so. You will be amazed at the 'coincidences' and what shows up — a surprising check in the mail, offers of assistance from strangers, ideas given to you by friends and acquaintances, or you just happen to meet Oprah and she wants to help you with your vision. Just saying. (Smile.)

We respond to the Divine Guidance from a relaxed state of mind, which keeps the energy free-flowing; and with each step, casually asking with gratitude, "*How does it get even better than this?*" Stress and an uptight feeling will just restrict the flow, just like putting pressure on a water hose. Less pressure, more flow!

The hardest part of *transforming* our life is **not** making the same choices we have been making for years, forgetting the past, and not getting caught up in *reacting* to our present day *charges*, identity and circumstances. We have to **keep our focus on what we want to create and experience**, and not on the stories of the past or on the 'what is' now. We have to not buy into fear and the stories of our mind, and not allow the I WILL *Force* of the intellect take over once again. By trying to address and *fix* the 'what is', or falling into old patterns of complaining to others about it, or licking our wounds and feeling sorry for ourselves, **we are just keeping that energy alive and expanding**. Be too busy *Being* this new person, leading your vessel from your *Spiritual Essence*, to get involved in the old stories and drama. As a recovering 'Ms's *fix it'*, I know how difficult it is to not **try** and control everything and make it ok again— but if you are not changing your old patterns and focus every day, then for the most part, you are **re**-living your past and will continue heading towards your inherited history. If you repeatedly think, feel and react the same way you did yesterday, you will continue to create and experience the same circumstances in your life— which will cause you to think the same thoughts, have the same feelings and have some of the same reactions— causing you to stay stuck on the same old hamster wheel, going around and around again.

"You must unlearn what you have been programmed to believe since birth.
That software no longer serves you if you want
to live in a world where all things are possible."
~Jacqueline E. Purcell

You can't take the old person that you were into the future with you, and you can't let others try to do that to you either. Wherever you place your attention, your energy **expands.** Whatever you hold in consciousness about yourself will be mirrored back to you in the world. That includes wrong beliefs projected onto you from others — so don't buy into them, and don't react to them. Do not give them any life force to live off of. So what happens when you change, but you still have the same friends? You no longer fit in with them, and they may start to resent you. They might lash out at you because they feel you are rejecting them and their life style, by changing your ways and no longer being their crutch. When these fearful friends try to come back into your mental household, they will unconsciously attempt to block the light and dislodge your Life Vision. If they succeed, the Divine energy will be diverted from the fulfillment of your vision and channeled through the negative thought patterns and vibration instead— causing the old false beliefs to be again externalized. "*As within, so without.*" You have a choice at this point; you can keep the approval of your friends and family and step back into your old life, **or** you can move forward to a new frequency and draw in new friends that match your new Life Vision. It is just like getting off the Drama Triangle: you have to be willing to be the *'persecutor'* to the others still living in it, to get off of it!

Your job is to stand guard to the door of your new identity, and to your heart and mind. Stay vigilant to the infinite possibilities of your vision and stay away from all of the emotional bait of what's *'known today',* that will attempt to drag you away. Do your *Visulating* **every day** and **act *'as if'* your Life Vision is so**. Don't get involved in the stories of your mind and what appears to be real, and eradicate those pesky negative thought rascals with your affirming mantras. Neither you nor anyone else have the right to blaspheme God's creation. As soon as you become aware of one of those intruders attempting to break in, start chanting one of your mantras — "*I Am Love*", "*I Am Pure Love*", "*I Am An Infinite Being*", or whatever mantra supports your vision, over and over again, until you feel internal peace once again.

To stay strong in leadership from your *Spiritual Essence* and to keep your cup in overflow, say it whatever chance you get— as you're working out, taking a shower, getting ready, driving or going to sleep. Connect to Source and just flood your *Being* with this truth to thwart the attempts of the band of thieves to steal away your bright light and vision. Reclaim your unity with the great **I AM** and its *Power* and its promise that "*whatever you shall ask in my name, that will I do.*" This will create a protective cover around your Life Vision, while maintaining the energy flowing in its right direction. To think health when surrounded by the appearance of disease, or to think riches when in the midst of the appearance of poverty is very difficult with the *intellect* and the mind. It requires the **Power** of your ***Spiritual Essence,*** aligned with your *A Team* and Source, having total **faith** that what you want instead is already *'in hand'*; and it requires taking action towards it *as if* it is already *'yours'*, and taking **no action** towards validating the *'what is'*! **Doing this**, and only this, **is what requires your *WILL* Power** — your ***Spiritual Self's WILL Power***!

No matter what the present day circumstance is, you have to keep a clear mental picture of your Life Vision continually in your mind, just as the sailor has to focus on the port to which he is sailing, no matter what the distractions around him are. Keep your eyes and the nose of your vessel towards your destination at all times! This can be the toughest requirement in creating and living out your Life Vision— but remember, it **is** possible to think greater than your present day experience, and vibrate it into reality. The history books are filled with names of people who have done exactly that: Ben Franklin, Thomas Edison, the Wright Brothers, Martin Luther King Jr., Mahatma Ghandi, and my all-time favorite, Walt Disney, just to name a few. And when we do this, our minds are no longer a record of our and our ancestors' past, but instead, have become **a map to our future**.

One woman was told by doctors she could never have a baby — that it wasn't physically possible. She chose not to buy into their prognosis, and instead she put these tools into practice. She visualized herself pregnant and the baby growing in her belly; she saw herself having to wear bigger and bigger clothes; she visualized the birth and felt the great love and joy she had for her newborn. She planned her baby shower and set up a baby registry. She even went out and bought everything she needed to have her nursery ready for her little one's arrival. And soon, everything she envisioned transpired; her daughter is the living example of what is possible when you don't buy into the limitations told to you by the world, and instead, you wholeheartedly visualize, expect and believe in another possibility of your soul's intention!

Another example of successful Visulating was achieved by a teacher who had a massive stroke that damaged the language center of her brain. She was told by doctors that she would never be able to speak normally again. She refused to accept this prognosis, and chose to put these teachings into play instead. Day after day, she mentally rehearsed speaking in front of her students, in her mind. She saw herself effortlessly having a powerful impact on her students, and felt the great sense of joy that she would feel for the gratitude that they would express to her for her teaching. I am happy to say she is now blissfully teaching students, easily and impeccably, once again!

291

In his book, **Grow Rich! With Peace of Mind,** Napoleon Hill shared how he used this awareness to get his son, who was born without ears and many of the vital parts required for hearing, to be able to hear. It started with Napoleon **fully believing that it could be so** and his **taking actions accordingly**, meaning that he didn't put his son in special schools for the deaf or teach him sign language, amongst much judgment and ridicule. Instead, he would speak to his son's subconscious mind every night when he would sleep, thankfully telling it exactly what he **expected** it to do, as if it were already so. Through his efforts and belief, his son's brain grew new auditory nerves to the inner wall of his skull, which allowed him to hear 65% of what somebody with ears and all of the usual equipment could, and he got by in life just fine!

The key is to not buy into the stories that others tell you or that your mind tries to tell you, based on your fears and programming, and **take actions in alignment with what you want to manifest instead**. All faith healers heal by not buying into the illusion of the disease, and instead, see the person as perfect, whole and as *Pure Love*. Faith healer Michelle O'Donnell wrote a book, called **Of Monkeys and Dragons: Freedom from the Tyranny of Disease,** which is basically about not looking at or buying into the *'Monkeys and Dragons'*, and that this is how she helps heal so many who come to see her. In fact, I was talking to Michelle about this right before I left on my trip that would find me falling off that cliff in Fiji. I had been getting this message delivered to me consistently as I had been grieving the loss of my mother, and I told Michelle, "I so wish I knew this before my mother was diagnosed—unfortunately, I did buy into the fear and was doing everything I could to try and fight the cancer. In fact, I probably even ruined an opportunity to change my mother's belief system that perhaps could've saved her life, which my step-cousin was trying to provide for her."

My step-cousin did a psychic reading on my mom and told my mother that she and her brain surgeon had a karmic relationship in another life; that she had saved his life in another lifetime and this was his turn to now pay back that blessing and save hers. My mother believed her, and that after the surgery the karmic payback was done and that she was now going to be fine. She believed that she didn't need to do any other protocol that we were doing for her healing, so she was refusing to complete them. I knew, from my fearful logical mind, that the middle of her brain was inoperable, and that we still needed to do procedures to get the rest of the tumor out. I thought I needed her to stop believing this and keep taking the physical actions to rid her body from the rest of the cancer, so I got someone else who was able to get through to her, to talk to her. Unfortunately, she understood and stopped believing in my cousin's story, and just gave up instead. In hindsight, with my greater understanding, I now see that her subconscious mind fully believing that karmic payback story may have just been the *key* her mind needed for its full healing.

So this was the theme of this particular trip — and obviously the message I was meant to finally get. It started off with that discussion in Lake Tahoe with Michelle, and it continued in a discussion I had with the monks right before I went on my little adventure to the other islands of Fiji. In the class they shared a true story about a man, wanted for murder, who escaped prison and knocked on an old lady's door in the middle of a thunderous rain storm, drenched. The little old lady did not react to his unkempt look and odd looking attire and said, "Come in dear, and get warm. It's miserable out there. You must be freezing. You don't even have a jacket. Why don't you go take a hot shower, and I will give you some of my late husband's clothes to put on. I will make you some hot food and drink to warm you up from the inside, while you are taking a shower." When he got out of the shower, they shared a nice meal together. He didn't talk much, but she told him about her husband and showed him pictures of her grandchildren. When they were done eating, he thanked her for her warmth and kindness but said that he needed to leave. She gave him her husband's coat, an umbrella, and told him to take care of himself and to try and stay dry. He then went to a neighbor's house and killed them, to try and hide in their home instead. Because she didn't fear him or see him as bad, and instead saw him as a beautiful soul in need of some help and treated him with love and kindness, he mirrored her vision and vibration back to her, as much as his vessel could.

I told you about all of the miracles I then had with those monks after my fall. What I didn't tell you was how I had to remember these teachings, and apply them, to keep the miracle going! The man who stayed with me while the rest got help and held me while I was hanging out with my mother and pets on the other side, and who was talking to me and taking care of me when I returned to the body, had his own profound spiritual experience through it, which he wrote about and shared with the world. In it, he shared his account of what happened with me and my fall. Since I could not remember anything about the fall, I wrongly forwarded the letter to all of my friends and family to keep them in the loop as what was going on with me in my travels. That was a huge mistake, and almost cost me my miracle! As I said, I was feeling pretty great after the monks prayed over me and by the time I left Fiji, but after I'd emailed my story to my community, they all called me to check on how I was doing upon my return. In their well-meaningness, they would tell me stories about what happened to them or someone they knew that fell and hit their head as well. As they did, I began to feel the fear and anxiety take over me. I started fearing that I would have brain trauma and the experiences that they shared, **and I began to**. I then started making appointments with neurologists who would tell me that there was nothing they could do for me, that it would just take time for all of the symptoms I was now experiencing to go away — if they ever did. And as they gave me this prognosis, the fear and anxiety would increase and so would all of my symptoms.

Until one day I remembered all of these teachings and said, "<u>NOOOO</u>! This does not apply to me! I had a miracle. I am perfect and fine, and I need to not buy into all of these stories of what *'should have'* happened to me. This does not apply to me, and I need all of these well-meaning people to stop feeding this story and belief to me as well! I need to not buy into their stories — their reflection. Their reflection in their mirror is different than mine, because we are different Beings with different vibrations and programming. **My actions need to be in alignment with my belief in my miracle**, not in these fears, no matter how my reality feels and appears at this moment. By focusing on what *'appears to be real'*, feeling all of that anxiety *as if* it is real, and taking actions in alignment to it being real, I am just enforcing that vibration to get mirrored back to me. That is not my truth, and that is not what I want!" So, even though I was still feeling all of the symptoms, I stopped seeing the doctors, and I told all of my friends and family, "Thank you for caring about me and checking in on me, but please stop asking how I am because the only answer you are going to get from me is that **I am perfect**! I had a miracle, and all that you have seen and experienced does not apply to me. **I am perfect and feeling great!**" And if they ever asked again how I was doing, I would just say I was doing great, and I would say it all again. Within a few weeks **I was experiencing my miracle once again**! Now that I had more *awareness*, I was able to make a **better decision** this time with my own life!

By the way, is any of this sounding similar to Dr. Hew Len's healing an entire mental ward in Hawaii? I'm just saying. Another great tool you can you use when these negative or fearful intruders come knocking at your door is Ho'oponopono — thank you, I'm sorry, please forgive me and I love you! I also learned through this experience, that *before I could see others as perfect and whole*, **I needed to see myself as perfect and whole!!!** And that is when I could truly be a healer like Dr. Hew Len and Michelle O'Donnell.

The clearer you become about your Life Vision and all of the emotions you would feel **when it is so**, the more you focus your attention and actions **on this only** and not on your past or present perceived *'reality'*. And the more you fuse this vision within your heart, thoughts, beliefs and body, the greater your **conviction** will be for its actual manifestation. With your **daily**

commitment to this *Visulation*, your mantras, and a total belief with grateful **expectation**, your new joy-filled, magical life will unfold and be revealed to the world— *inspiring* others to create their own Life Vision and let their bright light shine as well! And we will then have fulfilled this part of Marianne Williamson's famous quote, *"And as we let our own light shine, we unconsciously give other people permission to do the same. As we are liberated from our own fear, our presence automatically liberates others."*

So before we start creating our life vision, let's go back to the question this book started with: **So What is Your Marathon?** What is your dream that you just haven't been able to fulfill? What is your soul's mission and intention? Have you gotten in touch with that yet, now that we have reacquainted you with your *Spiritual Self*, and now that it is taking the lead? What would make your soul celebrate? Have you gotten more clear on that, as you looked at the patterns of your life and saw what the Universe has been preparing you for all along? I am so grateful that I was given a second chance to finally make mine come true, unlike my mom and so many other souls who passed before *transcending* their fear and programming. I am so grateful that I became helpless enough that the Divine could show me how. I am so thankful to know that I'm not a victim stuck in a video game, dodging asteroids coming at me all the time, as I once thought. And instead, I now know the programming language and how to change the game and create a better one!

And now you do, too. So what are you going to do? Are you going to choose a higher road led by your *Spiritual Self* or continue down the one led by your wounded *emotional child* and your fearful protective mind? Remember: the mind thinks, but the heart (which is where the *Spiritual Self* resides) knows! **You are an Infinite Being,** and there are an infinite amount of possibilities just waiting for you in the Quantum Field, waiting for you to choose a better train track that will lead you to them, than the track you have been on thus far. Without your *Spiritual Self* or without the Divine, the mind can only do a few things, but together they are capable of everything! In unison, they can create pure magic and what might appear to the world to be miracles! Together, the soul is not limited by the mind's limited programming, and it has the blessing of the Divine's *bird eye* assistance.

The Quantum Field contains **everything** your soul may want; it is an inexhaustible storehouse of riches that is constantly producing new forms of itself. To get to it, you just need to declutch and liberate your *Spiritual Self* from your mind's fearful programming, and know yourself as this **Pure Love** that is one with Source— an *Infinite Being* **worthy** of any chosen possibility, with a Divine back-up team that has a grander perspective, and with clarity

decide how you want your life **to be**. And just **declare it** — with certainty, and a knowing that it **IS**! You do not want, you do not hope, **you decide and intend**, then take some *right action* in accordance, and are grateful for it being so! What is the difference between the girl singing in a dive bar and the one who is filling stadiums with thousands and thousands of people? It is her confidence, courage and certainty of who she is, what she wants, her worthiness to receive it all and her taking a *stand*! **This person took their right to be chosen**, and they chose themselves. They didn't ask; they didn't wait for others' approval; they didn't let their life situation or others' opinions and limiting beliefs dissuade them; they decided it for themselves. And only after this decision, *and because of it*, the world noticed them and mirrored it back! The world conforms to the conception of yourself when you are clear and you take a *stand*. Suddenly people find themselves saying, "There's just something special about you. I can't put my finger on it, but you just have that *'It Factor',* and I just want to support you!"

> *Once you make a decision,*
> *the universe conspires to make it happen.*
> ~Ralph Waldo Emerson

Someone who makes a decision like this stays focused on their vision and intention no matter what the naysayers do. No matter what the current *'what is'* appears to be. And for the benefit and the progression of the world, we should thank God that they did. What would our world look like if everyone just followed the world's opinion? Would we have the technologies we have, or by the time we had them, if Thomas Edison believed the teacher who threw him out of school because "he had an addled mind and was unable to have the focus required to receive a primary education"? Would we be enjoying Beethoven's beautiful music if he listened to his teachers who told him that "he was hopeless and would never succeed as a musician"? What about if Fred Astaire believed his first directors, who told him he "couldn't sing, dance or act"? Could you imagine how different the world would be without Disneyland — the happiest place in the world? Walt Disney was told he "lacked imagination and had no good ideas" as he was fired by a newspaper editor. Steven Spielberg was rejected from the University of Southern California School of Theater, Film and Television three times. Elvis was told by the Grand Ole Opry concert hall manager that he "was better off returning to Memphis and driving trucks than trying to sing" and that he would never make it. Oprah was told that she "wasn't fit for television." Michael Jordon was cut from his high school basketball team because he wasn't a good enough ballplayer. Albert Einstein did not speak until he was four and could not read until he was seven, and his teachers told his parents that he was "mentally handicapped and unfortunately wouldn't amount to much." Abraham Lincoln was told that he was a bad engineer, a bad soldier and a bad lawyer, and was defeated in his first attempt in politics— but he didn't let any of that keep him from becoming one the most influential presidents and changing United States history! And, for those of us who love to travel, thank God that the Wright brothers never listened to all the people that told them that they were delusional when their first prototypes would not fly successfully.

"When writing the story of your life, don't let anyone else hold the pen."
~Brandy Faith Weld

So, what is the life you choose for yourself, free from your parents' and society's opinion? What do you choose in alignment with your soul's vision and intention? What has your heart always longed for? What has it always wanted to do, see or experience? My soul always longed for a world where there wasn't any competition, where no one purposely hurt someone in order to feel more powerful or better about themselves. A world where everyone was thoughtful, kind and thought in terms of 'we'. A world that understood that *together* we could get through anything, and in competition and separation we would just destroy ourselves. A world that understood that, at the core, we are all the same; that we all come from the same source and that we all have the same wants and needs— to matter, to be loved and to love.

It wasn't until I crossed over that I was shown that this world **could exist** in the Earth realm, if I would just *remember who I was*, **believe**, and *finally do my part* towards this vision — **by running my marathon**. By playing my role in the total health, success and wellbeing of the body of the Divine. Each one of us has our own role in the tapestry of the ***Divine Body*** that we are all a part of — **our own marathon to run**. It is only our wounding and programming and the defense of the fearful mind that has blocked this Divine energy from being able to express itself through you freely, thus far. It is all of the conditioning to get love and approval outside of ourselves, based on the social parameters we were programmed with. But the body needs both a healthy liver cell and a heart cell; and the liver cell can't try to adapt itself to be a heart cell, just as the heart cell can't adapt itself to try and be a liver cell. Trying to do so is self-destructive and doesn't serve anyone. It doesn't serve the cell in being its best expression of itself, and it certainly doesn't serve the body in its total health and wellbeing. We need to stop always adapting ourselves to try and get approval from others and **start** **being our self** in our Divinely purposed authentic expression! It's time for you to live your life by design according to your ***Essence*** and your soul's intention, and no longer by default or by someone else's story.

"Your time is limited, so don't waste it living someone else's life. Don't be trapped by dogma- which is living with the results of other people's thinking. Don't let the noise of other's opinions drown out your own inner voice. And most important, have the courage to follow your heart and intuition. They somehow already know what you truly want to become. Everything else is secondary."

~ Steve Jobs (1955-2011)

www.HealYourHeartFreeYourMind.com/Jobs

So, what's your marathon? What legacy would you like to leave behind? What does the Divine want to express through you, as you? If you could have the life of your dreams, if you had no worries about money whatsoever and you were free of any limiting thoughts or beliefs, how would your life be right now? What goal and mission would ignite your Spirit and set it on fire? What would your life look like if, when your soul gets to the other side, it would say, "Wow, now that was a life well-lived! I fully lived out my life intention and sang my soul's song!"?

Each one of us, each soul, has a unique song to be sung and expressed to the world. Living in the west, we just haven't been conditioned to know that truth. But in tribes in Africa, they are. In certain tribes, when a woman is pregnant, she goes out into the wilderness with girlfriends and together they pray and meditate until they hear the song of the child within her womb. They recognize that every soul has its own vibration that expresses its unique flavor and purpose. When the women collectively attune to the child's song, they sing it out loud. And when the child is born, the community gathers and sings the child's song to him or her. And as they grow, when the child enters education, when they pass through the initiation to adulthood, and later as they get married, the village gathers around them and chants their song with them. And if at any time during the child's life, they commit a crime or a hateful social behavior, the individual is called to the center of the village and the community sings and reminds them of their song. The tribe recognizes that the correction for anti-social behavior is not punishment, but love and the remembrance of their true identity. You may have not been brought up in a community that recognizes and conditions in your soul's song, but life is always reminding you when you are in tune with yourself and when you are not. When you feel good, what you are doing and thinking about matches your song, and when you feel awful, it doesn't. Your **Spiritual Essence** knows; it has been trying to communicate it to you and guide you towards it for eons. So let's connect to the Divine and back to our **Essence**, and let it share with us what its true song really is, that it wants to share with the world.

Find a quiet location and for at least fifteen minutes invoke your Divine in any way you choose to. Perhaps sing or listen to the Moola Mantra, or do an Energy Center or Love Meditation. When your mind feels quiet and you feel connected to Source through your heart or your crown, close your eyes, put your hands on your heart, and connect with your **Essence**, and ask, "Please show me the highest vision you have for our life, what is our soul's intention and song?", and just see and experience **your soul's vision**. Sight is the job of the eyes, but **vision** is the job of the heart and soul! See your **Life Vision** from this limitless perspective, as an **Infinite Being** with infinite possibilities that receives everything it intends effortlessly! Open yourself up to be available to what seems beyond your current capacity to imagine for yourself, and answer the call to greatness that wants to emerge through you. Don't resist what is revealed to you by saying, "No, that vision is too big for me." And don't hesitate to ask for anything you may desire, for as Jesus told us, "*It is your Father's pleasure to give you the kingdom.*" Trust that the Divine will work out the ***how*** for you. All you have to do is get clear, decide and stay focused on your vision, take some *right action* in accordance with it, and trust that the *Divine Intervention* will guide you through! Know that what we are meant to do is already living in our **Essence**, and is what has been seeking to express itself through us since it has come into this physical life. And it has nothing to do with what has been told to us by outside sources for so many years, about what we "*should be doing*". Look at the dreams of these kids, who are still in touch with their soul's intention!

www.HealYourHeartFreeYourMind.com/Kids

You are living a daytime dream. Whoever controls the beliefs, controls the dream. Society, your parents and ancestors have controlled the dream thus far. Now you have been clearing out *their* dream, and from this clean slate you are now going to create your own living dream. One of **YOUR** heart and soul's intention! Just like when you set your alarm to wake up from sleep because you have an appointment, you are now waking up from a bad dream that has been driven by fear, for the appointment your soul has made to share your gifts and be a beneficial presence to the world. So in this state of connection, write your whole **Life Vision** down below, considering all the different areas of life you wrote about in the last exercise. As you envision each area of your life, **feel** the emotions you would feel when you actually experience it. Use all of your senses to *speak the language* of your subconscious mind and the Universe. **See** the things you would see, **say** the things you would say, **hear** the words you would hear as if it were all happening now! And make your statements, **your declarations**, using the two most powerful words in the world — **I AM**, as much as possible. To inspire you and get you started envisioning, listen to these songs from the master at inspiring **Life Visioning** first:

www.HealYourHeartFreeYourMind.com/LV1

In fact, after watching that and before we create our **Life Vision**, let's first get clear on our **I AM** declarations that we want to be the foundation of our **Life Vision**, and our life moving forward. Making sure we are keeping our vision in the high octave of our soul's song, we declare: **I AM** love, blessed, abundant, happy, healthy, grateful, excited, playful, charismatic, confident, centered, creative, comfortable, inspiring, peaceful, awake, one with Source, infinite, fit, wealthy and fun— just to give you a few of mine!

I AM –

....

....

....

....

....

....

Now from these **declarations**, connected to Source and from the song of your **soul**, listen to this inspiration and then write out your new **Life Vision**, for all areas of your life, using all of your senses and from a place of gratitude **for it all being so now**! Instead of goal-setting, we are doing some **Soul-Setting**!

www.HealYourHeartFreeYourMind.com/LV2

I am so grateful that this is my wonderful life:

....

....

....

....

....

....

....

....

....

....

....

....

....

....

....

....

....

....

What kind of beliefs would this person need to have? How would they see the world? What new things would they start doing? *What old behaviors would they stop doing?* Who would they learn from and spend their time with?

....

....

....

....

....

....

....

....

....

....

....

....

....

....

....

....

....

....

....

....

....

....

....

....

If you don't design your own life plan, chances are you'll fall into someone else's plan. And guess what they have planned for you? Not much.

~Jim Rohn

Let's begin to put this **ShiftShaping System™** into play and *transform* our life into the high octave of **our** heart and soul's vision and intention, envisioned by our *Spiritual Self* and from a state of abundant receiving. To do so, we first need to strengthen our energetic *Being*– we want to unblock, expand, and strengthen each one of our Energy Centers (chakras). We are going to love each one of our centers back to full life! In the exercise below, create a powerful image for each one of your chakras that is pertinent for you and your vision, be it for energetic strengthening or for physical healing, and that represents strengthening, unblocking and expanding that region. For instance, you could create an image of an oak tree with deep roots for your base chakra, an image of your heart flowering and blossoming for your heart center, a picture of a clear and healthy thyroid for your throat chakra, and an image of a silver cord or like an umbilical cord to Source for your crown chakra. In the spaces below, write down in detail what each symbol you create means for you and that energy center, so that when we go through the meditation, all you have to do is imagine that symbol, and not get your mind caught up in all the rest. The subconscious mind will know what that symbol means and take over from there. And as we move these energy centers and strengthen them, we will discover even greater clarity on our soul's song and our Life Vision. Here is a diagram to remind you what area of the body each energy center governs:

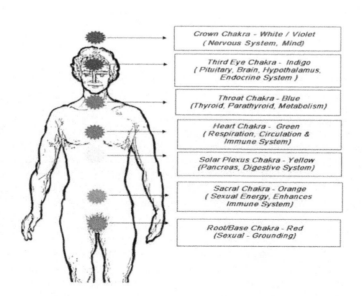

304

What healing and strong symbol and image do you have for your:

a. Base Chakra

....
....
....

b. Second Chakra

....
....
....

c. Third Chakra

....
....
....

d. Fourth Chakra

....
....
....

e. Fifth Chakra

....
....
....

f. Sixth Chakra

....

....

....

g. Seventh Chakra

....

....

....

We are going to use the visuals of these symbols for our *Energy Center Meditation* every morning as a part of our **Visulation** of our new present life, so that we can increase our connection to Source, increase our vibration, move out any blocks still residing in our Energy Centers, and get us deeper into a Theta hypnogogic trance state. This state bypasses the limited and fearful conscious mind and directly communicates with and programs our subconscious mind, naturally moving us into the love, gratitude and bliss state we need to feel to reset the *electromagnetic signature* we are broadcasting out to the Universe. Before you create your true **Life Vision,** we are going to do this meditation right now, which is going to ignite your new way of *Being* and **ShiftShape** your life into the one of your soul's intention. In this meditation you are going to hear and experience a special background music that uses sound technology to drop your mind into appropriate states of Theta, Alpha and Gamma, to greatly assist you in realizing your **Life Vision**. If you haven't already, download the *Expanding Your Energy Centers* audio to your MP3 player through the link below. Before you get started, make sure you go to the bathroom, drink some water and find a quiet and private place to go through this transformative inner journey to your soul's song and your **Life Vision**. Go to track #15 on the app, or you can download it at the following link:

www.HealYourHeartFreeYourMind.com/Expand

Now that you are more connected to your *Essence*, Source and the high octave of your soul's song, write out your new **Life Vision** as if you are sharing with your best friend, whom you haven't talked to for a long time, all the great things that have been happening for you the past year. See your friend through your own eyes, sitting across from you with a big smile on his or her face, excited to hear about all of the great news you have to share. Start it off with something like, **"I am so keyed up about all of the great things that are happening in my life right now; it's like my dream come true! I have had the most amazing year of my life!"** And then proceed to share, with great enthusiasm, all the amazing things that have been unfolding in your life in great detail. See it all happening through your own eyes and really feel all of the excitement about it in your body and Being! So we are taking the **Life Vision** we created earlier, and we are now creating a real life-like representation of that vision. Meaning, **we are sharing how our life is now AS this person**, and all the great things that have been happening in our life.

For instance, if you want to be a famous musician, you might share how your last concert filled up a stadium of over a hundred thousand people and the tickets sold out within 24 hours! Give your friend all the details of how it felt to be in front of the audience — what you saw through your eyes from the stage, what you felt in your body, what you heard all around you, what you were smelling, and **re-**live it as if you are there all over again! Tell your friend how the news of this resulted in you getting invited to have concerts in stadiums all across the world, that have also been selling out within 48 hours. And how all of this has led to talk shows, around the world, inviting you and your band to be a guest star on their show! Tell them in detail about one of your interviews and everything you experienced. Share how you just signed a multi-million dollar contract with Sony Records and all the great perks that have come with it! Give them all the details of one of those perks that most excites you. Tell them all about the interesting people that are coming into your life and all of the electrifying friendships and partnerships you are now forming. And express the exhilaration about a special meeting you had with one of your all-time idols! Etc...... Saying it all in the first person, of course, and ending it with, "And I am so grateful to the Divine for all of the blessings that have been bestowed upon me! I don't know how it's going to get even better than this, but I know that it will!"

So, you're not just stating a list of how you want your life to be as you did before, but you are actually giving your friend the specific details of all the exciting things unfolding in ALL areas of your life, now and in the past year. Share all of the unique emotions you are experiencing with each event, and really feel them in your body as you would when **re-living** a story in an intimate heart-to-heart conversation with someone who means the world to you! Create your **Life Vision,** incorporating your above **I AM** statements from this elevated state you're now in. Write your new life script now!

I am so excited about all of the great things that are happening in my life right now! I just had the most amazing year of my life! Let me tell you all about it!

....

....

....

....

....

....

....

....

....

....

....

....

....

....

....

....

....

....

....

....

....

....

....

So, every morning you're going to **ShiftShape** your life by *Visulating* your soul's vision by listening to this **ShiftShape Visulation**™. This daily tool is going to lead you through expanding your Energy Centers to raise your vibration and reconnect you to your *Essence* and Source; and then guide you through creating your **Life Vision** from this high frequency, unhindered by your conscious mind. And at the end of the night, right before you go to sleep, you're going to focus on all of your exhilaration that this **Life Vision** is happening now, and express your gratitude to the Divine and your *A Team* for all of the blessings you're receiving! This audio and these practices will bring your consciousness into the elevated state that is required for both the subconscious mind and the heart to change what they are broadcasting out, and for the Universe to respond more readily, and mirror back your vision into physical reality.

This *Visulation* will be approximately an hour long, and should be done preferably as you are just waking up and coming out of Delta/Theta. You will then get up from your *Visulation* **as this new person**, taking actions and making decisions from their perspective. How would this person walk, talk and carry themselves with others? What kind of choices would they make for themselves? How would they feel and what would they say about themselves and others? When making important decisions, you would just connect into your *Essence*, tap into this persona and ask, *what would this person, living this kind of life and having these kinds of beliefs system, do at this moment?* And then take action in accordance with that answer. We need to *Visulate* living this **Life Vision every day and every night**, in order to change from someone who is trying to remember all of the mechanics on how to drive a stick shift, to one who drives the car from point A to point B automatically, without a whole lot of thought to it anymore. This person is now able to easily think about other things while they are unconsciously driving the stick shift to their destination! And as we recondition this new state, this new *stand*, and become it, the actions and responses automatically unfold, and the Universe is automatically guiding you on the right track to your targeted destination. And your life **ShiftShapes** into the **Life Vision** that your soul has always intended!

So what are some of the *Right Actions* this version of you is going to do right away? What are the gifts you already have that will help support you in this Life Vision?

....

....

....

....

....

....

....

....

....

....

....

....

....

....

What are some things you need immediate help with, from the Divine and your A Team, in order to move towards your Life Vision?

....

....

....

....

....

....

....

....

....

....

....

....

....

Many famous names that we know have shared that they have used a similar method to **ShiftShape**™ their life into living their heart and soul's dream. You may recognize a few of the names, such as Jim Carrey, Will Smith, Oprah, Ellen DeGeneres, Bill Gates, Katie Holmes, Drew Barrymore, Anthony Robbins, Mariah Carey, Nick Cannon, Justin Timberlake, Tiger Woods, Michael Jordon, and Arnold Schwarzenegger — all of the many and various versions of his persona that he has created! This is what Arnold had to share about two versions of himself: "The mind is really so incredible. Before I won my first Mr. Universe title, I walked around the tournament like I owned it. I had won it so many times in my mind, the title was already mine. Then when I moved on to the movies, I used the same technique. I visualized daily being a successful actor and earning big money! It's all in the mind!"

Jim Carey shared that back in 1987 he used to sit in his car, overlooking Hollywood every night, visualizing having a very successful acting career in the movies. He wrote a check to himself for 10 million dollars "for acting services rendered," and dated the check for Thanksgiving of 1995. He carried it around in his wallet, and just a few weeks before that date, he was awarded a contract for 10 million dollars for his role in *Dumb and Dumber*! The lesson is— list an earlier date on your visualized check! Here is a blurb of a message he had for a college graduating class:

www.HealYourHeartFreeYourMind.com/Jim

It's one thing to idolize heroes.
It's quite another to visualize yourself in their place.
When I saw great people doing great things, I said to myself,
"I can be there."
~Arnold Schwarzenegger

So, let's get started now on your **Life Vision**! Go back and look over the symbols you created for your Energy Centers and read over your **ShiftShape**™ **Vision** you just created; then go to the bathroom if you need, grab some water, get back in your comfortable, quiet and sacred spot, grab your MP3 player with your headphones, and listen to track #16 to be guided on this **ShiftShape Visulation**™ to your new joy-filled, magical life! If you haven't downloaded yet, you will find it here:

www.HealYourHeartFreeYourMind.com/ShiftShape

To further cement your new magical future, utilize these two miraculous tools in **The Corroboration System**™. The *Mirror Method*™ and the *Collaboration Method*™.

For the *Mirror Method*, after you get up from your meditation, thrilled about your new exciting life, and while you are still in that energized vibration, I want you to have a conversation with your *intellect* in the mirror. Through the mirror, your *Spiritual Self* who is living this truth is going to share, as the captain of your vessel, everything that you guys have been doing and how fun and magical your life **Is**. You are going share in the excitement with your *intellect*, giving yourself a high five, a "*right on!*" a "*Thank you, Universe!*" and a, "*Wow, how does it get even better than this?*" Do this while you are getting ready for your day. And once you are ready for the day, go take an immediate action towards your vision, **as if it is so**, from this high vibration. Get the ball rolling and the energy moving in the right direction!

The *Collaboration Method* is a very powerful tool you use with a buddy. You partner with someone who has an understanding of *manifesting reality*. Someone who will validate and *be in agreement* with you about how fabulous your life **is going**, and celebrate it with you! You will share all the exciting things that are happening for you **right now** as if it *'were so'*, via one of the many communication tools we have. So you will share the *'exciting news'* via text, voicemail, an email, a social media message, a Yakit, or whatever the latest and greatest technology of the day is. Your buddy, *who is in on the gig*, will be in agreement with you and validate it for you with congratulations and praise. This is a very powerful **tool of agreement,** to multiply the energy of your vision and your clear signal and communication to the Universe, to fast-forward your soul's intention!

I am big into visualization. I have visualized every part of my career and thus far, all of it has come true. I don't worry about my opponent or their game. I worry about my game.

~Conor McGregor

These two powerful tools of the **Corroboration System** will cement your **Life Vision**, increasing the clarity of your *stand* and the **electromagnetic signature** you are broadcasting out to the Quantum Field, and the response you receive from it. Share this book with someone special to you and invite them to join your team in the *Collaboration Method*!

We are now crossing over the finish line of this particular marathon. We have learned how to *transcend* the programs that once limited us from even running the race, let alone winning, and we have learned all the tools to *transform* our life into the one that will allow us to win the race of our heart and soul's intention. And we have been **inspired** to live a life according to our **Soul's Song**– one that *inspires* us and encourages others to live their greatest dream and at their greatest potential!

And so the **Ninth Step** to Freedom is:

9. Return to the Love, your *Spiritual Essence*, one with Source that you Truly Be and create your life experience from this place instead. (*At cause.*)

   - From this place clearly **decide** what you want and how your life **will be**. And just **declare it** — with certainty and a knowing that it **IS**!

   - Daily connect to your *Higher Self* and *Source* and **Visualate**™ your idealized life **As So** with excitement and gratitude.

   - Daily, take *right action* towards it **As So** immediately, then let the *Divine Intervention* and guidance lead you to *receiving* it.

   - Take a clear **stand** and know and claim your worthiness to *receive* the abundance with full expectancy.

- Continually express gratitude for all of the guidance you get moving you toward your vision and then ask, "How does it get even better than this?"

- Every night, right before you go to sleep, focus on all of your excitement that this Life Vision is happening now, and express your gratitude for all of the blessings you're receiving!

- Do not buy into the story of the *'what is'*, do not react and try to fix it. Be more like the **Faith Healer**, not buying into the disease but instead, buying into the wholeness of your **Life Vision**!

- Guard the door of your mind from the mischievous thieving thoughts through your **daily mantras**.

- Use the *Mirror Method* and *Collaboration Method* to further validate and cement your **Life Vision**.

- Remember, because you were imprinted, you *used to be* the art – but now, **you are the artist who is consciously imprinting!**

- I recommend you purchase and listen to Michael Bernard Beckwith's **Trancendance** album as much as possible to continue your high vibration and integration of your true *Essence* at:

  www.agapelive.com/shiftshape

- I also highly recommend you create your own custom Mind Movie of your **Life Vision** to help you really use all of your senses to **ShiftShape**™ your life here:

  www.mindmovies.com/shiftshape

- Let Dr. Joe Dispenza tell you how and why MindMovies works so well to **ShiftShape**™ your life here:

  www.HealYourHeartFreeYourMind.com/Whymindmovieworks

Transcend*Transform*Inspire

Chapter Sixteen

Afterword

So we are nearing the end of our journey; yet we know it is never the end. A chapter may end, but a soul's story continues. It is just an ongoing journey of ***Transcending, Transforming,*** and expanding so that you can live an ***Inspiring*** life for yourself and for others. You now have been given both the *awareness* and the tools to do so.

Through this journey, we have become aware of why our life has been unfolding the way that it has. We have become informed of our subconscious programming, **how** the *cud* got there and how it has been unconsciously driving our life experience. We have learned **how** we can ***Transcend*** the programming and its effect on our life. **We have been awoken to how powerful our heart is and our thoughts are, and more importantly, the marriage of the two are, on our world!** We now have an even greater understanding of **why it is so very important** *to heal our relationships, our hearts and our subconscious programming.*

We have discovered how we have been living and participating in victim consciousness and how we have been abusing and imprisoning ourselves for so very long, by staying stuck and attached to our victim stories. More importantly, we have learned **how to stop** the self-abuse and to set ourselves free. We practiced powerful tools of forgiveness and learned that magic can unfold when we set our prisoners (including ourselves) free. We have gone through potent processes to heal our relationships and limiting belief systems, and learned a **powerful formula** to continue our healing and to achieve our goals. We have become aware of how our mind tries to distract us and sabotage our expansion, and we have uncovered the way to circumvent its tactics. We gained effective ways to bypass the limitations of our mind and access a *Higher Consciousness* with a greater perspective and more *awareness*.

We have become clear that one of the most important relationships we need to heal is the one we have with ourselves. That a lot of our suffering is because of the programming we received that told us to get love and approval outside of ourselves, from people who were also suffering and crying out for love because they were programmed and taught the exact same way. We learned how to **Transcend** that programming and reprogram ourselves with **Self-Acceptance** and **Self Love**, and *how to refill our own love tank from within and from Source*. We learned how important our parents are to our subconscious programming, whether we were brought up with them or not, and how healing our relationship with them is crucial to determining what experiences we will have in our life. We also discovered how our life partners are really our **Healing Angels** and how they are our greatest opportunity to **Transcend** the obstacles that keep showing up and have kept us from living the life of our desires. That we are more than physical partners, we are also spiritual partners in each other's growth and evolvement.

We uncovered that once we healed our subconscious programming, our victim consciousness and our hurts and limiting beliefs, we can stop living and experiencing life from our lower consciousness and the *concept* of who we are or used to be. Freed up from this debris, we can **return back to the Pure Love that we really are, and experience life from this *Power* filled place of love, peace and joy instead!** We can **stop** living life in *the effect* and **start living life** *at cause*.

We have come to understand we are not separate from the world and just affected by the things around us. Instead, we are interconnected with the world and all of the particles it is made of. We are always communicating with this *Field* and have a huge influence on our world, based on our feelings and what we are vibrating out through our heart, subconscious mind and our **Essence**. Until today, because of our lack of awareness, we have been unconsciously communicating with it in ineffective ways for our greater good. We are now reconnected to this **Essence** as who we are, and have taken charge of the vessel that we are living in, freeing our *intellect* of all of its burdens and worries of protecting this vessel, and the hurt, fearful child that has been trapped within it. We gave our child a voice and a safe place to heal and communicate its pain, and we gave our body and intellect a voice too; we created a treaty, trust and more internal peace for all. We created unity amongst the parts and faith in a trusted leadership that is for the greater good of all, and has a far grander perspective.

One of the biggest lies we have been told is that we are nothing more than physical beings defined by a material reality, devoid of dimension and separate from Source. Like everything in the Universe, we are made up of subatomic particles, and are implicitly interconnected beyond space and time. We don't need to be touching or even in close proximity in the Quantum Field to affect or be affected by some *'other'*. We are so much more than what we have been programmed to believe about ourselves. We are much more than our past, our identity and our knowledge. When we wake up and remember *who we really are and the power that is within us*, and that we are part of, we awaken to our *Spiritual Self* and begin to speak the **language of the heart** — *the language of love and gratitude*– and communicate more clearly with the Quantum Field. The Universe then responds, gives us feedback, and we realize what a direct and immediate impact we can have on our world. We recognize that what we truly hold in our **heart and in our Being** will be the truth of our reality. We now understand that we **are** an *Infinite Being* inter-related with the *Infinite Universe* that has *infinite possibilities* that are available to us when our thought intention is integrated with our emotions, and fused with the feelings of the **Love** that we are!

Now that we have awakened you out of the Matrix, cleaned up the viruses, uninstalled debilitating programs, installed Forgiveness, cleaned up your Heart Drive, emptied your Recycle Bin, upgraded your Operating System, reinstalled Love and its sub-file Self Love, re-installed Higher Conscious-ness, showed you where your *At Cause* files are, integrated your hard drive and showed you how to effectively utilize your cleaned-up powerful Operating System, it is time for you to live your life from who you **Truly Be**. Your Soul and the cells of your body are going to say, "*Finally, and thank God! We are so tired of all of that fear, limitation and negativity we have been bootlegged with for so very long. Let's finally* **LIVE** *and really express our unique expression of the Presence!*"

Your Soul has been wanting to retire the past and live its intention; but it hasn't been able to, with all of the generations of victim consciousness you have been carrying around, along with all the years of imprisonment with hurt, anger and pain. The soul has been trying to get your attention for years, shouting at you, "Wake up! Let's get on with it, or we're going to have to come back and do this shit all over again until we get it!" It is so happy it can now ***Transcend*** all of that *cud*, and truly create, live magically, and expand to its next greatest expression!

Staring at the blank page before you, reaching for something in the distance, release your inhibitions, only you can let it in. Drench yourself in the words unspoken, live your life with arms wide open. Today is where your book begins, the rest is still unwritten![24]

So now that you have the **pen in your hand,** let's create an exciting joy-filled, magical life story!

I will not die an unlived life.
I will not live in fear of falling or catching fire.
I choose to inhabit my days, to allow my living to open me,
to make me less afraid, more accessible, to loosen my heart
until it becomes a wing, a torch, a promise.
I choose to risk my significance
to Live.
So that which came to me as seed
goes to the next as blossom
and that which came to me as blossom,
goes on as fruit.

~ Dawna Markova

Now let's go run our marathon!

Transcend*Transform*Inspire

Next Steps.....

I once read an article called "*The Loneliest Whale in the World*" that really relates to this deep journey we have just been on and the Life Vision we want to live moving forward. The whale has been calling out at a frequency not used by any other whales in the North Pacific Ocean for the last 20 years. Usually whales sing at a frequency of 17 to 18 hertz, yet this amazing High Conscious creature sings at a whopping 52 hertz, and hence cannot be heard by her fellow whales.

The same goes for us; we all have different vibrations that resonate differently to one another. Each one of us has a unique frequency, like a fingerprint, that I call a **SoulPrint**. Some people resonate with our SoulPrint and others don't, which influences how well we understand and communicate with one another. And this frequency, this SoulPrint or electromagnetic signature constantly evolves as we do, and as we now consciously imprint our soul.

So as you have healed your *charges*, you may find that you don't resonate with some of the people you once used to. You may find that even with people you once felt very comfortable with, there is now a mutual feeling of being less at ease around each other. You are now vibrating higher than 18 hertz, so their 17 hertz no longer relates. As you continue to heal your *charges* and raise your vibration towards your Life Vision, your right tribe that aligns with that vision will be drawn to you. As Sir Isaac Newton cited when he discovered the Law of Gravity, matter is attractive in nature and like vibration will be drawn to its like vibration.

This work we have introduced to you to increase your vibration is deep, and the nature of the conscious mind is to avoid it and stay in control of what it knows. So you may find that you need some guidance and support to go through it effectively, and get to your next evolution to truly **Transform Your Life** into the one of your heart and soul's intention. We have a variety solutions to support you at www.HealYourHeartFreeYourMind.com/Programs, but the key ones you may want to consider right away are:

- Our bi-monthly group coaching teleconference program, where you can continue your learning and get all of your questions answered.

- Our eight day, all inclusive retreat to personally take you through this powerful and intensive internal journey of transformation.

- Once you are clear on your **Life Vision**, you can get a customized **ShiftShape**™ **Your Life Visulation** of your vision created by Bob Doyle (see Bio below), complete with advanced sound technology to imprint your **Life Vision** deep into your subconscious mind.

- Our Heal Your Heart ~ Transform Your Life Certification Program

Know that you are not alone in this, and that there is a community to support you through your journey. Stay connected with us and all of the opportunities we are offering to help support you in your healing and transformative expedition at:

- Our private FB group www.facebook.com/groups/HealYour Relationships
- Our Facebook page www.facebook.com/HealingYourRelationships
- Our Free Tools www.HealYourHeartFreeYourMind.com/Free-tools for healing
- Download our Free App called *Eternal Love* at www.AppCatch.com

This book is just a taste of what we do at our intensive 8 day retreat. Of course, there are limitations to what we can do through a book, that we don't have at our live events. The powerful vortex of energy we create there makes your healing happen quickly and in greater velocity. I am gratefully honored to have the opportunity be a part of your growth and healing journey, and I look forward to connecting with you personally as we continue our work moving onward.

With Much Love, Blessings and Grace,

Brandy Faith Weld

About Bob Doyle

Bob Doyle is the CEO of Boundless Living, Inc. and author of the #1 Best-selling book *Follow Your Passion – Find Your Power*. Bob has been teaching principles of **Living Life by Design** utilizing the principles of the **Law of Attraction** since 2002. He is best known as a Law of Attraction expert, and for his part in the movie and book, *The Secret*. He is also absolutely committed to opening up people to **all** aspects of their creativity and sense of play. Bob works with groups to help them clarify their vision, identify areas where they are stuck, and help them move powerfully into action towards their intended goal. You can reach Bob at www.boundlessliving.com.

ACKNOWLEDGEMENTS

I chose to write this on Thanksgiving Day because it is a day of recognizing all that you have to be grateful for. And I have so many people I feel grateful to.

I thank the many teachers that have crossed my path and provided the bridge of experience that has led to the powerful and empowering messages of this book. Some of them are teachers that I learned from through their books and workshops. And many others I learned from without their awareness. Some of them taught me by their example of what to be or what not to be or do, and others served as my Healing Angels. They were excellent mirrors, enabling me to SEE all of the stories, programming and wounding within me, that were driving my life experience. Each one of them has been a perfect teacher for me in their own way, and I am grateful to them all.

My journey of growth and learning started with my mother and father and continued on with other family members. As I grew, it continued further with friends, boyfriends, teachers, acquaintances and bosses. Each experience prodded me to look for answers, and led me to another book and another teacher. My first intellectual teachings were from the many personal development books that my mother would read, which spurred my curiosity for more awareness. Soon, my hobby and passion was growing and learning, and I discovered my own mentors and guides along the way.

Then the Divine stepped in, came calling with my first near death experience, 9-11, my mother's death, and my temporary crossing over to the other side, and became my ultimate teacher and guide. I am so very grateful for all of the teachings and awareness the Divine has led me through, and for being the best life partner one could ever have!

While it would take an entire volume to name everyone to whom I am grateful to for being a part of this healing and freeing journey, there are many people I would like to thank for helping me in the creation of everything you will experience around this book. I will start with my friend Tom McCarthy, who inspired me in so many ways in our journey together, and when he acknowledged me in his first book, *FIRE UP*. I also want to thank Brendon Burchard for giving me the belief that I could share my message in a bigger way. Also, Joe Vitale for showing me how I could better deliver my message. I also want to thank my wonderful friends and mentors in so many ways, Lynn Rose, Bob Doyle, David Corbin, Arielle Ford, Brian Hilliard, Jack

Canfield, Marci Shimoff, Dr. Joe Dispenza, Gregg Braden, Debbi Dachinger, Natalie Ledwell, Marcia Wieder, Tom Antion, Morgana Rae, TR Garland, Rich German, Nigel Henry, Margaret Irving, Marina Fleishman, Lisa Sadowski, Scott Harrell, Debbie Pomerantz and my book cover designer Rade Rokvic. I also want to thank Viki Winterton, Bill Froehlich, and my editor, Esther Faludi, for your help in bringing this message to the world in a better and grander way. I am so grateful to each one of you for all of your guidance, input and support in helping me both train for and finish my marathon!

In addition, I want to give an extra shout out of gratitude to both Bob Doyle and Lynn Rose for sharing your many talents with me to help produce the meditations that go along with this book. I also want to thank the Oneness University, its founders and all of its teachers for all that they have done to assist me in my healing and my awareness. I am eternally grateful for it all!

With Much Love and Gratitude,

Brandy Faith Weld

ABOUT THE AUTHOR

I grew up with a lot of victim consciousness. I would feel the world's pain, and I spent most of my younger years not wanting to be here. As I shared in my preface, I felt as if I only came here to be close to my mother. Because of this victim consciousness, I had my first near death experience in my 20s, when I thought I had a terminal disease. This fear that I was about to meet my maker sent me on a deeper internal journey searching for the Truth. This voyage made me realize that I wasn't a victim at all, that instead I was a powerful creator, and that I had been creating this sickness and all of the challenges in my life through this very same victim consciousness. Relieved and wishing I knew this as a kid, and knowing how different my life would be if I had, I became passionate about sharing it with others. I manifested an opportunity to do so under my safe corporate umbrella and began sneaking some of the teachings into our sales skills and new hire programs at Cisco Systems worldwide. I was very fulfilled at the time yet still playing it safe and small, afraid to leave my security blanket of Corporate America. Then a life-changing event happened for me and for many Americans: 9-11.

I took a vacation from Cisco and was assisting Tony Robbins at his last live Life Mastery event when the tragic event occurred. We were in Hawaii, six hours behind New York, so it was 3 a.m. when we got the life-changing call. Since most of the audience was asleep with their phones turned off, Tony broke the news to the audience of around 4,500 (mostly) Americans. As he broke the bad news, an attendee from Palestine got up and said, "I am glad this happened because now you Americans know how it feels." Then an Israeli man stood up and said, "You guys are the cause of the world's problems because you guys are raised to hate!" So here we were with the Middle East problem rising up in the middle of the largest tragedy to happen on the United States mainland soil. Tony handled it so perfectly that at the end, both men were on stage with him hugging each other, saying "I Love You, Man." They created an organization called *Passion and Action for Peace* right there, to bring what they just learned to their respective countries in an attempt to bring peace between the two. Almost the entire audience signed up to join and help; and at the end, we were all arm in arm singing Michael Jackson's "We are the world, we are the children," as we rocked together, side to side. It was a heart-opening, mind-blowing experience that made me realize what I really wanted to do is stop things like that from happening — people operating from hate, hurt, fear and separation, instead of realizing that at the core we are the same, and together we can get through anything— but that in anger, separation and competition, we will destroy ourselves.

This was the compelling event that caused me to leave my corporate security blanket and step out in faith to help people, at the spiritual and personal level, no longer limited by what I could share under a corporate umbrella. Still, due to my generation upon generation victim programming, I really didn't have the confidence to fulfill my vision when my work was ridiculed by people I cared about, because I still desperately needed others' approval. So I continued to try and stay safe and played small. I felt more confident when I was helping others with their dream, so it was easier for me to go for my vision when I was focusing on helping my mother make her dream come true. But since I never really did heal my childhood wounds and programming at a deep spiritual and subconscious level, I let both of our dreams die with her. (Because the healing I tried to do prior was with NLP, psychology, and with a rational and compassionate adult's mind. Again, you can't solve the problem with the mind, because of the mind's nature to deny and protect itself.)

So when my mother died, the hurt little girl who lost her mommy took over, and I experienced what spiritual teachers call existential suffering, and what Eckart Tolle (author of the **Power of Now**) refers to as the Pain Body taking over. From all the things that transpired within my family from my mother's death, I fell to my absolute lowest; I didn't want to exist. I became totally helpless, and that is when the Divine was really able to work its magic on me. Big Brandy, my mind, the ego, could no longer defend and hide. The healing started and the *awareness* began, but I still didn't want to be here, and I still longed to be on the other side with my mother. That was, until I did briefly join my mother on the other side. There I was shown the root of the human condition and the pathway out, and I was told that I had to come back and share it with the world. I came back different, with a new *awareness* and a new knowing. I was excited for the first time to now fully live, knowing that I was a spiritual being having a human experience. I felt a sense of urgency to get this information to as many people as possible before the winter solstice of 2012. I dedicated my life and worked feverishly within spiritual communities.

At the end of 2011, I was guided to move to Southern California, and it was there that I was shown that I needed to start sharing this information with the mainstream world to help stop the hurt and the bleeding that gets passed down, unknowingly, from generation to generation. So here it is, **my marathon!** Finally ran. I hope you will join me in this journey to true self discovery and total self love.

So what is your marathon?

Are you ready to start training for it?

If so, join me deeper in this powerful journey....

Transcend*Transform*Inspire

End Notes- Look below for more information about some of the things we shared with you in the book.

[1] For more information about The Institute of Heartmath and all of their studies go to: http://www.heartmath.org/research/research-home/research-center-home.html

[2] For more information about The Institute of Heartmath and all of their studies go to: http://www.heartmath.org/research/research-home/research-center-home.html

[3] For more information about this study: http://www.rexresearch.com/gajarev/gajarev.htm

[4] To learn about Dr. Emotto's work with water go to his website: http://www.masaru-emoto.net/english/emoto.html

[5] For more information: http://health.usnews.com/usnews/health/articles/050228/28think_2.htm

[6] For more information on these cases please read: A Change of Heart by Sylvia and Novak, 1997 and The Heart's Code: Tapping the Wisdom and Power of Our Healing Heart Energy by Pearsall 1998.

[7] For more information: http://www.whylovematters.com/

[8] For more information: The Secret Life of the Unborn Child; Thomas Verny: http://www.trvernymd.com/index.html

The Mind of Your Newborn Baby; David Chamberlain http://www.amazon.com/The-Mind-Your-Newborn-Baby/dp/155643264X

How the Brain and mind Develop in the First Five Years; Lise Eliot, PhD http://www.amazon.com/Whats-Going-There-Brain-Develop/dp/0553378252

Quantitative EEG and Neurofeedback; Dr. Rima Laibow

Is Your Brain Really Necessary; John Lorber: http://www.sciencemag.org/content/210/4475/1232

http://www.bibliotecapleyades.net/ciencia/ciencia_brain01.htm

http://www.nhahealth.com/science.htm

[9] http://www.amazon.com/Morris-Massey/e/B001KIE85E

[10] When Isaac Newton discovered the law of gravity, he also learned that gravity is always attractive. Every object in the universe attracts other objects. So Law of Attraction was discovered around the same time as the Law of Gravity. http://skyserver.sdss.org/dr1/en/astro/universe/universe.asp

11 http://health.usnews.com/usnews/health/articles/050228/28think_2.htm

12 The Matrix was a popular movie in the 80's. For more information about it go to:
http://en.wikipedia.org/wiki/Red_pill_and_blue_pill

13 Changes in the Brain Function of Depressed Subjects During Treatment with Placebo;
Leuchter; American Journal of Psychiatry 159; 122-129

14 http://www.nytimes.com/2000/01/09/magazine/the-placebo-prescription.html

15 http://www.what-is-cancer.com/papers/newmedicine/placeboandcancer.html

16 The Drama Triangle was originally created by Stephen Karpman in 1968.
http://en.wikipedia.org/wiki/Karpman_drama_triangle

17 http://www.sedona.com/Home.asp; http://www.releasetechnique.com/what-is-
releasing/lester-levenson/

18 You can find out more about what the Blessing is (Deeksha in Sanskrit) and find a local
place to experience it on the World Oneness Community site here:
http://www.worldonenesscommunity.com/page/find-deeksha-givers
http://www.onenessuniversity.org/index.php/what-we-offer/deeksha-oneness-blessing

19 For more information about Real Love go to Greg Baer's website at:
http://www.reallove.com/

20 For more information about Radical Forgiveness go to Colin's website at:
http://www.colintipping.com/strategies/radical-forgiveness-2/

21 For more information about Ho'oponopono please go to both Joe Vitale's website and Dr.
Hew Len's: http://www.mrfire.com/article-archives/new-articles/worlds-most-unusual-
herapist.html

http://www.self-i-dentity-through-hooponopono.com/index.htm

22 For More information go to http:/www.5lovelanguages.com

23 http://skyserver.sdss.org/dr1/en/astro/universe/universe.asp

24 Taken from Natasha Bedingfield and Danielle Brisbois"s song , *Unwritten*
http://www.azlyrics.com/lyrics/natashabedingfield/unwritten.html

34741476R00183

Made in the USA
Middletown, DE
29 January 2019